Memphis

An Architectural Guide

W9-CHG-616

Memphis

An Architectural Guide

*Eugene J. Johnson and
Robert D. Russell, Jr.*

Maps by Thomas Nathan

The University of Tennessee Press

Knoxville

Copyright © 1990 by The University of Tennessee Press, Knoxville.
All rights reserved. Manufactured in the United States of America.
First Edition.

The paper in this book meets the minimum requirements
of the American National Standard for Permanence of Paper
for Printed Library Materials. ∞   The binding materials have
been chosen for strength and durability.

Library of Congress Cataloging in Publication Data

Johnson, Eugene J., 1937–
    Memphis, an architectural guide / Eugene J. Johnson and
Robert D. Russell, Jr.: maps by Thomas Nathan.—1st ed.
          p.   cm
    Includes bibliographical references (p.   )
    ISBN 0-87049-655-7 (cloth: alk. paper)
    ISBN 0-87049-654-9 (pbk.: alk. paper)
    1. Architecture—Tennessee—Memphis—Guide-books.
2. Memphis (Tenn.)—Buildings, structures, etc.
I. Russell, Robert Douglass.
II. Title.
NA735.M39J64   1990
720'.9768'19—dc20   89-21501   CIP

*For Frank and Betty
and Joe and Irene*

Contents

Illustrations

Preface

This has been a labor of love. Born and raised in Memphis but having lived away for most of my adult life, I returned in the winter of 1988 to be the first Lillian and Morrie Moss Distinguished Visiting Professor in Art History at Rhodes College. I knew that little had been written on the architecture of the city, and I thought it might be interesting to write a brief guide to its buildings while I was in town. A year later there was this book, with around 550 buildings—a book that turned out to be far more interesting to research and to write than I had dared imagine. I, or rather we, hope the reader will find the same delight in discovery we found in learning about Memphis architecture.

I say "we" because this has been, from the very beginning, a collaborative effort. The primary collaboration has been with my colleague at Rhodes, Robert Russell. Together we offered a seminar on Memphis architecture to help teach ourselves the subject, and together we have driven endlessly around the city in search of good or interesting buildings. Once, cruising the streets with cameras at the ready, we were taken for "narcs." "Hello, officers," a man lounging on a corner of Trigg Avenue called out as we passed. Although we wrote some chapters individually and collaborated on others, we take joint responsibility (and blame) for the book's contents. Also we have done almost all the photography ourselves.

This is the first work to deal with the architecture of Memphis from the earliest remaining buildings to those of the present. That has been both drawback and opportunity: a drawback in that we have had little earlier work to fall back on, an opportunity in that we have been able to define the object of our study as we saw it.

We decided at the outset that this book would be critical. That is, it would evaluate both the good and the bad of what has happened in the city architecturally. As scholars we could do no less. The negative remarks found in some parts of this book are offered in a spirit of love, with the hope that some of the mistakes that have been made will not be made again. The praise—and it is ample—is offered in the same spirit, in the hope that some of the successes that have been achieved may be emulated.

From the many thousands of buildings we looked at, we selected a group that we feel are the best aesthetically, the most important historically, or the most representative of a widely built type. In a few cases, a building fits all three categories. Private buildings not readily visible from the street, even if they are of great architectural interest, generally have been omitted. Some users of this book will be disappointed that a favorite structure has been left out or that some particularly abhorred building has been included. With such inevitable reactions to our work we are sympathetic. All we could hope to do, to paraphrase William R. Moore's motto on his tomb in Forest Hill Cemetery (G-12), was the best we could.

We have not written a history of Memphis architecture. (Such a book would have required more years of work than we could devote to it.) That is, the reader of this book will not be able to follow the history of Memphis architecture chronologically. The guidebook format organizes the buildings according to where they stand in the city, rather than according to chronology or according to the careers of individual architects. For that reason, it may be useful to sketch here, in the briefest terms, an outline of the architectural history of Memphis.

Memphis is a city dominated by classical architecture. The classical tradition has sometimes been overturned by a particularly vigorous new style, but it has always reasserted itself, and with renewed vigor. The handful of great houses left from the 1840s and 1850s, such as the Massey House (C-2), the Hunt-Phelan House (C-11), or the Eli Rayner House (G-13), all have in common symmetry, clear geometric shapes, planar surfaces, and four white columns in the middle of the front. A new, unclassical style appeared in the 1850s, in the Italian Villa of Annesdale (F-16), that was asymmetrical, richly ornamented on the surface, and dominated by a single tall tower. After the Civil War, the great Victorian houses, such as the Woodruff-Fontaine House (C-3), continued the basic elements of this style, with even more lavish surface decoration

With the turn into the twentieth century, however, the classical style returned in full strength. One has only to point to the Laurence House on Anderson (F-92) to see a fine example of a deliberate revival of the four-columned plantation houses that had ringed the small city of Memphis in its early days. This revival of a local classical style was joined by others, such as the Raine House (F-30) or the Mann House (F-94), that revived other types of classically-inspired domestic architecture.

In the first half of the twentieth century, the city was blessed with a number of very talented designers, certainly more than might be expected. Before World War II, almost none of these men had succumbed to the blandishments of the modern movement in twentieth-century architecture, either as promoted in this country by the Prairie Style of Frank Lloyd Wright or in Europe by radical young architects such as Le Corbusier, Walter Gropius, and Mies van der Rohe. The best Memphis architects stuck very close to traditional architectural styles—not only the classical, but also the Tudor from England and the Italo-Hispanic from the Mediterranean. They did so not only because their clients wanted traditional architecture, but also because they simply liked it better. By the 1930s, some Memphis architects dealt well with the contemporary Art Deco style, but that style often used symmetrical, classical massing dressed in jazzy, angular, and therefore "modernist" ornament.

In Memphis, Art Deco appears only in certain kinds of public buildings, because most Memphis architects felt that "modern" was a style appropriate only to a restricted number of building types. In this way, they followed the nineteenth-century notion that each architectural style was proper in certain instances but not in others. An example would be the Gothic, which was frequently employed in churches but rarely, if ever, in department stores. In Memphis, the modern has almost never been considered appropriate for houses. In a city that puts much emphasis on home and family life, houses form the single richest treasure of fine architecture. But in Memphis, domestic architecture does not form a mother lode of modern design.

After World War II, twentieth-century architectural styles finally came to Memphis, in quality as well as quantity. At least one thing is clear about the architecture of the recent past. Most of the best Memphis designers have been deeply influenced by the Philadelphia architect Louis I. Kahn, whose work in the 1950s and 1960s constitutes one of the high points in the history of American architecture. It would be hard to pick a better man to follow. Memphis, however, remains slow to adopt changes in architectural style. Thus the most recent style, postmodernism, which was born in the early sixties and became dominant in America and Europe in the late seventies and eighties, as yet has produced few local monuments. And among the very best of the very recent buildings, there are still fine designs in a straight classical mode (K-11).

In our research, we encountered some interesting architects we feel we ought to single out. We can take no credit for bringing attention to the great trinity of nineteenth-century Memphis architects, Edward Culliatt Jones, Mathias Harvey Baldwin and James B. Cook. That is the accomplishment of Eleanor Hughes. But we have added, we hope, a few important buildings to the list of their works. We have also been able to identify a few buildings from the late nineteenth and early twentieth centuries designed and built by Robert R. Church, a real-estate entrepreneur and banker who probably was the south's first black millionaire. If it is true that he designed and built over one hundred buildings in his lifetime, as G.P. Hamilton, the historian of black Memphis, tells us, then Church certainly is a major figure in the history of African-American architecture.

We feel that possibly the most solid contribution we have made in this book is the reconstruction, at least in part, of the careers of some wonderful architects of the first half of this century. One of the most inventive of these was Neander M. Woods, Jr., the son of the minister of the Second Presbyterian Church. The house that Woods built for himself in 1909 at 1521 Peabody (F-50) is a memorable design, from a memorable decade in American architecture. On the basis of the visual evidence of this documented house, we have attributed to Woods several other houses of the years 1909–11, such as the equally splendid Parrish House on Vinton

(F-71). Woods' career in Memphis was brief. According to members of his family, he moved to Connecticut, where, presumably, his later work can be traced.

Another figure who has emerged with great clarity is George Mahan, Jr., who began to work on his own in the decade 1910–20, after an apprenticeship with Woods. Mahan could design almost equally well in almost any historical style, with the exception of the Gothic. His daughter told us that he always asked his clients what style house they wanted. One replied that she didn't care what the style of her house might be, so long as it was fancy. Mahan and his first partner, James J. Broadwell, produced an astonishing number of Italo-Hispanic revival houses in the 1920s, almost all of very high quality (E-48, for example). They also rang more changes, stylistically, on the bungalow than any other pair of architects we have had the privilege of getting to know. Of these bungalows, the Curtis King House in Morningside Park of 1917 (F-140) is particularly wonderful and, for that quintessentially middle-class house type, shockingly aristocratic.

An architect of remarkable versatility was J. Frazer Smith. His early houses of the 1920s (I-38) are typically eclectic in style, but in the thirties he concentrated his efforts on variations on a theme of southern classicism, from Williamsburg-inspired cottages for the middle class (F-25) to a book, *White Pillars*, on the antebellum architecture of the Middle South. In the same years, however, he was the principal architect of the Dixie Homes (C-38), a modernist housing project for poor black families, and he organized the Memphis Small House Construction Bureau to improve the design and execution of lower-cost houses in the city.

Alongside Woods, Mahan, and Smith worked several other highly talented individuals: Bayard Cairns, trained in Paris at the École des Beaux-Arts; Walk Jones, Sr.; Jones' partner, Max Furbringer, who wrote a little book about domestic architecture; and George M. Shaw, from whom we have one documented house of tantalizing distinction, at 1 East Parkway North (F-146). Later, in the late twenties and thirties, appeared Everett Woods, nephew of Neander; and Nowland Van Powell (who ultimately turned from architecture to marine painting). Then came Walk Jones, Jr., and Lucian Minor Dent, two architects who brought classical design to a very high level in the city around 1940 (see, for instance, I-20 and I-8, respectively).

With this book in hand, the reader can seek out the works of these men, come to know their individual styles, and assess their accomplishments while standing in front of their buildings. The brand of eclectic architecture that they practiced has been in considerable disfavor among architectural historians and critics for the last half-century or more. Recently, however, architectural historians have begun to take note of this great unstudied body of work from the first half of our century. We hope that the work of these Memphis architects will take its appropriate place in their studies.

Critical opinion is still divided over many of the Memphis buildings of the last decades, as it should be. We have our own favorites, which we hope may also become your favorites as you make your way around town with this book in hand. Memphis has a lot of good architecture to enjoy.

Eugene J. Johnson
Williamstown, Massachusetts
January 1989

Acknowledgments

This book would not have been possible without the generosity of Morrie Moss, who provided the endowment for Professor Johnson's visiting professorship in art history at Rhodes College. This professorship, in turn, provided the stimulus and the opportunity to write the book. Moss funds have underwritten the expenses of producing this volume, although we also have received help from research funds made available by Williams College. It is Morrie Moss's hope to make art available to a wide public rather than to an elite. We trust that this book will do its part in furthering his admirable ambition. We also would like to express our appreciation to the authorities at Rhodes, who cooperated with us unstintingly as we have sought to complete this work: the administrator of the Moss Endowment, Loyd Templeton; the president, James Daughdrill, Jr.; and its dean of academic affairs, Harmon Dunathan.

As our first collaborators, the students in the seminar on Memphis architecture that we offered at Rhodes deserve pride of place in our acknowledgments of help: Bob Barnett, Jeff Dillard, Adele Hunt, Luke Lampton, Toddy Peters, Greg Smithers, and Laura Wilson. All are direct contributors to this volume. After school was over, Toddy Peters went the extra mile, doing an additional month's work on the Downtown section. Her contribution thus has been doubly valuable. Another Rhodes student, Stacy Boldrick, not a participant in the seminar, devoted many hours to tracking down elusive names and dates.

A seemingly endless number of Memphians has made our work easier, pleasanter, and more exciting. Luckily, one of the city's leading architects, Thomas Nathan, came forward to offer to make the handsome maps found within these covers. His collaboration has been absolutely essential for the utility and beauty of the book. William P. Cox, an architect who knows more about the architecture of Memphis than anybody else, helped us get started on the project by taking one of us to lunch atop the 100 North Main Building. As our table revolved above the city, he threw out ideas, seemingly into the space of the city itself, that set us off in numerous profitable directions. Coming down to street level from that lunch, one felt a little like Moses coming down from Mount Sinai. Mr. Cox also graciously consented to read the entire manuscript in draft form. His comments were as invaluable as they were appreciated. Eleanor D. Hughes, who has done much to resurrect the careers of three of the city's greatest nineteenth-century architects, also was unstinting in her help. Dr. Jim Johnson and his staff at the Memphis and Shelby County Room, Memphis Public Library and Information Center, particularly Patricia LaPointe, have been endlessly cooperative, as have the staffs of the Burrow Library, Rhodes College, and of the Mississippi Valley Collection, Memphis State University Library. The directors of the city's two art museums, Bill Heidrich of Memphis Brooks Museum, and John Buchanan of the Dixon Gallery and Gardens, have also helped in many ways. Cathy Bruner and Lydia Henegar of the Memphis Landmarks Commission staff and Kim Isbell of Memphis Heritage took part in the seminar on Memphis architecture and provided us with information that otherwise we doubtless would have missed. Carl Awsumb, Roy Harrover, Lowell Howard, Walk Jones, Tom Nathan, Jack Tucker, and Zeno Yeates gave generously of their time to talk to us and answer questions. James Williamson kindly donated a copy of his *Central Gardens Handbook* to the cause. Two daughters of Memphis architects, Elizabeth Mahan Ballenger and Sue Cheek Smith Hughes, provided us with information about their fathers' important careers that fleshed out the picture of Memphis architecture with details that otherwise might have remained forever obscure. Oscar and Mary Jo Menzer helped on his work and on that of her father, Lucian Minor Dent. Sandy McNabb's study of the work of his father-in-law, Nowland Van Powell, although unpublished, is a model of what such studies might be. Powell's daughters, Jennie Powell Grehan and Helen Powell McNabb, made the manuscript available to us. R.J. Regan's grandson, Martin Regan, also volunteered aid. In addition, countless people phoned in with tips or gave us advice during brief conversations at cocktail parties, dinner parties, or whenever we could get them to stand still for a couple of minutes to answer questions. To all of these people we are extremely grateful, and to others too numerous to name here.

Thanks are due to Matthew Rohn for very helpful chats about American domestic architecture, to Charles Dew for guidance in the literature on southern history, to William Pierson for generously taking time to read the manuscript and comment on it, to Eva Grudin for sharing her research on the interest of black Americans in Egyptian art, to Ernie and John LeClaire for a fine job of printing our photographs, and to Greg Woods for editorial assistance. Leslie Nicholson Johnson has been a constant companion and advisor on the project. She spent days and days in the libraries, combing city directories and other materials for the facts we knew this book required. Her double training in art history and librarianship proved its worth at every turn. Without her, we might never have gotten the book together.

Guide to Using this Book

We have attempted to divide the city into manageable parts, which can be visited in any order the reader may choose. The locations of these eleven sections, designated with the letters A through K, are shown on the map of the city as a whole. Each section of the city has its own map, located at the beginning of the text for that part of town. Each building pointed out in the text is given a number. That number includes a letter denoting its section (e.g., A for Downtown), followed by a dash and the number it has been given in that section (e.g., 9, which is the number for Memphis City Hall). Every building is located on its section map by the number assigned to the building in the text. To make the maps easier to read, however, we have not repeated the section letter at each individual building location; it appears on the section map only once, in the title.

The individual entries for buildings contain: the building's name, its address, the name of the architect, if we know it, and the date of design and/or construction. Houses are given the names of the original owners, while public buildings are given their current names. If the name of a public building has changed, the original name is given in parentheses after the current title.

For most of the houses, the name given is that of the male owner. In the city directory, where we found the names, a house is always listed under the name of the male owner unless it belonged only to a female who was not legally attached to a man. In some cases it is possible to identify the wife's name from the city directory, but not always. A female living at the same address might be the wife of the male owner, but she might also be his mother, sister, daughter, grandmother, or cousin. It would require major research to set the record straight on this count. We hope that some-day someone will undertake such a study.

The date given for a building generally is the year in which it first appears in the city directory. Research for each annual volume of that publication was carried out during the summer that preceded its appearance. For that reason, our dates sometimes may err on the side of lateness rather than earliness.

The texts of the individual entries vary considerably in length. In some cases we give only a simple citation of name, address, architect (if known), and date. In others, we comment briefly on the building. In still others we have a bit more to say, and in rare cases we go on at some length. In general, but not always, the length of the entry may suggest the importance we attach to the building. We have quite deliberately chosen not to put stars beside the names of the "Ten Best" buildings in town. We prefer that readers make such choices individually.

Less than half of the buildings mentioned in the text are illustrated in accompanying photographs. This is a guidebook, not a coffee-table picture book. To illustrate every structure would have made the book too big to carry, and its price too high. One purpose of the photographs is to help readers choose, before setting out on a tour of the city, those structures they might most want to see. Once the buildings have been seen, the photos will serve as reminders of structures particularly enjoyed or disliked. They also offer the chance, in the field, to compare something already seen, but now halfway across town, with the building directly in front of you.

In a few cases, we have included photographs, accompanied by text, showing buildings that no longer stand. These structures are designated by the phrase "(Lost Memphis)." Mostly, they have been replaced by other buildings, thus the lost buildings are given the same number as what stands in their stead. Cities are dynamic; they change markedly over time. American cities have changed with a rapidity probably not exceeded in any other culture at any other time. As cities change, one moment is layered on top of another, a fact physically manifested in the way a new building is sometimes built on the foundation of an older one. We hope the "Lost Memphis" photos and descriptions will allow you to imagine how part of the city once looked and to create for yourself a kind of imaginary visual layering of the old and the new.

A majority of the buildings noted in this book are private houses. We want to emphasize the word private. Mention in this book in no way implies that a building is open to the public. For that reason, we have been very reticent in commenting on the interior arrangements of houses, and we have chosen not to publish a single photograph of the inside of a house.

Memphis

An Architectural Guide

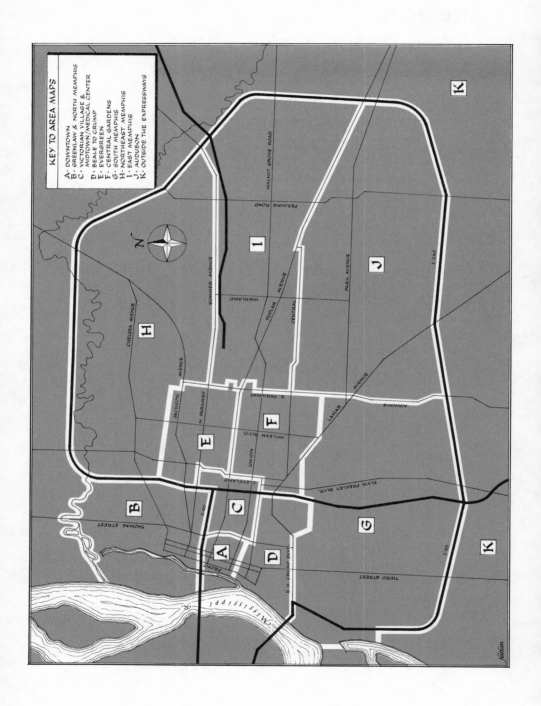

KEY TO AREA MAPS

A. DOWNTOWN
B. GREENLAW & NORTH MEMPHIS
C. VICTORIAN VILLAGE &
   MIDTOWN/MEDICAL CENTER
D. BEALE TO CRUMP
E. EVERGREEN
F. CENTRAL GARDENS
G. SOUTH MEMPHIS
H. NORTHEAST MEMPHIS
I. EAST MEMPHIS
J. AUDUBON
K. OUTSIDE THE EXPRESSWAYS

Introduction

A Brief History of Memphis

In 1820, *The Port Folio*, a Philadelphia magazine, ran an advertisement for the year-old city of Memphis, designed to appeal to disgruntled easterners and others wanting to relocate to the western frontier. It has been claimed, for no very good reason, that it was none other than Andrew Jackson who wrote the ad's text:

> The streets [of Memphis] run to the cardinal points. They are wide and spacious, and together with a number of alleys, afford a free and abundant circulation of air. There is [*sic*], besides, four public squares, in different parts of the town, and between the front lots and the river an ample vacant place reserved as a promenade. . . . This is the only site for a town of any magnitude on the Mississippi between the mouth of the Ohio and Natchez.

The literary style of real estate publicity has not changed appreciably in the last 168 years.

John E. Harkens's recent and slightly more dispassionate view of the early years of Memphis, put forth in his *Metropolis of the American Nile*, describes the situation in less glowing terms. Harkens argues that "from its founding in 1819 until about 1840, Memphis was a primitive and pestilential little mudhole striving to survive as a town." Since Memphis suffered its first cholera epidemic in 1826, the same year it was chartered as a city, it may be that the second description is the more accurate.

What is clear from the early civic propaganda is that, from the very beginning, Big Things were intended for Memphis. The way things have fallen out, neither Cairo, Illinois, at the confluence of the Ohio and Mississippi rivers, nor Natchez, downriver in Mississippi, have turned out to be great rivals, and primitive, pestilential little Memphis has become the great civic success story between Saint Louis and New Orleans.

The city's location on the fourth and southernmost of what are called the Chickasaw Bluffs—a series of high spots on the eastern bank of the Mississippi stretching from Kentucky down to southwestern Tennessee—has saved Memphis from the periodic floods that were a part of life along the great river until it was tamed in the 1930s. The natural advantages of the location were played up by astute citizens, who saw in civic growth the chance for personal enrichment. The mid- and late-nineteenth-century battles for railway lines came out well for Memphis.

The foundation of the city is well documented, and the original

Fig 1. William Lawrence, Survey Map of Memphis, 1819.

surveyor's map still survives (Fig. 1). Memphis was laid out on 1 May 1819 by William Lawrence, a young surveyor hired by the owners of the land on which the new city was to grow. John Overton and Andrew Jackson had acquired five thousand acres along the river a quarter century before and had been sitting tight on them. By 1819, Gen. James Winchester also had gotten into the act, and it was he who came up with the Egyptian name for the intended new city. The name "Memphis" was the only exotic part of the town, however, and the streets of the grid plan that was laid out along the bluff had such foursquare American names as "Front," "Main," "Second," "Third," and "Union." In the early 1820s, Jackson decided that participation in a land venture on the western frontier would be a liability during a presidential campaign, and so he traded his share of the land in what was now Shelby County to John C. McLemore.

Settlement in the early years was slow. There was a post office the year after the city was laid out, although the official charter of the city was not issued until 1826. That was also the year of the first cotton shipment out of Memphis, an event marking the intimate connection between Memphis and cotton that was to be a fundamental aspect of the city for the next century and more. The first newspaper set up in town in 1827, and another event, as prophetic as the first cotton shipment but more ominous, was the first yellow fever epidemic in 1828. There was a town hall of some sort in 1830, and the official census of that year put the population of Memphis at 633.

By the early 1840s, things were looking a little better. The population of

Memphis had risen to 1,799 in 1840, but there were more people than that on the bluff. In addition to the "city" of Memphis, to the south of Union Avenue there was a settlement outside the city limits, called, logically enough, South Memphis. This area was incorporated as a town in 1846, but it existed before the actual incorporation. Still further south was an even less clearly defined community called Fort Pickering. The original Fort Pickering had been built by the U.S. Army in 1798, near the present-day Frisco and Harahan bridges (D-28a and b), to establish an American military presence in the area after the Spanish, who had also built a fort, left in 1797. The American fort was not a success and was abandoned after a short time, but it became the nucleus of a civilian settlement.

In 1842 Memphis was strong enough as a civic entity to bring civilization—in the form of law, order, and taxation—to southwestern Tennessee. That was the year of the locally famous confrontation between the city, in the person of Mayor Spickernagle, and the forces of anarchy, embodied in a large group of flatboatmen who had occupied the city river landing and who were refusing to pay the wharfage charges. The altercation ended in the death of a flatboatman, several sore heads, and victory for Memphis. This exertion of civil control, combined with the decline of Randolph, Tennessee, to the north on the second Chickasaw bluff, near the mouth of the Hatchie River, established Memphis as the main commercial center of the central Mississippi. The popular application of the term "city" to Memphis dates from this time.

By the 1840s, Memphis was beginning to look like someplace. There are reports of more than thirty brick buildings in the town in 1843, and a

Fig 2. Memphis in the 1840s, seen from the Mississippi River.

surviving print (Fig. 2) shows a thriving river front of four- and five-story buildings, bounded on the north by the portico of the old Exchange Building and on the south by the grand neoclassical front of the Gayoso House (A-43), the city's most elegant hotel. By 1847, the city had begun to issue bonds in order to finance civic improvements, most notably the construction of new streets and the maintenance of ones that already existed. Public schools came to the bluff in 1848, as did large numbers of immigrants: Germans, Jews, Italians, and Irish. The Irish mostly settled around where the Bayou Gayoso fed into the Wolf River at the north end of town, in an area picturesquely called the Pinch Gut, or the "Pinch" for short. The name is supposed to have derived from the emaciated physical appearance of the inhabitants.

In 1849, Memphis and South Memphis agreed to merge under the name of Memphis, and the south city limit was moved from Union to Calhoun Street. There is a story that the name of Union Avenue resulted from the fact that it was the border between these two towns. It was the border, but it is also called "Union" on the 1827 map of the city, at a time when there was not yet a South Memphis. The unification of the two towns is the earliest example of Memphis' growth by merger and annexation, and it partly explains why the population of the city had grown to nearly 9,000 by 1850. In 1855 yellow fever struck the city again, but optimism was abounding, and the very next year the Greenlaw addition was advertised. This was the first expansion of the city north of its 1819 boundary of Bayou Gayoso.

It is important to realize that all this early development of Memphis was along the riverfront and on the bluffs to the north and south of the original town. Clearly, no thought was given to any eastward expansion. Memphis was a river city. It had the largest inland cotton market in the world in the 1850s, and most of the cotton came and went by river. There was a hinterland, but it had little to do with the urban developments along the river. It was not until the later 1850s that Memphis began to look in any other direction except up and down the Mississippi. In 1857, the railroad track connecting Memphis with the Atlantic seaboard was completed, and the first train arrived on the Memphis and Charleston Railroad. The new terminus was the first important railway station in town, and it was built at the beginning of an architectural boom. In 1859 about 1,400 buildings were put up in the city, and in 1860 even more structures went up. In the decade of the 1850s, Memphis' population grew from a little under nine thousand to more than twenty-two thousand, and the "city" of 1826 began really to be a city.

The boom quickly faded to an echo after the Civil War started. The citizens' sympathies were almost completely with the South, and in a burst of patriotism the city named the street which marked its eastern boundary "Manassas," in commemoration of the Confederate victory at the first Battle of Bull Run. After 1862, Memphis was an occupied city, but it suffered relatively little during the remainder of the war. There was a tremendous increase in population in the second half of the 1860s, and despite a third, more serious yellow fever epidemic in 1867, the population had passed forty thousand by 1870. Part of this increase was due to the annexation of the Greenlaw and Chelsea areas to the north of the city, and of Fort Pickering to the south, but much of it was absolute growth, as Memphis drew both civilian refugees and mustered-out veterans.

This growth overwhelmed the already inadequate public services of the city. By the early 1870s the Bayou Gayoso, the meandering creek which had formed a natural eastern boundary to the northern third of the town when it was established in 1819, had become little more than an open sewer and a breeding ground for mosquitoes. In late summer and fall 1873, a fourth yellow fever epidemic resulted in over 2,000 deaths. Scarcely had Memphis recovered from this when, five years later in 1878, the fever struck for the fifth time, resulting in the greatest disaster in the history of the city. Between the late summer and the first frosts in the fall, more than 17,000 citizens (most of them poor; anyone who could afford to leave left) contracted yellow fever, and nearly a third of this number—5,150— died.

Memphis ceased to function. Virtually all of the people who ran the city had left as soon as the epidemic began. The Protestant clergy, too, had abandoned the town, leaving only the Roman Catholic and Episcopal priests and nuns to care for the sick and dying. By the end of the year, the city was bankrupt, and on 31 January 1879 the city charter was repealed, and Memphis became the "Taxing District of Shelby County." By 1880 the population had declined nearly 20 percent from the level of a decade before, to 33,592. But the "pestilential mudhole" period of Memphis' development was nearly over.

In 1880, Memphis began to deal systematically with its civic deficiencies. The series of open cesspools, which was all that was left of the Bayou Gayoso, was covered over and made a part of a new, citywide sewer system. This "Memphis system," as it was called when it was not called the "Waring Sanitary System" (after its inventor, George E. Waring), was a completely new method of sewage disposal, based on continuous water flow. More than thirty miles of sewer line were laid in the 1880s, and more than fifty miles had been put in by the turn of the century. In 1881 electric streetcars were introduced, and in 1882 Main Street got streetlights. One of the most important discoveries in the history of the city happened in 1887, when it was found that Memphis was sitting on top of millions of gallons of the purest water in the world, and artesian wells replaced the Wolf River as the source of the city's drinking supply. Memphis had recovered enough so that by 1890 the population numbered more than 64,000, nearly double what it had been when the decade began.

Memphis' importance as a transportation connecting point was tremen-
dously increased in 1892 with the opening of the railway bridge over the
Mississippi built by the Kansas City, Fort Scott, and Memphis Railroad.
The Frisco Bridge (D-28a), as it is now known, was the only bridge south of
St. Louis, and consequently all the westbound rail traffic from the southeast and the central Atlantic seaboard funnelled through Memphis. In
1893 the city finally got a public lending library, to demonstrate that it
was cultured as well as rich. And the city charter, which had been revoked
in 1879 after the devastating fifth yellow fever epidemic, was restored to
the city the same year. In the early 1890s, the view of the city from the
river began to change noticeably. The Cossitt Library (A-63) was erected in
1893 and added a third tower along Front Street to the two already flanking the Customs House (A-64). In 1895, the city skyline went modern with
the construction of the first skyscraper, the Continental Bank Building
(now the D.T. Porter Building [A-19]). Just before the turn of the century,
in 1899, Memphis annexed twelve square miles of surrounding land and so
entered the twentieth century claiming a population of 102,320 (which
may have been overestimated by as many as 20,000), and with the city
limits at Vollintine on the north, Cooper to the east, and Trigg on the
south.

Boomtime continued through the first years of the twentieth century,
and the city acted ever more like a city. The Board of Park Commissioners
was established in 1900. Almost immediately it authorized the development of Riverside Park (G-3) and bought the 335 acres at the eastern edge
of town which were to become Overton Park (E-56). In 1902 the Parkway
system was begun, which was to provide a ring of roads around the edges
of the city. The city zoo (E-60) was begun, almost by accident, in 1906,
when a local baseball club chained its mascot, a bear, to a tree in Overton
Park. The first zoo buildings were opened by the end of the decade.

This was also the period of the Jim Crow laws, and Memphis stiffened
segregation by establishing, around 1905, two new black neighborhoods:
Douglass Park (H-4) in the northern part of town, and Orange Mound, east
of the city limits. (In the late nineteenth century, in contrast, in such areas
as Vance-Pontotoc, blacks and whites sometimes had been next-door
neighbors, or frequently had lived on adjacent streets.) Annexation continued as well, and in 1909 the Lennox area, bounded by Poplar, Cooper,
Central, and East Parkway, was brought into the city. The Parkways were
complete by 1910, and at the end of the first decade of the twentieth century Memphis had more than 131,000 people and three thousand automobiles.

The second decade of the century saw the beginning of the reign of the
automobile, an invention destined to alter the cityscape of Memphis as
completely as anything could. The three thousand cars of 1910 had
doubled by 1913, and just about the time that the Doughboys went "Over
There," the Harahan Bridge (D-28b) was opened next to the Frisco railway

bridge to let Memphians drive their cars over there to Arkansas. The term "Out East" began to creep into the local vocabulary, too, as annexation progressed inexorably inland. The Binghampton area, east of East Parkway, was brought into the city in 1919, helping to increase the population to 162,351 in 1920. In 1928, Highland Heights, along Summer Avenue, was annexed, and the next year more than twenty square miles of suburbs were incorporated into the city, with the result that Memphis entered the Depression with a population of more than a quarter of a million.

The 1930s were bad for Memphis, but things were not as bad here as they were in a lot of other places, and people continued to move to the city, putting added strain on already overstretched capacities. In 1934 the Memphis Housing Authority was established, and some of the best (from an architectural point of view) of the city's low-income housing projects, such as the Dixie Homes (C-38), were conceived. Local architects, singly and in groups, reacted to the housing crisis, and some extremely original— and often successful—solutions were worked out. By the time of Pearl Harbor, the population had risen from 250,000 to nearly 300,000, and many Memphians were living in much better houses than they had ever had before.

The automobile continued to condition the expansion of the city after World War II, and a second highway bridge over the river was begun as soon as the war was over. This, the Memphis and Arkansas Bridge (D-28c), was opened in 1949. As improved roads and more private cars made longer commutes possible, the city reached farther and farther out for new areas. Frayser, north of the Wolf River, was annexed in 1957, and in 1958 construction began on the ring of expressways which was to encircle the expanded city. The original intention of the freeway builders, fortunately not completely realized, was also to draw and quarter Memphis, with east-west and north-south expressways cutting the city into chunks. The north-south link was built, effectively separating the downtown area from the rest of the city, but in the 1970s, citizens' groups successfully forced a halt to the construction of the east-west continuation of Interstate 40, thereby preventing the destruction of much of Overton Park, the largest open space in midcity. Unfortunately, large areas of the residential neighborhoods east and west of the park were destroyed before construction was stopped, giving midtown Memphis a taste of what had happened to the downtown a decade before. Interstate 40 did result in the construction of the fourth Memphis bridge over the Mississippi in 1973. The Hernando de Soto Bridge (A-70), as it is popularly called (officially it is just the Interstate 40 Bridge) has become something of a local landmark, since it enters or leaves the city (depending on your point of view) just at the north edge of the downtown, rather than a couple of miles south, like the other three bridges. City officials have decided that its twin arches make a giant "M," which obviously stands for Memphis.

By 1960 the city population numbered almost half a million, and growth in the suburban areas was increasing at an even faster rate. But the 1960s were a bad time for the old parts of the city. The Memphis Housing Authority, which had been established in the Depression to coordinate civic housing projects, found that the social programs of Lyndon Johnson's Great Society had made huge amounts of money available for "urban renewal," and the directors of the authority felt pressured to come up with ways to spend that money. The noble ideals of the Great Society were not always subscribed to in Memphis, although the money offered through the U.S. Department of Housing and Urban Development scarcely ever was turned down. Under questionable leadership, the Memphis Housing Authority began what was essentially an all-out effort to destroy the nineteenth-century urban areas immediately to the east and south of the downtown. Until 1968 there was no congressional requirement that alternate housing be available to people dispossessed by urban renewal, and entire blocks, entire neighborhoods, were dynamited and bulldozed—simply, so it seems, to get rid of what was there: both the houses and their inhabitants. It was at this time that the area stretching east from downtown to the north-south strip of the interstate highway assumed its present devastated appearance. Most of the part of the city that had been built up during the boom years of the 1880s and 1890s was wiped out in the 1960s. But growth continued in other parts, and the area of Memphis proper, which had been just under 51 square miles in 1945, increased to 264 square miles in 1988. The population, which in 1960 stood at half a million, also increased to an estimated 652,000 in 1986.

The present fragmented city, then, is the result of a combination of longterm historical development and relatively recent conscious choice. The city, which for so much of its history has been a river city, is a river city no longer. For virtually the entire population, the Mississippi has been reduced to the level of a Sunday afternoon tourist attraction. Mud Island is the perfect metaphor for this. A sand-and-mud bar that developed almost overnight in the second decade of this century to separate the riverfront of Memphis from the Mississippi proper, Mud Island now is the site of a river museum and a scale model of the whole lower river (A-69).

In the 1970s and 1980s Memphis turned its back on the original reason for its existence. This is one reason that the downtown today stands so forlornly apart, facing away from the rest of the city. Another reason, ironically, is the original location of Memphis. The fourth Chickasaw Bluff has no counterpart on the western bank of the river. The Arkansas shore is low and subject to periodic flooding. Who remembers Hopefield, the town that tried to make it across from Memphis? A river city that cannot grow on both sides of its river must either remain small or grow in another direction. Memphis' success as a city doomed its relation to its river.

The urban tragedy of present-day Memphis is that it is now trying to be a city without a center. The downtown is cut off from its turn-of-the-century suburbs by the desolation of the urban renewal of the 1960s and the wall of subsequent interstate highways. These early suburbs, now called "midtown," in themselves really constitute a small southern town. Largely residential, they contain neither the manufacturing capacities nor the services one would expect in a city the size of Memphis. These have all moved farther out, to the east, southeast, and northeast. White flight, in the wake of the racial disturbances of the late 1960s, combined with new growth in newly developing suburbs and outlying independent towns, has caused a fundamental shift in the urban center of gravity. At the time of this writing, the latest word, according to the *Commercial Appeal*, the city's only newspaper, is that "the Hyatt Regency [a hotel—now called "The Omni"—at the intersection of Poplar Avenue and Interstate 240, at the eastern edge of the city (K-9)] is the maypole around which Memphis will revolve." As if bearing witness to the truth of this statement, the downtown is now becoming a yuppie suburb, with the old office buildings converted to upscale condominiums.

This book is not a sociological study of Memphis; it is a guide to its worthwhile architecture. And it is quite clear that very little that is worthwhile architecturally revolves around the Hyatt Regency, although that building itself is a fine one.

Memphis, like any living city, is a constantly changing organism. Our aim in writing this book has not been slavishly historical: we have not attempted to depict the city at a series of specific moments. Nor have we had any desire to become apologists for the largely tawdry and dull architectural effusions which ring the city in ever greater numbers. We began this book hoping to find works of architecture in the city worth sending the reader to see. We have ended by realizing that hope.

Robert D. Russell, Jr.
Memphis
January 1989

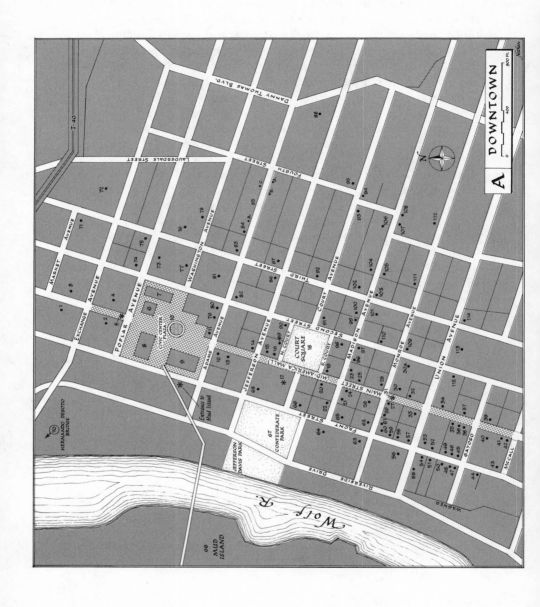

A   Downtown

A-1   Cook Convention Center

255 North Main Street
Louis H. Hagland, architect, 1970

A-2   Ellis Auditorium

255 North Main Street
Charles O. Pfeil, architect, 1920–24
George Awsumb, principal designer

Ellis Auditorium is a giant Italian Renaissance barn that houses two separate halls. They thriftily share the same stage, but that arrangement can be uncomfortable when something is happening at the same time in both. Part of the building sits atop Market Square, one of the four spaces left open in the original plan of the city. The west wing of the building is a large display area, dubbed "the Market" in compensation for the fact that the building obliterated a precious piece of open land. Pfeil wanted to win the competition for the auditorium commission so badly that he went to Chicago to find a talented designer for the job. He found Awsumb, who not only won the competition but also began a three-generation family of Memphis architects.

A-2

A-3 Holiday Inn Crowne Plaza

250 North Main Street
Taylor, Crump and Lindy, architects, 1985

A-4 Federal Reserve Bank

200 North Main Street
Schwarz and Van Hoefen, St. Louis, architects, 1969–70
Walk Jones/Mah and Jones, associate architects

A very cool, elegant building. The large-scale elements of the reinforced-concrete structural frame are covered in white marble.

A-5 "I Have Been To The Mountaintop"

Richard Hunt, Chicago, sculptor, 1977

A memorial to Dr. Martin Luther King, Jr., by one of the leading black sculptors of our day. Hunt produced an abstract mountain of Cor-Ten steel that rises directly from the pavement, so that we stand face to face with it and are even challenged to climb its treacherous surfaces (as teenagers try to do on their skateboards). The title, of course, comes from the famous speech King gave in Memphis, in the Clayborn Temple, the night before he was assassinated. The Hunt sculpture is not as rhetorical as the speech, but it makes its point eloquently.

A-5

Main Street (Mid-America Mall)

Gassner, Nathan and Browne, architects, 1976

The Mid-America Mall forms part of ongoing attempts to revitalize downtown Memphis. Main Street was closed to traffic, and a pedestrian mall—complete with fountains, trees, benches and works of sculpture—was laid out in an effort to attract shoppers back to a street that they had abandoned with abandon. The mall was completed in 1976 and dedicated—one fears appropriately—by President Gerald Ford. Ten blocks long, it begins monumentally at Civic Center Plaza and ends in a whimper at a parking lot across the street from the splendid, but presently vacant, Riley Building. The hyped name, Mid-America Mall, does not sit well with us. We are using plain old Main Street here.

Civic Center Plaza

Civic Center Plaza was the brainchild of the local chapter of the American Institute of Architects, who decided that the city needed a monumental center laid out according to Corbusian standards of urban design, which called for widely-spaced rectangular buildings, arranged asymmetrically. The city lacked both governmental office space and the architectural focus that a group of imposing civic monuments, placed around a square, can provide. Our tastes have altered radically, and what seemed wonderful in the 1950s and early 1960s doesn't seem quite so wonderful anymore. The plaza is bleak, even life-threatening on a cold, windy winter day. Few people really enjoy it, except the kids who play in the fountain when it's hot.

A-6 Donnelley J. Hill State Office Building

170 North Main Street
Gassner, Nathan and Browne, architects, 1964–5
Hagland and Venable, associate architects
Francis Gassner, principal designer

Of the Civic Center Plaza buildings, only this one measures up to the scale of the space. Gassner used very large exposed structural members to divide the building into multi-storied sections which read clearly from a distance and make the structure work as a grand piece of urban sculpture.

A-6, A-7   A-8

A-7   Shelby County Administration Building

160 North Main Street
Gassner, Nathan, and Browne, architects, 1969
Hagland and Venable, associate architects
Francis Gassner, principal designer

Gassner gave this building exactly the same articulation as that which he used on the individual stories of the Hill State Office Building, but he left off the large, superimposed framing members. The effect is to make the County Building a subservient, background building. But the County Building is not merely that; by forming the northeast corner of the plaza, it gives the space a clear edge.

A-8   Clifford Davis Federal Building

167 North Main Street
A.L. Aydelott and Associates, architects, 1961–63
Thomas Faires and Associates, associate architects

This is the least successful building of the Civic Center group. The small-scale exterior changes in color and materials are fussy, and they compromise the large scale the building needs to dominate the space around it. The lobby, however, should not be missed. The Op Art effects that Aydelott achieved with colored stones arranged in geometric patterns can cause dizziness in the weak. What doesn't work on the outside works almost too well inside.

A-9

A-9   Memphis City Hall

125 North Main Street
A.L. Aydelott and Associates, architects, 1966

Aydelott designed this skeletal structure as if he were working with large wooden planks attached to each other at right angles, although he actually used concrete covered with marble. On the piers that rise from the plaza level, he faced two sides with black marble and two sides with white. Because the black visually disappears, the piers look as if they were made of two very thin white boards. The marble didn't stick to the building very well on the first try, thus its local sobriquet, "Marble Falls." All was put back, however, at a cost of several million dollars. The north lobby contains portraits of the mayors of Memphis.

A-10   Civic Center Fountain

Gassner, Nathan and Browne, architects, 1976

From a large circular basin that provides a great wading pool for street kids, the fountain shoots a single stream of hundreds of gallons of water over one hundred feet in the air. The spectacle of the great jet is magnificent, but on breezy days it has to be shut down to avoid giving the city a shower.

A-11   E.H. Crump Building

(formerly North Memphis Savings Bank)
110 Adams Avenue
Max Furbringer, architect, 1901

This thin building, with nicely bulging bay windows, now looks a bit awkward as a corner element of a plaza whose scale is far bigger than it is. One is thankful, however, that it still stands. Originally a bank, the building became the insurance company office of E.H. Crump, mayor of Memphis from 1909 to 1916 and the leader of the political machine in Memphis until his death in 1954. For a long time, then, ultimate political power in Memphis was housed in this building rather than in any official government structure.

A-12   Claridge Hotel

109 North Main Street
Barnett, Haynes and Barnett, St. Louis, architects, 1924
Jones and Furbringer, associate architects

This steel-frame sixteen-story building with limestone on the first three stories and red brick on most of the remainder, has some rather thin ornament spread around its top. The large and ornate lobby, with splendid coffered ceilings, was remodeled in 1954. The Claridge ceased to operate as a hotel in 1968 and now serves as an apartment building.

A-14

A-13   99 Tower Place

99 North Main Street
Thorn, Howe, Stratton and Strong, architects, 1968

A-14   Jack's Food Store #1

76 North Main Street
1880

The flank of this commercial structure is strikingly similar in design to Henri Labrouste's Bibliothèque Sainte-Geneviève in Paris. In both, a long row of masonry piers supports a series of round arches, with roundels in the spandrels. Even though this building had no pretension to being "great architecture," it was still very thoughtful about its urban situation. The long side is a real addition to the cityscape, even though that side is not as important commercially as the Main Street front.

A-15   B. Lowenstein and Brothers Building

72 North Main Street
Mathias Harvey Baldwin, architect, 1882

Richly varied in rhythms and materials, this is one of the great remaining commercial structures of the nineteenth century in Memphis, and probably Baldwin's finest building.

On the long Jefferson Avenue side, there is a clever play in rhythm

A-15

between the cast-iron and brick piers, which shift from two to three both horizontally and vertically. Although the brick and cast-iron are mostly in the same plane, the darker metal elements seem to recede, while the lighter masonry seems to stand forward. On the top floor, the small free-standing cast-iron columns actually do move forward, to make that floor visually and physically lighter. The engaged columns of the second floor, on the other hand, make that floor seem much heavier. The central bay, wider than the others, picks up speed rhythmically as it climbs from four bays on the second floor to five bays on the top. As the facade wraps around the Main Street corner, rough stone is used to give the Main side greater heft and elegance. Here almost all the detail is in cast iron. A steel structural frame is introduced on this side to allow the wide spans of the three bays.

In the post-World War II period, the exterior was covered in "modernizing" panels. To install them, large amounts of the original cornices and other projections were removed. But even in its ruinous state, the building still exerts its quirky power.

A-16 Lincoln-America Tower

(formerly Columbian Mutual Tower)
60 North Main Street
Isaac Albert Baum of Boyer and Baum, St. Louis, architect,
1924

Here Cass Gilbert's Woolworth Building of 1912 in New York has been scaled down to Memphis size. Its twenty-two stories of steel frame are encased in concrete for fire protection. The concrete, in turn, is covered on the outside in creamy-white glazed terra cotta. To increase the building's visual sense of verticality, there are more vertical elements in the facade than there are actual steel structural elements holding up the building. The reveals on the pilasters show where the steel frame can be found: four on the pilasters that actually cover steel beams, and three where the pilasters are only for visual effect. The exterior window frames originally were painted green to match the tile of the roof.

The twenty-first floor, in the tower, held the office of Lloyd T. Binford, president of the company. From this aerie he had a wonderful view of the city which he served (or persecuted, depending on your point of view) as the eagle-eyed head of Memphis's board of film censors. Under Binford's notorious rule, Memphians were not allowed to watch any film by Charlie Chaplin, whose morals Binford found loose. After Ingrid Bergman's affair with Roberto Rossellini, her movies suffered a similar fate. Binford was a staunch advocate of family values. The models for the bas-relief on the facade were his three children and the son of the company secretary, George W. Clayton.

A-16

A-17 "Ascent of the Blues"

Arman, sculptor, 1987

Pianos and guitars not quite building a stairway to paradise.

A-18 Court Square

MMH Hall, architects for redesigning, 1986

Intended as the site of the courthouse, Court Square was one of four public squares marked off on the original city plan of 1819. Of these, it is the only

A-19

that still exists. In 1821 a log-cabin courthouse, which also served as a
church and meeting house, was built here. This was surely the first major
public building in the city, even if its appearance could have been nothing
but modest. The fountain in the center of Court Square, designed by James
B. Cook, was donated by fifty citizens in 1876 to celebrate the United
States centennial. It is undoubtedly still the nicest fountain in town. At its
top is a replica of Antonio Canova's statue of Hebe, cupbearer to the Greek
gods. The bandstand to the north has octagonal columns and capitals that
are reminiscent of fourteenth-century Italian civic architecture. Its modern
base, while sturdy, is not quite compatible stylistically.

A-19   D.T. Porter Building

(formerly Continental Bank Building)
10 North Main Street
Jones, Hain and Kirby, architects, 1895

This, the first steel-frame skyscraper in Memphis, was built by the Continental Bank and then sold in 1898 to the heirs of Dr. D.T. Porter. After the
yellow fever epidemic of 1878, the city charter was revoked, and Memphis
became a taxing district. Porter, a merchant and banker, stepped in bravely
to run the affairs of the city at the lowest point in its history. Under his

able direction, the city came back. Porter died in 1898, and his will directed his heirs to provide a memorial to him. They bought the bank, then the tallest building south of St. Louis, and renamed it in his honor.

Unfortunately, since it is one of Edward Culliatt Jones' last buildings, the Porter Building fails visually. Jones was an architect trapped in older ways when times were changing, and it is clear that he could not shift easily into the new skyscraper mode younger architects had invented in Chicago and St. Louis in the decade prior to this design. The Court Avenue side is quite consistent, and there is even a nice Renaissance palazzo effect on the top two floors, but the architectural elements are applied to the Main Street facade in an illogical way. On this side, Jones tried to give the Porter Building the asymmetrical vitality of his great houses of the 1870s and 1880s, but his attempt foundered on the rigid rectangularity of the skyscraper's steel frame. Jones left the east and south faces windowless; he expected skyscrapers to be built next to them.

Those who delight in historical trivia will thrill to know that, at the time of its construction, the Porter Building was the tallest building in the world to have a circulating hot-water heating system. It also had one of the first elevators in the South, and visitors paid ten cents to ride to the top to see the view. The building was renovated in 1982–83 and turned into apartments. The original thick slabs of marble that were used as stall dividers in the restrooms were reused for staircase steps in the penthouse.

A-20 Kress Building

9 North Main Street
1927

The facade, designed by an unknown Kress company architect, features a wild replay of Florentine Renaissance motifs in terra cotta, particularly those developed by the Della Robbia family, but with certain changes. The swags are oversized; eagles, those all-American birds, appear among the fauna; and the color is far gaudier than anything a fifteenth-century Florentine, who would have enjoyed a bit of color, might have imagined. The first Kress dime store in the country opened nearby on Main Street in 1896.

A-21 Tennessee Trust Building

79 Madison Avenue
Shaw and Pfeil, architects, 1904–1907

Most Memphis skyscrapers that were designed by local architects rather than by out-of-towners have a strongly developed base formed by the ground floor and the mezzanine. Above the base rises a simple shaft composed of office floors that are treated more or less identically. All this is capped by an elaborately developed topknot that includes at least the two upper floors. In the Tennessee Trust Building, the ground floor and mezzanine are rusticated, and there is an elaborate double cornice around the top. Arguably, this is the first skyscraper to put these ingredients together in this way in the city. While the design is not entirely original—other architects in other cities had done it earlier—it caught on strongly in Memphis.

The Tennessee Trust was the first building on Banker's Row (Madison between Front and Second) to exceed the four-story height traditional for banks in the city.

A-22   State Savings Bank

72 Madison Avenue
Wiseman, Bland and Foster, architects, 1955

A small building, at the old bank scale, that looks something like the chimney at Frank Lloyd Wright's Falling Water. Fortunately, the parcel of land occupied by the State Savings Bank was not available when the overbearing garage next door was built, and so the garage was forced to wrap around the bank.

A-22   (Lost Memphis) North side of Madison Avenue

between Main and Front Streets

The financial heart of Memphis in the late nineteenth and early twentieth centuries was this stretch of Madison, lined with bank buildings that competed eagerly with each other in architectural pretension. Perhaps most remarkable of them was the Bank of Commerce Building, by Edward Culliatt Jones and Mathias Harvey Baldwin, which stood on the northwest corner of the alley that intersected the block at the halfway point, where the State Savings Bank now stands. The elaborate cornice, with overlapping pointed arches, was one of the most convincing statements of these architects' apparent conviction that it's what's up top that counts. This splendid streetscape has been replaced by the blank side wall of the Lerner Shop between Main and the alley, and by the grimly modern garage and office building that occupies the corner of Madison and Front. The only break in this dreary scene is the State Savings Bank.

A-23   Lane, Smith, Goff and Stroud Offices

(formerly Mercantile Bank Building)
109 Madison Avenue
1904

The only small-scale bank left from the days when Madison was Banker's Row has a classical front of austere mien. Almost the only relief from the elegantly simple detailing are the bronze palmettes and wreaths in the Doric capitals of the pilasters.

Bankers often used classical facades to convey the idea of institutional probity behind them. Probity, however, is not guaranteed by pilasters. In 1914 it was discovered that the Mercantile Bank's president, C. Hunter Raine, had lost $1,050,000 of the bank's money on the stock market. Raine, who had built one of the city's greatest houses at the corner of Central and Willett (F-30), was forced to trade the neo-Colonial splendor of his residence for a jail cell. One wonders if W.J. Dodd, the Louisville architect who designed Raine's house in 1904, also designed this handsome building.

A-22a

A-22b. Madison Avenue in 1988 and c. 1890.

A-24

A-24   Mednikow Jewelers Building
1–3–5 South Main
1937

This lively Art Deco building has a single second-floor room copiously lit by large panels of glass and glass brick, but the space, strangely, has remained unrented since the building first opened. Memphis is fairly rich in Art Deco structures, and this is one of the best.

A-25   Commerce Title Building
(formerly Memphis Trust Company Building,
then Bank of Commerce and Trust Company Building)
12 South Main Street
Hanker and Cairns, architects, 1904, 1914

The original 1904 structure is the south half, to which the north half was added as a mirror image in 1914. The joint between the two parts is still clearly visible. The Commerce Title Building has a very elaborate ground floor (the columns of which were wrecked in the 1950s in a sad modernization carried out by Hanker and Heyer), a modestly articulated shaft of office floors, and a richly detailed upper area, where the large-scale columns of the base are repeated. The orders switch from Ionic below to Corinthian above. The top here gets a much greater play than on the contemporary Tennessee Trust, and the south side is enriched by a large number of three-sided bay windows that increase the amount of light entering the spaces behind them.

    In Thomas Hines' biography of the great Chicago architect Daniel Burnham, a 'Bank of Commerce and Trust Company building' is listed among his commissions of 1904. It can't be this building, which was built for the Memphis Trust Company and opened October 1, 1905. The Bank of Commerce and Trust Company merged with the Memphis Trust Company on October 30, 1905, and the building was renamed after that. It may well be that the Bank of Commerce and Trust company had commissioned a design from Burnham in 1904, but then decided not to build because of the upcoming merger and the new building that came with it.

A-26   Brinkley Plaza

(formerly B. Lowenstein and Brothers Department Store)
80 Monroe Avenue
Hanker and Cairns, and Emile Weil, New Orleans,
associated architects, 1924
Antonio Bologna, architect for renovation, 1986

Over the dark ground floor, now jazzed up with gilded ornament, rises the two-story mezzanine, marked off with columns. The top floor has a modest balustrade, and above that is a Sullivanesque cast-metal cornice that is the best part of the building. Brinkley Plaza clearly was designed with the Brodnax Building across the street in mind. Both have the same white color, beveled corners and general sense of scale. Together they make one of the most unified street corners in town.

Lowenstein's went out of business in 1967. The building was renovated in 1982 and renamed Brinkley Plaza after R.C. Brinkley, who built the original Peabody Hotel in 1868 on this site. The hotel remained here until the new Peabody opened at Second and Union in the 1920s.

A-26a. Jones, Mah, Gaskill and Rhodes Offices

ninth floor, Brinkley Plaza
Jones, Mah, Gaskill and Rhodes, architects, 1987

The sequence of space and light in these offices is well worth a detour off the street. The elevator opens onto a long, transverse hall capped by a barrel vault covered in paper that imitates gold leaf. (Francis Mah likes metallic surfaces. Witness the silvery splendors of his sanctuary of the Anshei Sphard-Beth El Emeth Synagogue [I-49].) The lunettes at the ends of the vault are faced with mirrors, so that the gold seems to go on forever. Glass block walls, which provide a completely different sense of surface and light, screen this entrance area from a low, dark, reception space. This, in turn, is separated by heavy, round concrete piers from a two-story space surrounded by galleries and brilliantly lit by a four-sided monitor. At the north end is a glass elevator, and at the south, in a dimly-lit room, are the computers. The whole has a sacral character. The elevator, placed where the altar would be in a church, accomplishes the Elevation of the Architect instead of the Host, and the computer room is treated as if it were a treasury.

A-26a. Jones Mah Gaskill and Rhodes Office, Brinkley Plaza, Elevator Lobby and Central Hall.

A-27   Brodnax Jewelers Building

39 South Main Street
1900

Because the first three floors of the Brodnax Building were used as show rooms, they had taller ceilings and bigger windows than the top two floors, which held offices. The windows are very close in design to so-called "Chicago windows," invented in that city to fit the new steel frames of the great skyscrapers that went up around 1890. Chicago windows had a large pane of plate glass in the center, flanked by two smaller double-hung windows that could be opened for ventilation. The extra-tall openings on the Brodnax second and third floors, however, were the wrong shape for pure Chicago windows. The architect solved this problem by stacking a smaller Chicago window on top of a larger one. The shorter top floors, however, have Chicago windows modestly heightened by the addition of window transoms. The Brodnax Building has a lot of ornament, but none of it is obviously derived from an earlier architectural style. For that reason it is historically quite remarkable in the city. Whoever the architect was, he was clearly aware of the latest ideas in major architectural centers such as Chicago.

A-27

A-28 William Len Hotel

110 Monroe Avenue
1930
Carl Awsumb, architect for renovation, 1983–4

A good example of Art Deco design, even if the exterior is a bit flat. The lobby has been well restored, complete with striped piers, decorated coffers, and etched glass. The flat lotus-leaf designs on the exterior of the building are carried inside to become a main decorative motif that appears on light fixtures and even on the elevator doors. Inside are two murals painted by James Mah in the 1980s. These show people in startlingly real 1930s scenes, as if they were actually inhabiting the lobby.

A-29 Chamber of Commerce Building

(formerly Business Men's Club)
81 Monroe Avenue
Shaw and Pfeil, architects, 1910

Another good example of the tripartite school of skyscraper design that took root among local architects. Shaw and Pfeil enriched the base with stone, from which rather plain pilasters climb up to a very heavy cornice at the top.

A-29

A-30a

A-30 National Bank of Commerce Tower

1 Commerce Square (southeast corner of Main and Monroe)
Roy P. Harrover and Associates, architects, 1968–70

A-30a. National Bank of Commerce Building

Second Street and Monroe Avenue, southwest corner
Hanker and Cairns, architects, 1929

This building takes the scale of this part of Main Street up another step, both in terms of height and of the size of the individual elements of the composition. The tower is very simple. Horizontals and verticals, all the same width, are covered by the same flat masonry surface. A certain relief is provided in the bevels around the windows, and the top is made thicker to give the building a strong edge against the sky.

The tower rises out of a surprising sunken plaza, into which one descends to enter the building. The point of this descent is made clear after one walks past the elevators inside and enters the grandest public space downtown, the lobby of the National Bank of Commerce Building, completed by Hanker and Cairns in 1929. Harrover brought his own entrance down to the level of this earlier building, which sits downslope from Main at the corner of Monroe and Second.

At the instigation of their client, Hanker and Cairns bought the plans of the Mellon Bank in Pittsburgh from McKim, Mead, and White in New York and modified them to fit the Memphis site and program. While the major elements of the Mellon Bank are here, they have been simplified to create a single clear space that in some ways may be more powerful than the original. The proportions are based on the Golden Section favored by the ancient Greeks, or at least on a three-by-five plan that comes close to the Golden Section in proportion. (The ratio of the Golden Section is 1 to

1.618.) The steel frame of the building is encased in huge marble columns (everything above the columns is plaster) set wide apart to open up the space. In the bank of 1929, this sense of openness was carried so far as to put the president's office, in the northeast corner, behind glass walls, so that, whatever he was doing, he was always visible. The skylit ceiling of the center was raised one floor by Harrover, who took out the original glass skylight to open up the interior space even more and to increase the amount of daylight entering.

Hanker and Cairns' steel vault for the bank can be found by descending the stairs that lead from the lobby to the Second Street entrance. The view of the vault is blocked until the last minute, when its enormous round door is revealed. The door itself bristles with giant bolts, wheels, gears, hinges, and locks, to the point that it suggests the essence of physical safety, an idea all banks want to suggest to their customers, but which few carry through as well as Hanker and Cairns here.

The exterior of the Hanker and Cairns building is a fine piece of banker's Beaux-Arts. The walls are marked by severe, unfluted Doric pilasters that rise beween nobly ample windows set high enough off the street to offer no temptation to robbers. The entrances, on the other hand, are given the full treatment of large, free-standing Doric columns, set into the plane of the wall. Above the great cornice, a double attic story puts a secure lid on this monument to the sober safekeeping of wealth.

A-31 Fountain—"The River"

Main Street south of Monroe Avenue
John Seyfried, sculptor, 1976

The idea for the steps in this fountain must have come from Lawrence Halprin's fountain in Portland, Oregon, but this one doesn't have the same sense of fun, because the steps are too large for people to play on them or in the water comfortably. The real river, in sculpture, is better served by the Riverwalk on Mud Island.

A-32 Lemmon and Gale Wholesale Drygoods/ Memphis Queensware Building

58–62 South Main Street
1881

One of the several good commercial Romanesque buildings in town. Compared with the more sophisticated rhythmic patterns of B. Lowenstein and Brothers at Main and Jefferson (A-15), however, the rhythms here are much more straightforward. The machicolated attic, a bit of fortress architecture unexpectedly erupting on Main Street, gives the building a certain romantic air.

A-33

A-33 Memphis Business Journal

(formerly Farnsworth Building, then Three Sisters Building)
88 Union Avenue
E.L. Harrison and Noland Van Powell, architects, 1927
Antonio Bologna, architect for addition, 1987

This is a subtle building that achieves its sense of height by stepbacks in wall planes, by setbacks in the massing on top, and by using bricks that grow lighter in color as they rise from bottom to top. The entire central section is recessed by the thickness of one brick; this makes the corners of the building seem stronger and the center weaker. Two structural steel piers are embedded in the large corner piers, and two in the recessed center. These latter two are covered by black glass at ground level, so that they disappear visually and make the building seem supported only at the edges. On top, the Art Deco stonework drips down the walls like angular icing. The same pair of architects, Harrison and Powell, collaborated three years later on the city's finest Art Deco structure, Fairview Junior High School (J-1).

A-34   Magevney Building
88–90 South Main Street
1902

The facade has a basic structure of three piers, two at the sides and one in the center. Between them, terra cotta ornaments hold the windows in place. The most remarkable of these ornaments are two outlandishly tall colonettes that rise from vases of acanthus leaves and turn into *fasces* made of bundles of the skinniest columns imaginable.

A-35   A.S. Barbaro Building
99–101 South Main Street
After 1899

The southern half-block of Main between Union and Gayoso has more largely intact nineteenth-century buildings than any other part of Main Street. This would be a good place to concentrate preservation efforts, to bring these splendid storefronts back to their original glory. Only the north half of the original Barbaro Building facade is visible, but the cornice can still be seen running under the newer facade on the south. The north edge of the facade is marked by a peculiar pilaster with its edge and capital turned out on a diagonal. There are also diagonally-set strip frames around the windows. This is a building of some originality.

A-36   Sammy's
103 South Main Street
c. 1905?

A Renaissance-style building with elaborate fan reliefs in the arches and two winged horses in relief in the center. Above these are a somewhat Moorish horseshoe-arch cornice with rosettes, and Gothic cast-metal capitals in the attic. The cast-iron panels on the sides at street level were made by Scherpe and Koken of St. Louis. The ornamental metalwork on Memphis buildings of the nineteenth and early twentieth centuries was often brought in from larger cities.

A-37   102–110 South Main Street
1870s?

This group of five buildings is connected by one facade, probably built in the early 1870s. The facade starts on each end with single brackets under the cornice. Toward the center, the brackets are paired, and finally, in the center, the brackets are clumped in bunches of three. The facade covers buildings which may not have been built at the same time, and which subsequently have been remodeled at different times. The part of the fa-

A-35

cade at 104–106 was remodeled by Hanker and Heyer in the 1950s by covering it with a marble collage. From the alley side, number 106 appears to be the oldest of the five buildings, and it retains a pair of cast iron columns that formed part of its loading dock.

A-38 107–109 South Main Street
c. 1900?

A beautiful Renaissance storefront with cast-iron panels and an entire cast-iron second story. Even in their less than perfectly preserved state, the ribbons in relief give this facade a wonderfully lively quality. One wonders if beribboned apparel for ladies may once have been sold inside.

A-39 Jolly Royal Furniture Company
(formerly Black and White Store)
122–132 South Main Street
Hanker and Heyer, architects, 1947

The name of the store for which this building was built dictated the architects' choice of colors. Hanker and Heyer clearly did some careful looking at the Art Deco Mednikow Jewelry Store (A-24) a few blocks up the street. They managed to transfer some if its verve into their design, even if by 1947 Art Deco was a movement past its prime.

A-40   Goldsmith's Department Store

123 South Main Street
1901
Nowland Van Powell, remodeling architect, 1957

The fifties was a decade peculiarly intolerant of old buildings, especially if the old ones dated from the nineteenth or early twentieth centuries. Goldsmith's modernized itself in 1957 by entirely covering its building of 1901 in pink porcelain panels, "the biggest panel wall job south of Chicago" in its day. The original facade with two-story columns is still there, *sub rosa*, so to speak. On the Gayoso Street side, the series of arches with "negative" or recessed voussoirs puts some sparkle in an otherwise plain facade.

A-41   Majestic Theater

145–149 South Main Street
1915

A typical early-twentieth-century glazed terra cotta facade.

A-42

A-42   Riley Building

157 South Main Street
1891

The capitals of the pilasters on this Romanesque commercial building are decorated with Hiberno-Saxon interlaces that come straight out of eighth- and ninth-century manuscripts made in Irish monasteries. The egg-and-dart moldings over the windows roll into volutes, and at the top, hefty engaged columns suddenly pop out of the plane of the wall. Engaged columns that behave similarly occur on the Gallina Building by B.C. Alsup on Beale Street, also of 1891 (D-10).

FRONT STREET

A-43   Goldsmith's Warehouse

(formerly Gayoso Hotel)
123 South Front Street

The Gayoso Hotel had one of the most complex architectural histories of all the buildings in Memphis. The first hotel on the site, with a handsome Greek Revival portico, was designed by James Dakin of New Orleans in 1842. It was almost certainly the first building in Memphis by an architect of distinction. In the years before the Civil War, the porch, visible from the river, gave the city one of the two porticos that framed the otherwise undistinguished row of brick structures that lined Front Street. (The other portico, of less architectural distinction, was attached to the Cotton Exchange Building, which stood on the northeast corner of Front and Poplar, where the Ellis Auditorium now rises.)

In 1855 the owner of the Gayoso, the real estate entrepreneur Robertson Topp, decided to enlarge it. On that addition a number of architects worked, including two locals, Hammarskold and Foster, and, in a capacity yet to be defined, the Cincinnati firm of Isaiah Rogers, the most distinguished hotel architect in America in his day. Rogers was responsible for the Tremont House in Boston as well as number of other significant hostelries. Apparently Rogers sent James B. Cook, an Englishman briefly in his employ, to Memphis to oversee work on the Gayoso, and Cook ended up spending the rest of his life in the city. The addition of 1855–57, to the south of the original part, was graced on each floor by wrought-iron balconies that overlooked the river. Both parts of the Gayoso house can be seen in the print reproduced here (A-43b).

The Gayoso burned in 1899, and Cook was called in to design a new hotel, which was built in the next two or three years. This, the present building, was shaped something like a slingshot, with a short handle reaching Main Street and a very broad, squared-off "U" opening onto Front

A-43a

A-43b

The Gayoso.

A-43c

through an elaborate screen of columns. That screen, which we illustrate in an old photograph (A-43c), is now gone. To that building Charles Oscar Pfeil added a gaudy Second Empire porch that once fronted on Main Street, in an attempt to reorient the building from the river to the principal commercial street of the city. After the hotel closed, Goldsmith's bought the building and converted it to mercantile purposes, expanding the store area into the Main Street wing and converting the rest to warehouse space. Sadly, almost none of the architectural or artistic delights of the building are left, inside or out.

COTTON ROW

Front Street was the center of the cotton business, the central business of Memphis. Cotton merchants had to be near the river, on which cotton was shipped in and out of town. The merchants needed buildings with wide openings on the ground floor, so that bales of cotton could be moved in and out easily, and they needed large windows in the upper floors, where the visual work of classing cotton took place. The cotton buildings that still stand along Front all share these characteristics. They also share the characteristic of being largely utilitarian structures. Their owners felt little need to proclaim their power and prestige through elaborate facades. Instead, through the frugality of their architecture they suggested to the world that they were reliable businessmen. When they spent money on architecture, it was on their houses, such as the mansion Noland Fontaine lived in on Adams (C-3), or the one his partner Napoleon Hill built at Third and Madison (A-102 [Lost Memphis]).

A-44   Frost Block

> Corner of Hotel Avenue and Front Street
> 1899

The cast-iron piers were made locally by the Chickasaw Iron Works.

A-45   Perkins-Golden Co. Building

> 116 South Front Street
> 1899

A-46   Johnson Building

> 110–114 South Front Street
> c. 1900

This building was built in several different phases. Number 114 is the original part, and it may have been built as early as 1880. Numbers 112 and 110 were added to the north, and then the two stories on top were built across the ground floors of all three.

A-47   Vergos Building

109 South Front Street
c. 1893

A-48   Stewart Building

105 South Front Street
c. 1900

A-49   Allenberg Building

104 South Front Street
1871
Hnedak-Bobo Group, architects for renovation, 1987–88

The handsome new interior, behind the restored old facade, is dominated by a vertical space that features top lighting and a nice play between a curved wall, set with square panes of glass, and a curved metal staircase placed on axis.

A-50   The Butcher Shop

(formerly Joseph N. Oliver Building)
99–101–103 South Front Street
Alsup and Woods, architects, 1904

The original function of this building as a cold-storage warehouse seems belied by the exuberant Beaux-Arts facade, where rustication and quoining have a field day. Here one probably senses the hand of Alsup's young partner, Neander M. Woods, Jr., whose even more exuberant stone houses in the Central Gardens form one of the most original groups of buildings in the city. (One also suspects that either Alsup or Woods, who split as partners in 1908, may have been responsible for the more restrained building at 427–435 South Front Street [D-23], where many of the same visual devices are at work.) The upper cornice, bearing the dates 1860 and 1909 and the apposite word, "Excelsior," was added later, presumably in 1909. The contrast between the pretensions of this structure and the plainness of the surrounding cotton buildings makes the deliberate simplicity of the latter all the clearer.

A-51   Riley Building

89–91 South Front Street
1903, with later additions

A-49

A-50

A-52   Murff Building

88 South Front Street
1880s

A-53   Cotton Exchange Building

84–86 South Front Street
Mahan and Broadwell, architects, 1925
C.G. Rosenplaenter, associate architect and civil engineer

In the Cotton Exchange Building, the hub of activity along Cotton Row, the buying and selling of cotton take place. This building is the fourth that the Cotton Exchange, organized in the 1870s, has used. The first was rented space on Front Street, the second and third stood and still stand at the corner of Madison and Second, and this last marked a return to the street that is the center of the cotton trade. Mahan gave this building a flatness typical of his work when he was doing a large building. There is also a mixture of styles, from relatively classical arches and engaged columns on the ground floor and mezzanine to a rather Gothic arcade at the top. This building, like other skyscrapers by local architects, puts the architectural activity at the top and bottom, but it does so with a restraint that borders on timidity.

A-54   Howard's Row

(group of cotton buildings perpendicular to Front Street)
77–81–85 South Front Street
c. 1843, with later additions and alterations

These buildings, known collectively as Howard's Row, are apparently the oldest commercial buildings still standing downtown. From the alley just south of Union one can see clearly that the very simple backs of the buildings are older than the facades one sees on the street. The Front Street fronts are the result of a rebuilding, caused by the widening of that street in the 1920s that took several feet off the old buildings.

A-55   Timpani Condominiums

35–49 Union Avenue
Jack Tucker, architect for renovation, 1974

This is the first group of old buildings downtown to be rehabilitated, and Tucker did the job well by not trying to make the buildings more than they actually are: good-looking, tough commercial structures with little architectural pretension.

A-53

A-56 Fire Station
65 South Front Street
A.L. Aydelott and Associates, architects, 1967

A-57 Weathersby Building, and Armisted and Lundee Building
66–70 South Front Street
1890

The building is broken up nicely into three sections on the long south facade on Union by pairs of pilasters that frame round arches. Instead of placing a keystone in the center of each arch, the architect took portions of the brick out, leaving a void that implies a keystone—a clever use of a negative space.

A-58   A-59

A-58   Reichman-Crosby Company
>   60 South Front Street
>   1875, facade c. 1910

The building was probably constructed around 1875, but it got a new front early in this century. The first floor of this elegant building has been altered, although the southern third still shows the original cast-iron piers. Elaborate shell niches over the second-floor windows give this building a richness of architectural detail unusual for the street. Reichman-Crosby was not a cotton firm, but a mill supply house; perhaps that fact accounts for the difference.

A-59   Hart Building
>   48 South Front Street
>   B.C. Alsup, architect (?), c. 1899

Architecturally, this was the fanciest building on the block until Reichman-Crosby got its new front. Above the straightforward second floor is a curious top floor that has two windows with huge stone lintels in the center. To the sides of these windows appear two strong round arches that have no relationship to the actual structure of the building as it rises from the ground, even though their shape suggests that they perform an important supporting function. The inner end of each arch is actually set over a void in the structure below. B.C. Alsup played a similar game with stone

A-60

arches and cast-iron street level supports in his Gallina Building on Beale Street in 1891 (D-10), and so it is entirely possible that he was responsible for this facade as well. Originally, a steeply-pointed pediment rose over the center of the facade, but now it is gone.

A-60   Mid-South Cotton Growers Association Building

44 South Front Street
Walk C. Jones, Walk C. Jones, Jr., architects, 1936

This restrained Art Deco building has concrete walls finished to a remarkably high degree of smoothness. Into this elegant surface, abstract classical elements are incised in the shallowest of grooves to pick up shadows in the most circumspect way. For years this building was used in advertisements for the Portland Cement Association as an outstanding example of what could be done in concrete construction. Contrast this treatment of concrete with the same architects' proto-Brutalist work on the National Guard Armory four years later (J-2).

A-61   Little Tea Shop

67–69–71 Monroe Avenue
Estes Mann, architect of remodeling, 1955

Mann had to deal with three doors in one small facade. He put the one in the middle dynamically off center, under an asymmetrical marquee that makes very discrete use of neon. Mann's interior unfortunately has disappeared in a later restoration, but the good southern cooking that has come from this kitchen since 1918 has not.

A-62   Shrine Building

66 Monroe Avenue
Jones and Furbringer, Hanker and Cairns, associated architects, 1923
Antonio Bologna, architect for renovation and reconstruction, 1976

The Al Chymia Shrine Temple wanted a multi-purpose building that would house its own headquarters and provide rental income. Ground-floor storefronts and then professional offices, treated on the exterior as all alike, took up the first eight floors. These supported the Shriners' quarters not only economically but also literally. The temple proper began on the ninth floor with a billiard room (should one say pool hall?), which required only the daylight provided by small windows. (Many of these small windows have been replaced by larger ones, to light apartments now located where once the Shriners shot pool.) The two-story, segmentally-arched windows of the next level mark a large, two-story auditorium. The floor above the arches was given over to a lounge, with an elegantly coffered

A-62

ceiling and a library with flat groin vaults reminiscent of the buildings of Sir John Soane. The top floor housed a restaurant with great views of the river. The vaguely Spanish cupola that once rose over the center of the south facade unfortunately had to be removed for structural reasons. Until one understands what went on in this building, the changes on the exterior seem capricious instead of suggested by the functions inside. Below ground, there is a handsome swimming pool.

Struck down by the Depression, the Shriners moved out in 1936, when they could no longer meet their mortgage payments. In the recent conversion to apartments, supervised by Antonio Bologna, much of the original interior of the Shriners' floors was preserved.

A-63a.   Cossitt-Goodwyn Library

A-63   Cossitt-Goodwyn Library

33 South Front Street
Office of Walk C. Jones, Jr., architects, 1958 (front)
E. L. Harrison, architect, 1924 (rear)

In 1958, the first Cossitt Library building was torn down and replaced by the Jones wing, a modernist box raised on pilotis once covered in small blue mosaic tile but now painted beige. The glass upper floors are shaded from the sun by vertical louvers set on angle. These too were originally blue. The old building was one of the few great monumental structures in the city. Unfortunately, the new lived up all too well to the criticism often launched at modern architecture—that it could not be monumental. Behind the modern box, and uncomfortably joined to it, is the red sandstone addition that E.L. Harrison, undoubtedly helped by Nowland Van Powell, put onto the red sandstone original structure. On the north, west, and south facades of this wing two little colonettes and a gable cleverly unite paired arches that rise over the windows. This design surely was Powell's idea. All of the ornament is made of cast stone, except for a small portion of carved stone on the northeast corner, which is very easy to pick out.

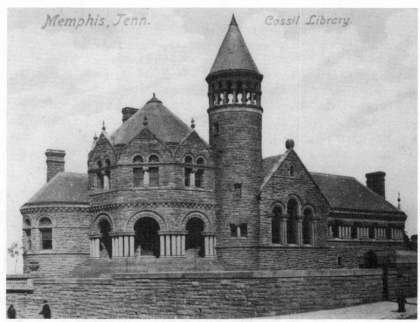

A-63b. Cossitt Library, 1893

A-63 (Lost Memphis) Cossitt Library

M.L.B. Wheeler, Atlanta, architect, 1893

The loss of no old building in Memphis is more regrettable than that of the Cossitt Library, an imposing Romanesque structure of great power and dignity. Set grandly back from the street on a broad terrace, it welcomed readers with a triple arched portal broken into three planes that related to the street corner and the two streets that intersected there. To the north rose a round tower topped by a light gallery. To the west, a great terrace was built over the bluff, so that the view of the library from the river, still an important view in the 1890s, was of a building of strength. The library tower and the two towers of the Customs House next door formed three great verticals that marked Memphis as a special event in the thousand miles of horizontal landscape along the lower Mississippi.

Before 1893 Memphis had no public library. The building was given to the city by the daughters of Frederick Cossitt, who had lived in Memphis for a time before moving on to New York to make a great fortune. With the erection of this prominent monument, culture and learning seemed at long last to occupy an important place in the city.

A-64 U.S. Customs House, Courthouse, and Post Office

1 South Front Street
James G. Hill, architect, 1876
James Knox Taylor, architect for addition, 1903
James Alexander Wetmore, Supervising Architect of the
Treasury, architect for rebuilding, 1929–30
Eason, Anthony, McKinnie, and Cox, architects for
restoration, 1960
Thorn, Howe, Stratton and Strong, architects
for remodeling, 1983

James Hill's Customs House (A-64b) stood proud on the bluff. Its two towers marked the presence of the city for passersby on the river, while the stacked porticos on the east front made a dramatic backdrop to the bustle of bankers on Madison, of which the building formed the visual terminus. Although the towers are gone, parts of Hill's Italian Villa Customs House still lurk inside the present building. The banded columns of its original lobby are partly hidden behind the lobby windows of the 1929–30 post office.

Taylor did nothing in 1903 to change the first structure's appearance from Madison, and relatively little from the river. He simply added a stone block of a building to the west, between the towers, that looked as if it could have been there from the beginning. This block is still visible in the center of the west facade.

Wetmore in 1929 was faced with the need to enlarge the building considerably, and he did so by tearing down the tops of the towers and embracing the old buildings in new spaces, enfolded in a great wall of granite, on the south, east, and north (A-64a). On the east he applied a row of paired columns based on those of the East Front of the Louvre in Paris. Sen. Kenneth D. McKellar was responsible for the existence of this colonnade.

A-64a

A-64b

When he saw the preliminary designs, he told Wetmore to add columns to
the building, so that it would harmonize with the Shelby County Courthouse and the new Bank of Commerce. The senator's taste in civic architecture seems to have been developed at the feet of the City Beautiful
Movement.

The grandeur of the lobby matches that of the facade. In the lobby,
Wetmore cleverly set his columns and the post office windows opposite
them in a complicated pattern that hides the fact that the intervals on his
facade don't line up with the columns of Hill's interior of 1876, which can
be glimpsed behind the windows. For many years the feet of Memphians,
mailing letters and packages, wore grooves in the marble floor of this space
that is grand enough for ancient Romans. Now the lobby is limited to
"authorized personnel." If you aren't "authorized," some grim-faced civil
servant will glare at you if you dare come in to look. Go in and glare back.
The public post office has been shoved into a cramped, ugly space on the
north side of the building. *Sic transit gloria populi.*

A-65   Union Planters National Bank

> 2 South Front Street
> McKim, Mead and White, New York, architects, 1924
> Hanker and Cairns, then Hanker and Heyer, architects for
> addition and remodeling, 1937

The original portion of this building can be seen in the first five bays coming up Madison from Front. The four bays to the east are a later addition.
In the center of these first five bays is the original door, and above that is

A-65

an elaborate coat of arms with swags and ribbons. The cool Beaux-Arts architecture of McKim, Mead and White is more that of Madison Avenue, New York, than Madison Avenue, Memphis.

A-66 Falls Building

> 20–22 North Front Street
> John Gaisford, architect, 1909–12
> Bullock-Smith and Partners, Knoxville, architects for renovation, 1984

The Falls Building was designed to stack the cotton men of Front Street vertically, since space for their lateral expansion was limited. The very wide windows of the Falls Building were designed to let in as much light

A-66   A-68

as possible, to facilitate the classing of cotton. On top of the building there opened, in July 1914, the Alaskan Roof Garden, named for the cooling breezes that blew in from the river. Here the orchestra leader, W.C. Handy, conducted the premiere performance of his own composition, "St. Louis Blues," in November 1914. The Depression shut the Alaskan Roof Garden down, but the idea of dancing on a roof came back in the late thirties with the Plantation Roof atop the Peabody Hotel. The renovation of 1984 turned the Falls Building to face the great greensward created by the destruction of all the buildings on the block to its north to make way for the Morgan Keegan Tower.

A-67   Confederate Park

1908

In the 1819 plan of Memphis, the waterfront slope up to Front Street between Jackson and Union was given to the city as a "Public Promenade." Of this promenade, only Confederate Park still stands unencumbered, probably because of its inglorious early history as the city dump. Garbage was carried here by citizens, then transported on a barge to the middle of the river to be scattered on the Father of Waters. The originator of the idea for the park was Robert Galloway, then chairman of the city Park Commission. Galloway wanted to install a "crumbling stone wall and silent cannon" as a memorial to the defeated Confederacy, despite the fact that no fortress had ever stood here, and despite the fact that the ninety-minute Battle of Memphis, which took place on the river in front of the city, was not a particularly glorious chapter in Confederate military history. The park actually boasts a statue of Jefferson Davis, a plaque inscribed with the Ten Commandments, and artillery from World War II set behind thin stone walls that don't even come close to Galloway's idea of a ruined fort.

A-68   Morgan Keegan Tower

50 North Front Street
Norman Hoover of 3D/International, Houston, architect, 1986

The Morgan Keegan Tower, the first large office building erected downtown after the Bank of Commerce tower, is a building that never made up its mind what it wanted to be. Four different schemes are at work, and they don't necessarily hang together. Basically the tower is a standard developer's box, lit by the square windows that have become one of the clichés of the postmodern movement. A huge diagonal has been sliced off one corner of the box to open up splendid views of the river to the southwest. This is a bold stroke that makes visual sense both inside and out. (It isn't clear, however, why the ground floor of the slice needs a great truss system, while the floors above it do not.) The descending terraces of the offices above the slice are a third idea. With their sloping glass roofs, they seem motivated by the fact that the offices under the sloping roofs of Johnson and Burgee's Pennzoil Building in Houston turned out to fetch a higher rent than the offices inside standard straight walls. Idea number four is the off-center tower, complete with pediments with circles in them, another *sine qua non* of commercial postmodernism. Visible from afar, this tower clearly is the monumental part, and it supposedly makes a contextual comment on the nearby tower of the Lincoln America Building. The Morgan Keegan topknot, however, holds nothing more important than mechanical equipment; the architectural forms with the most inherent meaning and highest visibility merely screen air-conditioning ducts.

This is clearly a Texas building, a minor eastward sally from the *glitz-krieg* being waged in Houston and Dallas. It seems something of an alien creature in Memphis, unless one argues that it is as confused a structure as Memphis' first skyscraper, the nearby Porter Building. The architects have insisted that the building is sensitive to its site, but one doubts that sensitivity to the Porter Building is what they had in mind.

A-69   Mud Island

Riverwalk and River Museum
Roy P. Harrover and Associates, architects, 1974–82

The island descriptively called Mud was dumped on Memphis' doorstep by a ship that ran aground and stayed too long. When it finally moved away, it left behind a sandbar that grew into the pile of dirt one sees today—or almost that pile. To create the Riverwalk, the top of the island had to be raised eighteen feet with silt dredged from the river. On this accidental sandbar now rises one of the finest architectural designs in the city's history.

For many years no-one knew what to do with Mud Island. At one time, there was a landing strip for private planes, but that had to go when the Hernando de Soto Bridge made landing from the north, on a site where the prevailing winds are from the southwest, impossible.

The visit to Mud Island begins on Front Street in a tough, buff-colored,

A-69a. View of Central Tower

mildly Brutalist building where you buy your tickets and board the elevated car, hung from a rugged steel trestle, that takes you over to the island. The car comes in high, so that you have to descend to get to the action. Escalators take you down, aiming your gaze at horizontally framed views of small fragments of the river which the whole island is designed to explain.

When you get down to ground level, the view of the river is blocked by an earth berm that forces you to concentrate on one of Mud Island's two principal attractions: a model of the river itself, cut into the concrete pavement. River water flows through at the same level as the river stage in Memphis on that day. Depth is shown abstractly, through the use of contours. The principal cities and towns along the river are represented by plans carved in slate, while the bridges that cross the river appear as stainless steel bars wide enough to walk on. If you turn right on arrival at the river model, you walk upstream into a flowery courtyard where the river systems that feed the Mississippi are represented vertically in wall reliefs. These reliefs are at a much smaller scale that that of the river model. (At the same scale, they would have become skyscrapers.) The only confusing

A-69b. View looking south

detail here is the relief that shows the Tennessee and Cumberland Rivers, which both flow north to meet the Ohio. These rivers had to be turned upside down on the wall to make their waters flow the way gravity dictates.

South of the courtyard in which you first encounter the model, you find the map of the city of Memphis. Memphis has city limits that encompass an enormous area; this map makes clear just how large that area is. From the terrace above the map of Memphis, you can enjoy one of the most interesting views in the whole complex. From there the river model and the map of Memphis with its bridges can be seen alongside the real thing, with the actual bridges rising out of the river far to the south.

Of all the views in the park, this is the one that makes Harrover's accomplishment clearest. He was actually making a huge piece of sculpture: an abstract representation, at a different scale, of a form occurring in nature. Basically, there is no difference between Harrover's representation of the river at a reduced scale and a one-foot-tall bronze sculpture of a human figure. Both have simply reduced the size of the original. Both also, of course, have abstracted the form that is being represented. Indeed, all sculpture, even the most seemingly realistic, abstracts the forms it purports to imitate. This statement is as true for Harrover's Mississippi as for Michelangelo's David (although the David is larger, not smaller, than life).

All of this effort is expended in the service of helping us to understand the river. Explanatory texts, written by the architect, line the banks of the river model. They contain more information than most of us can take in on one visit, so that repeated visits to the Riverwalk continue to offer new knowledge. You also learn simply by observing the course of the river. Like any good piece of sculpture, this one doesn't tell you everything at once. At the south end of the walk, past New Orleans and Lake Pontchartrain (with its fountain), lies a large pool of water representing the Gulf of Mexico. Here you see exactly how complex the delta of the Mississippi is, and you come to understand why it is so hard to navigate. And here, at long last, Harrover allows you a full view of the river, which looks far greater than the Gulf of Mexico at your feet.

The museum is best experienced as a series of surprises which a guide book should not spoil. There is much to be learned inside about the history of the river and the people who lived and worked on it. In the museum, Harrover had fun building part of a riverboat at actual scale. At the end of the museum, in the last room, he again lets the river itself win out over everything else.

The buildings are very much background buildings—that is, they call attention to the Riverwalk more than to themselves. Harrover saw the problem of designing these buildings as a difficult one. Too small in scale, they would have been dwarfed by the piers and trestles of the Hernando de Soto Bridge and by the skyline of the city. Too large in scale, they would have dominated the experience of the Riverwalk. He chose to do anonymous buildings that are bulky and uningratiating in detail—no Steamboat Gothic frippery here. One may long for a lighter touch in the buildings—after all, this is a place to have fun, as kids do when they wade in the river model. But Harrover did manage to find an architecture that was neither too big nor too small.

The idea for the river model was suggested to Harrover by a retired colonel in the Army Corps of Engineers. The corps itself, near Vicksburg, had built an indoor model of the river in order to study its behavior. That model, however, has neither the cities and towns nor the educational paraphernalia that the Mud Island model includes. Models of geographical phenomena or of cities occurred with some frequency in the architecture of the late 1970s and 1980s, but Harrover's design, fixed in general principles in 1974, may take pride of place historically over the others. In any event, it is a highly original idea that does considerable justice to its subject, one of the great rivers of the world. It is curious that Memphis, which has in the Riverwalk an original idea in which it can take great pride, treats Mud Island with less than the honor due it. Certainly out-of-town architects often put Mud Island first on their list of places to see in the city.

A-70   Hernando de Soto Bridge

> Charles R. Wolff, Jr., of Hazelet and Erdal, Engineers,
> Louisville, chief engineer, opened 1973

The fortuitous looping "M" shape of the central arches of this handsome bridge inspired a local citizen to have them bedecked with lights, so that a large, glowing city initial spans Old Man River at night. When large tows pass beneath, however, the lights have to be put out, so that the tow pilot will not be confused by them and run his barges into the piers. That's why the lights go on and off from time to time.

MARKET AVENUE

A-71   St. Mary's Catholic Church

> 155 Market Avenue
> James B. Cook, architect, 1864–74, steeple (now destroyed)
> 1901

The occupying Union Army helped to lay the cornerstone for this church that was to serve the German Catholic population of the city. Memphis suffered little during the Civil War. The river Battle of Memphis, on 6 June 1862, lasted only ninety minutes, and afterwards everyone who had come down to the bluffs to watch it went about their business. The prosperity of the city was never threatened. Indeed, Memphis profited to no small extent during the war from illegal north-south trade. Thus the construction

A-71

of a major church could be undertaken while the war was still going on. The interior, intended to rival that of St. Peter's Catholic Church (A-83), built a decade earlier, has the same disposition of a tall nave flanked by pointed-arched arcades that lead into aisles only slightly lower than the nave. But the whole is thinner at St. Mary's, and the church is even quite a bit smaller. Cook, an Englishman, simply may not have had it in his heart to do a truly splendid Catholic church. The brick exterior, on the other hand, suggests Calvary Episcopal, whose Gothic tower of 1848, based on English parish church architecture, Cook must have found sufficiently to his taste to emulate at St. Mary's.

A-72 Lauderdale Courts Public Housing

234–274 North Lauderdale Street
J. Frazer Smith, chief architect, 1935–8
Edwin B. Phillips; Everett Woods; William J. Hanker; George Awsumb; Walk C. Jones, Jr.; R.J. Regan; and W.C. Lester, associate architects

The white public housing units that act as companions to the black Dixie Homes (C-38) farther east on Poplar, the Lauderdale Courts share the Dixie Homes' ground-hugging character and some of the same axiality in plan. Market Street, grassed over, forms the central spine that leads from a group of three-story buildings that front the downtown along Third Street through a mix of one- and two-story buildings to the low focus of the ad-

ministrative building on the east side of Lauderdale. This terminus of the
axis is framed by two rows of buildings arranged in half-polygons, with a
curving plantation of magnolias in between. To each side of the main axis,
small courts are developed, or else the buildings are placed to shape minor
cross-axes. The buildings define spaces between them loosely, so that the
whole project seems simultaneously broken up into small, humane areas
and all of a piece. There is little surface modernity on the buildings, which
are marked by an inexpensive Georgianism of proportions and details.
Elvis Presley lived in Lauderdale Courts when he first moved to Memphis.

POPLAR AVENUE

A-73   Shelby County Office Building

157 Poplar Avenue
A.L. Aydelott and Associates, architects, 1959
Zeno Yeates and Associates, associated architects

Local government finally stepped into the twentieth century, architecturally, with this office building for Shelby County. For that reason, and because Aydelott was in many respects the father of modern architecture in
Memphis, the building is historically important. Behind the design, of
course, stands the full weight of the career of one of the great architects of
the century, Le Corbusier, and particularly his Swiss Dormitory at the
University of Paris of 1930, although Aydelott may have been looking at
Corbusier through the filter of Paul Rudolph's Jewett Art Center at Welle-
sley College, finished the year before this building was designed. Aydelott

A-73a

raised the main slab of the building high on thin, Corbusian *pilotis*, but he cheated a bit on Corbusier's principles by tucking considerable space in beneath. The elevated slab is encased in aluminum screens that were guaranteed by Alcoa not to be hospitable to roosting pigeons. They haven't been. The screens, hardly innocent of the ideas that Edward Durrell Stone was propounding in the fifties, are too thin to do much as sun breakers, but they are highly decorative. They also are the reason that the building is known locally as the Bedspring Hotel.

A-73   (Lost Memphis) Temple Israel

Poplar Avenue between Second and Third, south side
James B. Cook, architect, 1884

Among the greatest losses of buildings from the nineteenth century was this grand synagogue, with a huge horseshoe-arch portal squeezed between two tall towers that ended in bulging, open tops. The religious buildings by Cook that have been preserved do not necessarily show him at his best, as this building surely did. The building was abandoned by the congregation for a structure of equally high quality, Jones and Furbringer's temple at the corner of Poplar and Montgomery (C-43).

A-73b

A-74   First United Methodist Church

204 North Second Street
Jacob Snyder, Akron, Ohio, architect, 1887–93

Pepper Memorial
Sunday School Building

Hubert T. McGee, architect, 1924

As each religious group built a new church downtown, the architectural ante was raised a bit. The Methodists weighed in with the first all-stone church, built in materials that had to be brought in from a considerable distance. They chose an architect from Akron, who brought to Memphis the so-called "Akron plan," which involved building a Sunday school structure adjacent to the sanctuary. The partitions between Sunday school and sanctuary were moveable, so that on special days, when greater crowds could be expected, both parts could be united in one interior. Much of the original interior has been compromised in later remodelings.

A-74

A-75

A-75   First Presbyterian Church

166 Poplar Avenue
Edward Culliatt Jones, architect, 1884

The First Presbyterian Church has lost Jones' splendid wooden spire, (see photo) which has been replaced by a masonry tower inferior both in height and in architectural quality. The church itself is raised above a Sunday school floor, the common practice in Memphis churches of the nineteenth century. While the interior has suffered from remodeling, it is noteworthy for the decorative wooden beams Jones placed on the ceiling to hold some very newfangled accoutrements—electric lightbulbs. The bulbs have been replaced by chandeliers of dubious shape that have destroyed the integrity of Jones' design, in which he sought, successfully, to integrate new technology and older decorative forms.

A-76   Shelby County Criminal Justice Center

201 Poplar Avenue
Mahan and Shappley, architects, 1981

The forbidding mien of this building should encourage the renunciation of lives of crime, but there is no evidence that it does.

WASHINGTON AVENUE

A-77   Shelby County Jail

Washington Avenue, north side between
Second and Third Streets
Jones and Furbringer, architects, 1924

This jail, on the other hand, seems less fearsome. It is also no longer in use. The jail is a well-organized long building that does its duty to the urban landscape by looking good from Second and Third streets and to itself by having a grand entrance in its middle.

A-78   Trinity Lutheran Church

210 Washington Avenue
James B. Cook, architect, 1874–88

This modest church, with Sunday school rooms below and sanctuary above, has been unfortunately refaced with Permastone. The construction of Trinity Lutheran took a very long time for such a small building, because of the yellow fever epidemics of the 1870s. Many of the Germans in Memphis fled the fever and never returned, and so the Lutheran church was particularly weakened by the epidemic.

A-77

ADAMS AVENUE

A-79 **Fire Station #1**

118 Adams Avenue
Jones and Furbringer, architects, 1910

A-80 **Police Station**

130 Adams Avenue
Shaw and Pfeil, architects, 1911
George Mahan, Jr., architect for addition, 1959

The classical revival fire station was the first building of its type in Memphis. The original brick pavement can still be seen in front of the building. Both the fire station and the police station next door show local architects' responses to the classical style of the newly-built Shelby County Courthouse to the east. They also show the clear intention of the city's mayor, E. H. Crump, to build, for the first time in its history, a group of monumental public buildings, and to elevate the status of the fire and police departments, whose backing Crump needed, by giving them noble quarters.

A-81   Shelby County Courthouse

140 Adams Avenue
James Gamble Rogers and H.D. Hale, Boston and New York,
architects, 1906–1909
William Rhyne, sculptor
William H. Beaty, architect for renovation, 1987ff.
Hnedak-Bobo Group, architects for interior restoration,
1987ff.

The Shelby County Courthouse represented a major attempt by local government, and indeed by the whole city, to put a handsomer architectural face on things than Memphis had previously enjoyed. The first courthouse had been a log cabin, and the most recent one before Rogers and Hale's was a rented hotel building.

Made of blue Bedford limestone, the courthouse occupies a whole block with the serene classical confidence only a child of the City Beautiful Movement can muster. The most generous part of the very generous exterior is the south face, which has a colonnade stretching the entire length between the two corner pavilions. There is also an elaborate sculptural program, including six seated figures, each carved from a single block of Tennessee marble, representing Wisdom, Justice, Liberty, Authority, Peace, and Prosperity. This building says "Good Government," and says it well.

The south lobby, as long as the outside colonnade, is covered in colored marbles, including one with lively apple-green veins. The building surrounds a handsome courtyard of yellow brick with stone trim. Each of the four wings of the courthouse contains four courtrooms, two to a floor. These are expressed in the courtyard by projecting polygonal bays. The architects turned a particularly neat trick at the cornice line by joining the pairs of multi-sided bays under one strong horizontal.

A-81

The courtrooms are under restoration, some being returned to their original appearance. Some of the original elevators, in their Neo-Grecque steel cages, are also still to be seen. The four staircases, located in the angles of the courtyard, are lit by what may be the largest double-hung windows in captivity.

A-82   Calvary Episcopal Church

102 North Second Street
Rev. Philip Alston, designer, 1843
James B. Cook, architect for renovation, 1881
D. T. McGown, architect for renovation, 1953
Charles Shipp and Robert Browne, architects for additions, 1980

Calvary Episcopal Church Parish House

Jones and Furbringer, architects, 1905

Calvary Church, the oldest surviving public building in the city, has not had a simple building history. The minister who designed the church in 1843 had only a modest grasp of structure; the roof collapsed within a few

A-82

years. This original building, a simple box with pointed-arched windows, consisted of the present nave of the church. The flat east wall of 1843 had perched high up in it the pulpit, reached by a staircase on the outside of the building. The tower was added in 1848, and the east end was added in 1881 by James B. Cook. Cook removed the flat ceiling that had covered the nave and replaced it with the present open-timber roof that gives the church much more a sense of being a real English parish church than it had originally. The 1950s alterations were largely to the altar area, which received the elaborate relief of little niches that it now boasts. At the same time, a passageway decorated with similar forms was added to connect the narthex to the parish house. In 1961, the stucco that had covered the walls (for no-one knows quite how long) was removed to reveal the brick you now see.

A-83   St. Peter's Catholic Church and Parish House

190 Adams Avenue
Patrick C. Keeley, New York, architect, 1852
Antonio Bologna, architect for restoration, 1986

Keeley was the architect the Catholic Church in America chose to make hundreds of church designs to be sent all over the nation, as needed. In that way, the Church was assured of having better designs than were available from local architects in many parts of the country in the mid-nineteenth century. Good architectural design was one means for the church to present itself as an established body, worthy of respect, in a sometimes hostile Protestant land. Certainly Memphis had seen few imposing

A-83

churches before 1852, and St. Peter's made a strong mark on the cityscape. The stucco of the exterior is drafted to look like stone, and the whole exterior, with its crenellations and twin round towers, looks fortress-like, as if the Church wished to project an air of impregnability here on the wild banks of the Mississippi.

The interior is first-rate. The Gothic elements are handled knowingly, and the tall space of the nave, flanked by almost equally tall aisles, has the kind of heavenward ambition that one expects to find in a Gothic building. The stained-glass window over the entrance is one of the best in the city. Dedicated to sons of the parish who lost their lives in World War I, the window curiously was made in Munich, Germany, in the heart of the land of the Hun. The composition, straight out of early seventeenth-century paintings, features a panoply of Dominican saints (more males than females), kneeling warriors in uniform, and a dog, right in the center of everything, holding a lighted torch in its mouth.

A-84   Magevney House

198 Adams Avenue
After 1833

A simple wooden cottage, the Magevney House preserves for us, better than any building still left in town, an idea of what the city must have been like in the first decades after its founding, and indeed up until the period after the Civil War, when such modest frame cottages gave way to the more pretentious masonry structures one sees just to the east on the same street. Presumably, this is the earliest building listed in this book.

A-85   Nineteenth-Century Houses

200 Block of Adams Avenue

This block of Adams contains a few of the remaining houses in Memphis of the well-to-do, rather than the fabulously rich, of the second half of the nineteenth century. Each has its charms, but we like the ones at 246 and 253 in particular.

A-85   (a) Fowlkes-Boyle House

208 Adams Avenue
1850s

A-85   (b) First James Lee House

239 Adams Avenue
Joseph Willis, architect, 1869–70

A-85c

A-85   (c) John S. Toof House

246 Adams Avenue
Mathias Harvey Baldwin, architect, 1873–6

Of the four houses here on Adams, this is probably the best as a work of architecture. The raking cornice over the front door is splendid, as is the play of windows in the gable.

A-85   (d) Mette-Blount House

253 Adams Avenue
Edward Culliatt Jones and Mathias Harvey Baldwin, architects, 1872

An aggressive keystone in the arch of the main door rises up into the second floor. This idea is repeated three times in the way the keystones of the second-story windows push up into the attic.

A-86 Memphis Branch, Federal Reserve Bank of St. Louis

Jefferson Avenue and North Third Street, northwest corner
Mauran, Russell and Crowell, St. Louis, architects, 1929
Jones and Furbringer, associate architects

A-87 One Memphis Place

200 Jefferson Avenue
Bologna and Associates, architects, 1985

A glassy black box with a few zigs and zags to enliven the surface. The
building has been hard to rent, and so local wags have dubbed it "One
Empty Place."

A-88 Blue Cross/Blue Shield Building

85 North Danny Thomas Boulevard
O.T. Marshall, architect, 1969

A very taut-skinned rectangular building, in which the glass of the windows has been brought up right into the plane of the masonry of the facade. The "attic story," created by the skillful later addition of two al-
most-all-glass floors at the top, suggests that this is basically a classical
building with all decoration removed. The effect of the whole depends
almost entirely on proportions and disposition of parts, the same proportions and disposition of parts that Jones and Furbringer used in their
nearby Masonic Temple on the corner of Court and Fourth (A-95). Indeed,
in this design Marshall may have been making a deliberate comment on
that older building.

A-88

A-89   B. Lowenstein and Brothers Wholesale Store

North Court Avenue
H.J. Hain, architect, 1897–98

Hain was associated with E.C. Jones in the design of the Porter Building across the square, and then he struck out on his own. Here he presents us with a rather classical tall building with strongly-marked corners and restrained decorations, including the wreaths to each side that echo, in reverse curves, the arches below them.

A-90   Burch, Porter and Johnson Offices

(formerly Tennessee Club)
130 North Court Avenue
Edward Terrel, Columbus, Ohio, architect, 1890
Awsumb and Williamson, architects for renovation,
1983–84

On the outside, the building combines several architectural styles from around the Mediterranean basin into something that can be called Hispano-Mooresque without going too far wrong or slighting the building's quirkiness too much. The exterior is well-preserved, except for the filling in of the balconies over the main entrance, an act that compromised that

A-90

section of the facade seriously. The bay immediately to the west of the door has a really splendid variety of window shapes that bleed into one another. The circular motifs introduced by the horseshoe arch of this bay and by the round corner turret are played out on the interior in a number of circular rooms, including small card rooms, private dining rooms and the round ballroom on the top floor, the dome of which is visible from the Second Street side.

Awsumb and Williamson handled the renovation of the building to the west of the Tennessee Club in a very sensitive way. The new windows have been recessed behind the original facade to show that the inside is new but the outside is old. To the west side of this building, they added a shallow new space that takes its cues, in terms of curved shapes, from the outside of the old club.

COURT AVENUE

A-91   Welcome Wagon Building

(formerly Commercial Appeal Building)
145 Court Avenue
Shaw and Pfeil, architects, 1907

The more important facade of this building is the narrower one, because it faces Court Square. The architects solved this problem by giving the narrow side the greater relief of a pair of Ionic columns, instead of the flat

A-91

pilasters they applied to the longer flank. To give the longer side coherence and variety, they broke it into five sections, with those at the corners and center projecting slightly.

The building begins with a rusticated basement that carries two floors organized by the giant orders of columns or pilasters. On the pilasters of the Court Street side they glopped cast-stone ornaments at the top and bottom to emphasize the pilasters' verticality. That verticality is carried up into the attic story by the application of additional heavy cast-stone ornament there. In most of their large downtown buildings, such as the Business Men's Club (A-29) and the Tennessee Trust Building (A-21), Shaw and Pfeil followed the same procedure of using applied ornament, generally derived from no particular historical source, to hold their buildings together vertically. Of their downtown buildings, this is the most sophisticated and complex.

A-92   Dermon Building

Court Avenue and North Second Street, northeast corner
Pfeil and Awsumb, architects, 1925

This building contains more architectural variation than first meets the eye. The central pavilion is wider than the other bays. These others may all seem alike, but they aren't. To strengthen the corners visually, the architects used wider piers. This move forced them to set the windows between the piers closer together. Yellow and green terra cotta ornaments

A-95

placed against brown brick set the building apart coloristically from the rest of the city. The Dermon Building has one of the first cast-in-place, steel-reinforced, concrete-frame structures in Memphis.

A-93 American Legion Building

251 Court Avenue
Thomas Faires, architect, 1955

A Frank Lloyd Wright Prairie Style house converted to a downtown American Legion headquarters, built on the site of the first house Jefferson Davis lived in when he came to Memphis after the Civil War to go into the insurance business. The other house he lived in in Memphis, also on Court Avenue, was torn down to provide part of the expansive parking lot across the street from a telephone building.

A-94 Nathan, Pounders, Evans and Taylor Offices

(formerly A.N. Kellogg Newspaper Company)
265 Court Avenue
Jones and Furbringer, architects, 1905–1906
Gassner, Nathan and Browne, architects for renovation, 1968

The building gets its power from the relentless rhythm of round brick arches marching down the Fourth Street flank.

A-95 Masonic Temple

272 Court Avenue
Jones and Furbringer, architects, 1914

The Masonic Temple brings together a host of materials that might seem uncontrollable: a granite base; white Roman brick and brown brick walls; yellow cast-ceramic ornament; green glazed terra cotta; bronze door, lamps, and transom; iron balconies; cast-stone cornice; and yellow-veined marble panels in the attic. Even these may not quite be all. Jones and Furbringer brought them under control, however, through the simplicity and clarity of the structure and its proportions. The building is a plain rectangular box, subdivided into smaller elements by the application of ornamental bands which give the structure an extraordinary richness of texture and color. The short side, which has the principal entrance, is enriched by the three-dimensional effects of the columns and the porch beneath them, as well as by the grand staircase marked by bronze lamps. The principal view is from the southwest, where the two street fronts can be viewed simultaneously. The Scottish Rite Temple on Union (C-15), opposite Forrest Park, was the architects' warmup for this building, which is one of their very best. The Blue Cross/Blue Shield Building (A-88), nearby on Jefferson, may be a modern comment on it.

A-96   119 Madison Avenue

1917

This Gothic tile-front building fits very well, in terms of scale, with the Banker's Row buildings that used to line this street.

A-97   Second Goodwyn Institute Building

(formerly Commercial Bank,
then First National Bank Building)
127 Madison Avenue
James Gamble Rogers, New York, and Neander M. Woods,
Jr., architects, 1909
Jones and Furbringer, architects for addition, 1929

This slender skyscraper rises from a thin, conservative lower level marked by round arches and pilasters. One suspects that the classical hand of Rogers was more active here than the hand of Woods. To the south, along Second Street, the arches of the base were continued in the later addition by Jones and Furbringer.

This building and the Exchange Building across the street, designed a year later by Woods on his own, make a fine pair of buildings on an urban corner. Their stone bases are about the same height, and they use the same color scheme of red brick and white cast-stone ornament in the office stories of their towers. Even the detailing of the stone ornament in the horizontal floor slabs is analogous. When the First National Bank (now First Tennessee Bank) acquired the land occupied by the original Goodwyn Institute Building to build its present headquarters at Madison and Third (A-101), the Goodwyn Institute was given this, the bank's old building, as part of the deal.

A-98   Exchange Building

9 North Second Street
Neander M. Woods, Jr., architect, 1910

At nineteen stories, the Exchange Building was the tallest in the city for almost twenty years. Woods, on his own, became more exuberant and daring than he had been across the street in partnership with the older and more famous Rogers. Classicism still shows up in the triumphal arch that forms the entrance from Second. This arch is then echoed high up in the giant order of engaged columns on the top floors. The recessed central portion of the facade and the flanking wings terminate in the hefty French chateau, vaguely seventeenth-century in shape, that forms the surprising roofscape. Indeed, the Exchange Building has the fanciest skyscraper top in

A-97a
and
A-98a

town. Green tile was originally intended for the roof, instead of the actual copper. This was the first major office building in the city that deliberately turned its back on the river. The view from Main Street shows none of the rather lavish articulation of the walls that one sees from Madison or Second.

The Exchange Building was a joint venture of the Memphis Merchants Exchange and the Memphis Cotton Exchange. It replaced the four-story, Romanesque, Memphis Cotton Exchange that had opened on the same site in 1885.

A-98 (Lost Memphis) Memphis Cotton Exchange Building

Madison Avenue and Second Street, northwest corner
Mathias Harvey Baldwin, architect, 1883–85

This was the second great commercial structure that Baldwin built in the downtown area, the other being the Lowenstein's store at Main and Jefferson (A-15). This one was more complex in terms of the play of planes on the facade and more straightforwardly classical in its detailing. On the wider Second Street front, three bays projected forward at both corners to

A-98b

form two large Palladian motifs. The central bay of these three was pulled forward still farther, and this projection continued up four stories into the big dormers that came out of the roof. The triangular shapes of the dormers were taken up in the pediment placed over the main door. Over all of this pushing and pulling of planes rose a complex roof with pyramidal forms over the two ends. Woods may have kept Baldwin's roof in mind when he designed the roof of the building that replaced this one.

A-99   First Marx and Bensdorf Building

> 152 Madison Avenue
> Jones and Furbringer, architects, 1913

This small building, at original Bankers' Row scale, is faced with cast glazed-ceramic panels that give the building considerable sculptural richness.

A-100 Leader Federal Building

> 158 Madison Avenue
> Office of Walk C. Jones, Jr., architects, 1961–62
> Francis Mah, principal designer

A-101a

A-101 First Tennessee Bank Building

165 Madison Avenue
Office of Walk C. Jones, Jr., architects, 1961–64

This building adapts Mies van der Rohe's Seagram Building in New York, of the mid-1950s, to Memphis circumstances. Mies' bronzed-steel frame and purple glass were replaced by less expensive materials, but the building is similarly set back on a plaza, lifted off the ground on square piers, and capped at the top by a band of metal panels that replace the glass windows below. The First Tennessee building was the first tall building in Memphis of a truly modernist cast. South of the tower, a low wing containing the bank lobby extends to Monroe.

Inside the spacious lobby are exhibited the works of art that comprise the First Tennessee Heritage Collection, composed of images related to the history of the state. Carroll Cloar's *Historic Encounter Between E.H. Crump and W.C. Handy on Beale St.* (1964), is a painting not to be missed, if only for its wonderful view of the Old Daisy Theater (D-13). Behind the long row of tellers' cages is a mural on the themes of the history and geography of the state. This is the work of a Memphis artist, Ted Faiers, that was completed by Betty Gilow after Faiers' unexpected death. It is one of the very few examples in the city of a large work of art commissioned by a business for the enjoyment of the public.

A-101b

A-102a

A-101 (Lost Memphis) Goodwyn Institute Building

165 Madison Avenue
Alsup and Woods, architects, 1904–1907

The Goodwyn Institute was established by the will of William A. Goodwyn (d. 1889) as a cultural center for the city. Inside the building, an auditorium for lectures was located behind the giant order of columns on the facade, and there was also a reference library. These spaces and their activities were supported by the rental of the other parts of the structure. Alsup and Woods here produced an even more elaborate fantasy on a Beaux-Arts theme than the one they produced at about the same time for the Oliver cold-storage building on Front Street (A-50). The columns from the facade still survive on the front of a house on South McLean (F-97). When the First National Bank acquired this site for its new building, it traded its old building at Second and Madison to the Goodwyn Institute. The institute was subsequently disbanded, and its library was merged with the collection of the Cossitt Library on Front Street.

A-102   Sterick Building

Madison Avenue and Third Street, northeast corner
Wyatt C. Hedrick, Fort Worth, architect, 1928–30

The Sterick Building was financed by Hedrick's father-in-law, R.E. Sterling of Houston, as a real estate venture. The building's name is a combination of their names. At 365 feet tall, with twenty-nine floors above ground, it became the tallest building, not just in the city, but also in the South. For this design, Hedrick helped himself liberally to the massing and details of Eliel Saarinen's runner-up entry in the Chicago Tribune Building Competition of 1921. In his design, Saarinen had tried to create a modern Gothic style appropriate to skyscrapers, and his design had a wide influence in this country, even though he didn't win the competition.

The Sterick Building has not been treated perfectly by time. In 1947 the nine-foot cast-stone Gothic spires had to be removed from the thirteenth, twenty-eighth and twenty-ninth floors, because repeated lightning strikes had split them. The original color was the light gray of the building's limestone and granite stonework and of the cast-concrete panels that covered most of its upper floors. It was painted for the first time in the sixties, and in 1982 it was sandblasted and painted the present unfortunate pale yellow with dark brown and maroon trim. The roof was originally green. At the time of this writing, a new owner intends to restore the original color by painting over the yellow, brown, and maroon.

A-102b

A-102 (Lost Memphis) Napoleon Hill House

> Madison Avenue and Second Street, northeast corner
> Edward Culliatt Jones, architect, 1880

The Hill House was Memphis's gaudiest and finest example of robber-baron Victorian. Hill had been in San Francisco before coming to Memphis to make his fortune as a cotton merchant and financier, and it may be that memories of the architectural bravura he had seen there persisted in this house. For Hill, Jones produced a truly baroque design, perhaps based in part on Lucas von Hildebrandt's Belvedere Palace in Vienna. A three-bay porch, with an elaborately curved central arch, stood in front of a bold three-story tower from which two arms advanced to embrace the porch. The chimneys atop the arms stood like sentinels guarding the tower.

A-103 Scimitar Building

> Madison Avenue and Third Street, southeast corner
> Chighizola and Hanker, architects, 1902–3

When the Scimitar Building was built by Napoleon Hill, he owned all four corners of Madison and Second, including the site of his own house. He apparently wanted this structure to complement his house, for it looks more like a large New York townhouse on Fifth or Madison Avenues than an office building. From the windows of his house, or from his grand front porch, he could admire his own initials carved into the Madison Avenue facade. There is a winning detail under the cornice: a row of lions drooling *fleur-de-lis.*

A-104 Boatman's Bank

> (formerly Commercial and Industrial Bank Building)
> 200 Madison Avenue
> Gassner, Nathan and Browne, architects, 1974

Outside, this building has the geometric purity of a child's triangular building block. Inside, however, things aren't so simple. You walk from the sidewalk into a jungle: a conservatory that surprisingly turns the inside into the outside. Light for the plants comes through the south-facing sloping glass roof held up by boldly-scaled steel trusses. Beyond the plants is a simple four-story concrete office-building facade that has the remarkable effect of making you enter the building again before you can find the real inside. Low steps lead up through this facade to the banking room, which is treated as if it were a portico.

   This building predates the energy crisis; the shape with the sloping glass roof was dictated by a desire for a particular kind of spatial experience rather than for heat gain. That spatial experience is one of the most interesting in the city.

A-105 S.C. Toof Company

> 195 Madison Avenue
> George M. Shaw, architect, 1913

This brick building with terra cotta ornament is the earliest but least successful of the three Egyptian Revival commercial buildings in Memphis. Shaw was a better architect than one might suspect from the Toof Building; witness his first-rate Crawford House at the corner of Madison and East Parkway (F-146). The fifth floor of the Toof Building was added in 1926.

A-106 Hickman Building

> (formerly Medical Arts Building)
> 240 Madison Avenue
> Tietig and Lee, Cincinnati, architects, 1925–26

The only really good Gothic office building in the city. Four different patterns of terra cotta panels run diagonally across the front of the building to achieve great variety at small expense. This riot of Gothic tracery covers a standard concrete frame building. On the seventh floor, a pinnacle, added over the windows, leads up to the Gothic spires above the windows of the top floor. The top two floors appear to have curved windows, but this is an illusion created by curved ornamental window casings. Only the mezzanine-level windows are actually curved, because they are too close to the ground to get away easily with the trick used up top.

   The ground floor was remodeled in 1952 by the architect J.H. Perrell, and the terra cotta was replaced by slabs of red and black granite, which have suffered badly by being within reach of passersby.

A-104

A-107

A-107 Central YMCA Building

245 Madison Avenue
John Gaisford, architect, 1909

Although this was the first building in Memphis to be constructed entirely
of reinforced concrete, what is striking about the exterior is the lavish use
of ornament, all of which is made of cast ceramic, the same versatile material Gaisford used in the Lenox School (F-121). From a distance, the very
well-made ceramic easily passes for much more expensive carved stone.
Second Empire ornament runs riot on the ground floor and engulfs the
arches of the top floor with florid abandon. The contrast with the plain
walls of the second through fifth floors is extreme. William Howard Taft,
our most opulently upholstered president, appropriately dedicated the
building in October 1909, with twenty-seven state governors in atten-
dance.

A-108 Offices of Mockbee, Coker, Howorth, Architects

257 Madison Avenue
Mockbee, Coker, Howorth, architects for remodeling, 1986

A sensitive adaptation of an old building. By pushing back the ground-floor windows, the architects created a porch deep enough to hold a spiral staircase that leads up to an office and apartment. While the staircase and metal frames for the downstairs window and door look very modern, they are separated from the sidewalk by a wrought-iron fence that convincingly looks the age of the building. Thus the whole front plane of the building remains old in appearance, with the new kept behind.

MONROE AVENUE

A-30a National Bank of Commerce Building

Monroe Avenue and Second Street, southwest corner

See description above.

A-109 Leader Federal Building

(formerly Second Marx and Bensdorf Building)
42 South Second Street
Hanker and Cairns, architects, 1928

The south side of Monroe at Second offers a third pair of downtown buildings that work well together visually. In the Leader Federal Building we have a Corinthian response to the Doric Bank of Commerce across the street. In this case, as in the case of the First National Bank and Exchange buildings a block to the north, the same designer was responsible for both structures, and so one can say that it was all carefully planned. Cairns balanced the simpler but three-dimensional Doric order of the bank with the richer but flat Corinthian pilasters of Leader Federal.

A-110 A.R. Taylor Company

(formerly Clapp and Taylor)
18 South Second Street
c. 1890?

A good solid stone Romanesque Revival commercial building.

A-111 Salvation Army Building

(formerly YWCA Building)
200–202 Monroe Avenue
George Awsumb, architect, 1949–51

This is one of the city's last gasps of classicism as it succumbed to the attacks from modernism. While Awsumb tried to make the YWCA graceful and gracious with its courtyard and wrought-iron trim, he succeeded only in making it look a bit glum. Symmetry is not always everything. Actually, Awsumb was generally much happier when working in a medieval style.

A-112 H.T. Bruce Building

260 Monroe Avenue
Edward Culliatt Jones, architect, 1903

This posthumous work of Jones has a stretched-out, flat castle facade broken up into eleven parts. The high central pavilion has a single large arched entrance, pairs of arches on the second floor, and triple-arched windows on the third floor. The attic that rises over all this has a double sawtooth frieze. The central part is the only one to have three stories. From the center, a progressive low-high-low-high stepping down to the outer corners takes place. The relief here is very thin; the differences in wall plane between the bays is never more than one brick in thickness. Now painted yellow with brown trim, the building originally was the dark red-brown color of the brick underneath. Cornerstones at each end bear the date, "May 20, 1903"; Jones had died the year before. This castellated livery stable brings to mind the castellated Tennessee Brewery (D-26), but the two hardly seem the products of the same architectural sensibility.

UNION AVENUE

A-113 Peabody Hotel

149 Union Avenue
Walter Ahlschlager, Chicago, architect, 1925

The large new Peabody Hotel opened on 2 September 1925, its outside walls modestly decorated, particularly toward the top, by some Spanish ornament. Architecturally, the best part of the building is the lobby, which is ample in size and as handsomely detailed as a Chicago architect's dream of an oversized Spanish hunting lodge could make it. The center of it all is a fountain, wishfully Bernini-esque, made of a single block of Travertine. In 1932, the hotel manager, Frank Schutt, returned from a hunting trip with some live ducks, which he put in the fountain. The ducks have become a tradition. Each morning they descend from their roost on the roof and

A-113. Peabody Hotel, c. 1925.

waddle proudly across a red carpet from elevator to fountain. At cocktail time they make an equally incongruous retreat. Ever since it was built (with the exception of a few bad years when the hotel went bankrupt), the Peabody lobby has served as the living room of the city, and even as the crossroads of this part of the world. The restoration of the Peabody in the 1980s to its original splendor gave the downtown a real boost. There is nothing fake here, only a genuine 1920s Spanish fable.

Other worthy parts of the hotel are found on the top floor. The sleek Art Deco Skyway, with a circular dancefloor covered by a low dome lit by concealed lights, was added by George Mahan, Jr., and Nowland Van Powell in 1938. You can imagine Fred and Ginger dancing here, although they never did. Powell alone was responsible for the outdoor Plantation Roof. He capitalized on the *Gone with the Wind* craze and provided summertime diners and dancers with a deliciously fake, Tara-in-the-sky backdrop.

There are also some elegantly turned-out rooms on the lobby level and the mezzanine, particularly the ballroom, which boasts a plethora of Renaissance ornament.

A-114 Radison Plaza Hotel, west wing

> (formerly Hotel Tennessee)
> Union Avenue and Third Street, southeast corner
> Hanker and Cairns, architects, 1927–28

A-115

A-116

A-115 Commercial Buildings

87–91 South Second Street
After 1899

These are the last two all-cast-iron storefronts left in town. There once were many more like them.

A-116 (Lost Memphis) Central Baptist Church

398 South Second Street, between Gayoso and Beale
Edward Culliatt Jones, architect, 1868–85

Somewhere in the present wasteland of parking lots that lie to the south of the Peabody Hotel once stood Jones' most audacious church tower, which was also, in its day, the tallest one in the city. The sanctuary behind was simple, but in the tower Jones let forms burst out on top of each other with an energy that must have stunned passersby in the street below. In the nineteenth century, Memphis had more than ninety churches, all located in or near the downtown area. Of those, fewer than twenty still stand.

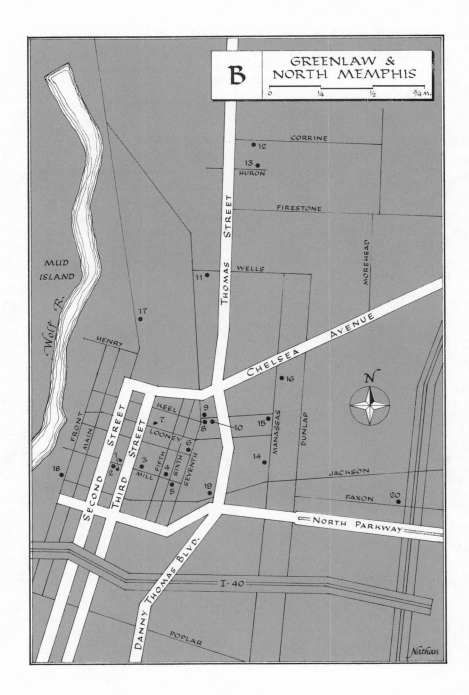

CORRINE

12

13
HURON

FIRESTONE

MOREHEAD

MUD
ISLAND

WELLS

11

Wolf R.

17

HENRY

CHELSEA   AVENUE

16

N

KEEL   9

FRONT   7

MAIN   LOONEY   8   10   15   MANASSAS   DUNLAP

SECOND   STREET   G   14

THIRD   STREET   1   3   FIFTH   4   SIXTH   SEVENTH

18   2   MILL

JACKSON

5   19   FAXON   20

NORTH   PARKWAY

DANNY THOMAS BLVD.   I-40

POPLAR

Nathan

B   Greenlaw and North Memphis

This part of the city, bounded on the south by Interstate 40, on the east by Interstate 240, on the north by the Wolf River, and on the west by the Mississippi, is largely residential, giving way to industrial wastelands as you head north. Chelsea, Jackson, and North Parkway are the three great east-west arteries, and the only north-south through street of any consequence is Thomas, as U.S. Highway 51 is called as it passes through this part of Memphis.

If fine houses are what you are after, or even once-fine houses, then this is the wrong part of town. Almost since its initial development, this has been staunchly working-class Memphis. It's true that the Greenlaw brothers had grand ideas when, in 1856, they laid out this first official addition to the original city north of Bayou Gayoso. (This bayou was what anyone outside of Memphis and Louisiana would call a creek. Don't spend any time looking for it; it long ago disappeared without a trace, save as a wiggly line on old maps and a memory in the minds of some oldtimers.) Greenlaw's addition, as it was called in the nineteenth century, was to have shady streets and granite curbs. The appeal was obviously to the carriage trade. The shady streets still remain, but if there were ever any granite curbs, they must have disappeared along with the bayou.

Greenlaw, strictly speaking, comprises the thirty or so blocks within the area bounded on the west by North Main, on the north by Kerr, on the east by Seventh, and on the south by Auction/Jackson. The most striking thing about this subdivision is that it continues the original grid plan of the plan of 1819 without deviation. It is the clearest extant evidence that the expansion of Memphis was assumed to be northward, at least through the middle of the nineteenth century. The Greenlaws were banking on this assumption, as they hawked their suburban vision of cobblestone streets shaded by sycamores and lined by those granite curbstones. They found takers, but for every two-story house built, ten cottages were put up. This working-class housing continues to give the neighborhood its character.

B-1   Shotgun Houses
500 Block of North Third Street
1890s

Because of the way the neighborhood developed, its architectural significance is often more apparent block by block than house by house. For example, the row of shotgun houses on the west side of the street here

B-1

B-2a

B-2b

shows clearly that even the humblest type of Memphis house could be given something "fine." Although these structures are in sad shape, their builder (not architect) knew what was selling downtown and adapted it to what could be built here. The gingerbread decoration is well done and almost makes one forget that behind the trim is an absolutely irreducible basic house.

The shotgun—one room wide and two or more rooms deep, with a porch across the gable-ended street front—is a common house type for poor blacks and poor whites all over the South. Both W.C. Handy and Elvis Presley were born in one. Apparently the type was first developed for slave quarters on plantations in Haiti, by fusing a traditional house type of the native population of the island with a house type common among the Africans brought to Haiti as slaves. Free Haitian blacks lived in shotguns as well. Many of these free blacks immigrated to New Orleans in the early nineteenth century, and they seem to have brought the shotgun with them. From New Orleans it spread throughout the South.

B-2   (Lost Memphis) Cottages

100 Block of Mill Avenue
1890s

On the south side of this block between Main and Third stood a really nice collection of cottages. They burned down as this book went to press. A few steps up the economic ladder from the shotgun, these houses gave their builder a chance to put up some fancy stuff. Since there was obviously no impetus to maintain any sort of architectural or stylistic "purity," these houses often had a wonderful craziness in their decoration. Large parts of this entire neighborhood must have looked like these. Unfortunately, large parts of this neighborhood now look like the present condition of this block.

B-3   Greenlaw Community Center

190 Mill Avenue
Lindy and Associates, architects, 1981

Greenlaw is not the sort of place one goes to see the glories of the past. For that reason, very few people are screaming to preserve it, especially as a specimen nineteenth-century subdivision. It has coherence as a neighborhood, and the residents are still trying to maintain something of its individuality. This Greenlaw Community Center, the newest structure in the area, reflects very clearly an architectural response to the neighborhood's problems. Its design is obviously based on World War II bunker architecture; the cast-concrete structure is covered by a layer of brick where it is not buried in the ground. The idea seems to be that no-one will try to spraypaint grafitti on a building if it has to be dug out of the ground first. Likewise, windows can't be broken if they aren't there.

This pragmatic approach continues on the inside. The building is laid out to accommodate what someone decided the local folks would use, not what might be "good" for them. Sporting facilities dominate, and there are no books or chairs in sight.

B-4   Cottage

> 274 Mill Avenue
> c. 1861

This is probably the earliest structure left in Greenlaw. At this writing, it is boarded up and covered with threatening signs. Even in this condition, however, it shows how well simple cottages were built back then.

B-5   G.T. Carter House

> 301 Mill Avenue
> 1905

One of a very few largish houses in Greenlaw that has been maintained in decent condition. This brick two-story townhouse has a three-bay front, uninteresting sides (because townhouses were supposed to be built in rows on narrow lots, and the sides wouldn't be seen), and a flat roof. It looks as if it might have strayed from Adams or Vance into another part of town.

B-5

B-6

B-6 George C. Love House

619 North Seventh Street
1889

This is another of the big houses in the neighborhood that is still in good shape. It is worth comparing it to 301 Mill. The general layout of the facade is about the same: three windows upstairs, and two windows and a door on the ground floor. But this is an uncompromisingly suburban—if not rural —house, while the Mill Street brick two-story fits much more readily into an urban setting. Both look a little out of place now.

The Love House has just about the right amount of decoration to be elegant without being pretentious. It would be nice to think that Love had more taste than Mollie Taylor or Elias Lowenstein, whose houses were built on Adams and Jefferson at about the same time, but he probably only had less money. There is a feeling of stability that comes from the horizontal elements of porch balustrade, porch roof, and clapboard siding. The tall, thin windows, on the other hand, especially the floor-to-ceiling ones at ground level, balance all the lateral effects with their strong verticals. The paint job is called "authentic," but that doesn't make it any less questionable. The only thing missing is the rocker on the front porch.

B-7 Cottages
200 Block of Looney Avenue
1880s and 90s

This is a particularly nice group of cottages. The carved panels in the gables and the wrought iron foundation vents show that attempts at architectural elegance were not restricted to the rich.

B-8 Walsh House
686 North Seventh Street
1899–1901

B-9 Louis Sambucetti House
700 North Seventh Street
1906

These two houses were not, strictly speaking, a part of the original Greenlaw development; they are on the wrong side of Seventh for that. 686 is a rather fine neoclassical townhouse with a projecting semicircular entrance porch matched at the roof by a pediment. The institutional addition behind the original house, mercifully, is not very noticeable.

700 is now the Holy Name Convent. It was an ostentatious house. When it was built, there was no question as to what kind of neighborhood it was in: pleasant but working-class, not one filled with mansions. This house has always stood out from its surroundings. It is vaguely Beaux-Arts in massing and detail, especially in the curved porch with its stone balustrade on the Keel Avenue side. The house unfortunately is built of the ugly greyish-brown brick popular in Memphis around the turn of the century.

B-10

B-10 Cottages

600 Block of Keel Avenue
1890s

Turning east on Keel between 686 and 700 North Seventh, one comes to what must be one of the most completely preserved stretches of turn-of-the-century cottages left in the city. Obviously the Greenlaw idea spread all over this part of town. The houses have been kept up very well, and the time-warp effect here can be overwhelming.

B-11 Shotgun Houses

500 Block of Wells
1931

No-one is ever completely safe from classical architecture; the block of shotguns between Thomas and Seventh shows that graphically. This is one of the best collections of this kind of house anywhere in the city—an uninterrupted block of identical houses with two varying porch treatments. There are alternating brick piers and, believe it or not, stumpy columns topped with Ionic capitals! The effect is a bit comical, but the response here is likely to be a chuckle, rather than the groan elicited by some of the obnoxious misuses of the classical orders one sees in new houses being built around town, especially in the city's eastern reaches. Be the structure a two-or three-room shotgun or a million-dollar French Pretential, the message is the same: someone wants to say, "This is a *house*, not a shack."

B-11

B-12　Wonder Snacks

(formerly Belz Building)
653 Corrine Avenue
1938

Even out here in the industrial wilds, you can find traces of architectural awareness, like the Art Deco doorway on this otherwise undistinguished building.

B-13　Roinco Manufacturing Company

(formerly GMC Parts Warehouse)
670 Huron Avenue
1949–50

Originally built as a GMC parts warehouse, this long, low Art Deco building reflects Memphis' extended fascination with that style. It is very similar to another GMC building at 660 South Third Street (D-42).

B-14　Humes Junior High School

659 North Manassas Street
Pfeil and Awsumb, architects, 1923–24
George Awsumb, principal designer

Humes is a fine example of the architectural eclecticism which is a dominant feature of many of the city schools that were built in the first three decades of the twentieth century. This one is a combination of vaguely Venetian and Tudor Gothic styles. The original 1924 building is the only part of the school with architectural distinction. The central entrance pavilion, which projects slightly from the flanking wings, has a big Tudor doorway topped by some strange polygonal buttresses that jump into the air as oversized finials at the level of the roof. These finials then march outward in both directions along the roof of the wings and corner pavilions. The main doorway is also echoed in a pair of smaller, Tudorized entrances, one going into each corner block of the school.

　　The brick surface of the building has a subtle but lively diaper pattern all across it, somewhat like the Doge's Palace in Venice. Two inspirational inscriptions, prominently inserted into the facades of the corner blocks, make sure no-one forgets that this is a school.

B-16

B-15 Missionary Baptist Church

(formerly the Salvation Army Temple Church)
733 North Manassas Street
1954

Most Memphis churches, especially the more modest ones, follow traditional ideas of church architecture. This is a modest building, all right, but its octagonal plan is rare for these parts. For a building built in the fifties, this plan is particularly a surprise, because the Colonial mode, which never used octagonal plans, was the dominant one for Memphis churches at that time.

B-16 Porter-Leith Children's Center

850 North Manassas Street
1856–1929

Built as an orphanage, this complex of buildings expanded over a period of fifty years or so in the late nineteenth and early twentieth centuries. The smaller building to the north of the main structure (on the left when viewed from Manassas) is the original one, dating from 1856. The main building, the work of Edward Culliatt Jones, is at the center and carries the date of 1875. This three-story brick block with a handsome polygonal tower in the center is strong enough to act as a pivot for the other buildings of the orphanage. The excessively heavy cornice of the tower is explainable by the fact that originally the tower was topped by an elaborate Victorian cupola, massive enough to put the cornice in its place. Built in a day when charitable institutions could be, and even would be, expected to be housed in handsome buildings, Porter-Leith still has something recognizably institutional about it. It's not just that the detailing is all brick, instead of stone or stucco. A comparison of this with other Jones buildings shows that he exercised restraint here, especially in the window treatment, no doubt considered fitting for a charitable home.

To the south is the Gould cottage, designed in 1927 by Hanker and Cairns and named after the New York millionaire, Jay Gould.

B-17 Shotgun Houses

> 980–984 North Second Street
> 1920s

As if to prove that bad taste knows no class barriers, these shotgun houses from the 1920s recently have been outfitted with second stories beneath mansard roofs, a "design feature" borrowed from cheap swinging-singles apartment complexes of recent years.

The shotgun is never fine architecture, but as a practical response to economic realities and the Memphis climate it is eminently reasonable. Its one story is surmounted by a steeply pitched roof that provided an attic as a buffer zone between the occupants and the sun. The room arrangement is basic: one opens into another, and you can see out the back door while standing at the front. Thus, given the one-room width and the windows on both sides, any breeze at all can be felt inside the house. These "upscale" shotguns have managed to wreck the simple functionality of the original design of the house without becoming any better in the process.

B-18 Memphis Humane Shelter

> Auction Avenue and Front Street
> Furbringer and Ehrman, architects, 1936

The Depression produced a flurry of architectural projects related to the public health of the city; not the least of these was the dog pound. Rabid dogs caused a serious problem in the city in the thirties; over eight

B-18a

hundred cases of rabies were treated in a three-year period. The dog pound was designed to take care of that problem. It was also a rather elegant Art Deco structure, of no mean price, funded by the Federal government, which seems not to have been able to resist the blandishments of Sen. Kenneth McKellar when he wanted something for his constituents. (He also secured the funds for the great public housing projects of the same years.) The high price of the pound became a minor national issue, and the *New York Times* (Lord forgive it) labeled it a "Boondoggle." Inside, captured stray dogs were separated by sex in two rows of sanitary, commodious pens. A dog had three days here. Each day, if unclaimed, it moved closer to the gas chamber. If Bowser was not claimed by the third day . . .

B-18   (Lost Memphis) Old Shelby County Jail

Corner of Auction Avenue and Front Street
James B. Cook, architect, 1868

Don't look for the jailhouse anymore. The present iron fence is all that was left when it was demolished to make way for the dog pound. The old jail, built by James B. Cook, Memphis' British-import architect, incorporated his patented (by Queen Victoria, no less) device for making a jail escape-proof. There was double wall construction, with the space between the walls filled with sand. An enterprising inmate who managed to dig a hole in his cell wall would end up with a cell full of sand. As the level of the sand between the walls dropped, monitors, something like giant toilet-bowl floats, would set off alarms, and the sandy escapee would be caught in the act.

B-18b

B-20

B-19   Hurt Village Public Housing Project

Thomas Street, corner of Auction and Jackson Avenues
A.L. Aydelott and Associates, architects, c. 1954–55

The four housing blocks closest to the corners where Auction and Jackson
run into Thomas were designed by Aydelott. There is no question about
which they are, since they are the only buildings in the housing project
that show any sense of architecture at all. Aydelott was thinking about
early-twentieth-century European housing ideas here, and no doubt he had
looked carefully at the nearby Dixie Homes (C-38), too. The red-brick
rectangles with their concrete staircases at the ends show similarities to
both prototypes. The humane character of the Dixie Homes, however, is a
bit lacking.

B-20   Epworth Methodist Church

North Waldran Street and Faxon Avenue, northeast corner
Jones and Furbringer, architects, 1923

Jones and Furbringer transformed a single Palladian window into almost
the whole side of a building here. The curve of the roof may suggest the
Mission Style, but it is really a response to the shape of the window below.
This very inventive building, certainly one of the firm's finest, at the time
of this writing is threatened by a proposal to widen the nearby interstate
highway. Widening the highway may well be necessary, but tearing the
church down to do so is not.

C   Victorian Village and Midtown Medical Center

This area of the city offers the most striking contrasts between old and new: between the few remaining houses of the nineteenth century on Adams and Poplar and the ever-burgeoning complex of modern buildings that makes up the Memphis Medical Center. On the west, the area has been cut off from downtown by the insertion of Danny Thomas Boulevard, which was an attempt to solve the problem of north-south circulation that has plagued the city for most of its mature life. To the east, I-240 cuts a never-to-heal slash that severs continuity with the expanding city beyond. In the late nineteenth century, and even the early twentieth, this was a prime residential area. Great houses stood where many of the city's modern institutions now rise, particularly on the site of Methodist Hospital on Union, and on the sites of the William R. Moore School of Technology and Memphis Technical High School on Poplar. I-240 also took out its share of buildings of quality. There is hope that the medical center will grow westward, and the downtown eastward, so that the Berlin-1945-look-alike gap between the two may someday be filled. Much of the wasteland of parking lots that occupies this territory was created by the shockingly thoughtless urban renewal programs carried out by the Memphis Housing Authority under the directorship of Walter Simmons, whose chief qualification for that position seems to have been that he was a bookkeeper for the authority before becoming its director.

VICTORIAN VILLAGE

This two-block section of Adams Avenue contains easily the most accessible and best-known collection of High Victorian (that is, late-nineteenth-century) upper-class mansions in town. The name "Victorian Village" is misleading. Eight houses—and they are all that are left—do not, under any circumstances, constitute a neighborhood. The fact that these few houses represent most of the last surviving shreds of nineteenth-century domestic elegance in the city is a sobering one. Standing in front of these houses, however, it is not difficult to imagine the street as it once was: lined, all the way down to the center of town, with the grand houses of cotton factors and lawyers and merchants. The street is the basic urban element, and there is still something of the old street to be seen here, despite the unfeeling intrusions.

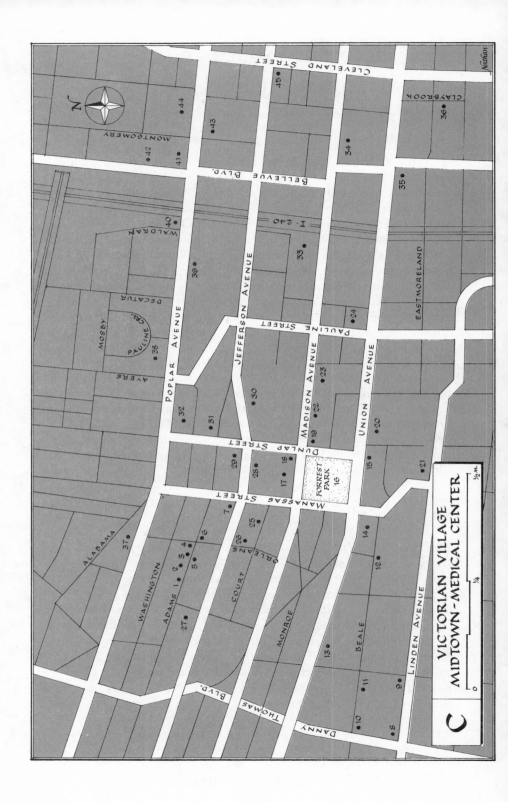

VICTORIAN VILLAGE
MIDTOWN-MEDICAL CENTER

C

Today it is easy to think of Victorian Village as something quaint and picturesque, and maybe even a bit phony, like Disneyland or Beale Street. The architecture is picturesque, but it was always meant to be so. Moreover, the houses and much of their contents are real. Even though these houses have very little to do with the way we live in the late twentieth century, they still present to us, with remarkable fidelity, daily life as it was lived by the upper orders in an earlier Memphis.

It is bitter irony that the Memphis Housing Authority is directly across Orleans from the Goyer-Lee House—bitter because of what the Housing Authority did, literally in the shadow of one of the surviving "great houses" of Memphis.

C-1   Mallory-Neely House

652 Adams Avenue
c. 1852–1890s

This is the most authentic late-nineteenth-century house in the city, and probably one of the most authentic late-nineteenth-century houses in the country. Although it is now a museum open to the public, this was a real home, where the late "Miss Daisy" Mallory, daughter of the man who gave it its final form in the 1890's, lived until her death in 1969. She made

C-1

very few changes. Most museums are places where authentic items are brought together from other locations. This, on the other hand, is a house that grew naturally and then became a museum after the fact. It is worth a visit, if only to see the interior, which preserves the reality of late-nine-teenth-century life in a way no restoration ever could hope to equal. Enter the Mallory-Neely House, and you enter a time warp.

The house began before the Civil War as a relatively modest single-story affair. It grew in the late 1870s and early 1880s, gaining a second story. In the 1890s, it received a third story, the rear ell with the kitchen was annexed, and the entrance tower was heightened—to get a view of the river, it is said. The ensemble combines elements of Italian Renaissance architecture, particularly the round arches of the main entrance and the porch, with the commanding tower of a High Victorian mansion.

C-2   Massey House

664 Adams Avenue
1844–49

The one-story clapboard Massey House gives the best idea of early Adams Avenue. The house is simple and elegant, restrained but not austere. Although small, it has a complicated and beautiful double portico with eight columns set in two planes. The central four columns protrude and support the pediment, while the others retreat and expand laterally to hold up the extended entablature of the large porch. Smaller, and hence more expensive, clapboards are used across the front facade, while wider and cheaper ones appear on the sides and back.

Like most of the Adams houses that are still privately owned, this one was restored by a law firm. Lawyers are about the only people able to afford these places nowadays. The house has recently been bought by the City of Memphis and will become the offices of City Beautiful Commission.

C-2

C-3

C-3   Woodruff-Fontaine House

680 Adams Avenue
Edward Culliatt Jones and Mathias Harvey Baldwin,
architects, 1870–71

This is the only one of the really big Adams houses that was built all at one time to a single overriding idea, and the house shows it. There is a coherence here that scarcely falters, an architectural tune played out with almost no false notes.

The steep mansard roofs of the tower and the main block give this house a more clearly French character than its neighbors have. Jones and Baldwin were sure enough of themselves to leave the brickwork exposed, and they created some very beautiful effects in their uses of setbacks and reveals, especially in the treatment of the third story of the entrance tower. The gentle asymmetry of the facade is held in check by the strength of the vertical lines of the quoins that rise along the tower edge from ground to elegantly detailed mansard roof. There is also a delicacy in the ornament that bespeaks the hand of Baldwin, whereas Jones was probably more responsible for the gutsier forms on the Goyer-Lee House next door to the east. The interior is spacious and elegant, and furnished with objects of the period. There is a false door downstairs (it leads nowhere) that is signed on the back by all the workmen who built the house. Some came from Canada.

C-4 Goyer-Lee House

690 Adams Avenue
1848
Edward Culliatt Jones and Mathias Harvey Baldwin,
remodeling architects, 1871–73

Another plain Adams house that got fancy when the neighborhood went upscale after the Civil War. When you look at the Orleans Street side, it is easy to see how the house grew northwards. The effect is a lot like a telescope opened up. This view also makes very clear that the street front was what really mattered to the owner and the architects; the rich effect given by the main facade is hardly the same as the rather plain one given by the flanks. To cover up the presumably patched nature of the added-onto exterior, the street front was given a layer of stone, while the sides and back were either stuccoed or left as bare brick.

C.W. Goyer, the owner in 1871, must have liked what Jones and Baldwin had built next door the year before, and he opted for a similar design, so that by 1873 three of the first four houses west of Orleans on the north side of Adams had great three-story entrance towers. The narrowness of the original house of 1848 did not allow the tower to be placed in the center of the facade, as Jones and Baldwin had been able to do next door, and so it was moved to the side. To make up for the asymmetry of the tower and the plainness of its lower floors, Jones and Baldwin gave it a particularly dazzling top, with a mansard roof, lifted on overscaled brackets, that swoops up from a square base to an octagonal finish. This pair of architects seems to have shared something of Michelangelo's delight in hefting great weights into the air.

C-4

C-5

C-5   Mollie Fontaine Taylor House

679 Adams Avenue
1886–90

Noland Fontaine built this house across the street from his own as a wedding present for his daughter. Austerity is not a characteristic of any of the big Adams Avenue houses, but, compared with this one, the houses on the north side are restrained. The porch contains enough decorative elements for a house twice this large, and its effect is almost that of stiffened macramé made by a giant inspired by some of the more curious elements of Chinese and late baroque art. There is no tower here. Instead, the tall central gable tries to match the vertical ambition of the three great sentinels across the street.

Although the architect, mercifully, is not known, the keyhole pattern around the ventilator and window in the gables of the street facade bears a distinct relation to similar "Moorish" decorative patterns on the Tennessee Club downtown (A-90), a building of c. 1890. One may reasonably wonder if there may be some connection here, or perhaps it is only the case that they share a particular stylistic phase of late Victorian architecture.

C-6   Pillow-McIntyre House

367 Adams Avenue
1852

A voice from an earlier, more restrained era, speaking softly on the edge of the late Victorian bombast of Mallory, Fontaine, Goyer, and Mollie Fontaine Taylor, the Pillow-McIntyre House is a standard pre–Civil War house of the region, with a two-story, four-columned portico attached to a basi-

C-6

cally cubic block. The capitals and bases, typically, are metal, while the slender column shafts are wood.

C-7   Elias Lowenstein House

756 Jefferson Avenue
1890–91

The Lowenstein House, slightly removed physically from its kinfolk on Adams, also has had a somewhat different history. It was occupied by the family until 1920, when one of them turned it into a house for single women who had moved to Memphis from the country to find work. Now a halfway house, it continues to serve an important social purpose.

The outside of the Lowenstein House has a strong Romanesque bent, particularly in the low, round arches and in the meatiness of the proportions. Inside, some of the original surfaces still exist, particularly walls glopped with swirls of plaster thick enough to make DeKooning jealous. Here is palpable opulence indeed. The carved wooden transom screen in the entrance hall does an astonishing imitation of basketry, and in the southwest corner of the front parlor is a small stained-glass window featuring a Scotsman in a kilt (!).

C-7

C-8   Universal Life Insurance Co.

480 Linden Avenue
McKissick and McKissick, Nashville, architects, 1949

Memphis has three Egyptian Revival commercial buildings. The Universal
Life Insurance Co. is the most modern in feeling, because its Egyptian
forms are handled with an Art Deco simplification, particularly in the
flattened lotus blossom capitals of the inset porches on the west and south
sides. The naturally flat patterns of Egyptian art take to this kind of
simplification readily, so that the building is satisfying as both an evocation of the old and a statement about the new.

This white marble building, built for a black company, is a late evocation of the interest black Americans developed in the 1920s in ancient
Egyptian art. For these blacks, ancient Egypt, located in Africa and ruled
by men and women of color, was their antiquity—a civilization older than
those of Europe. Marcus Garvey once asked what were the British doing
while blacks were building the Pyramids. The former Mississippi Boulevard Christian Church (D-62) is an earlier example of this deliberate use of
Egyptian motifs in the service of black pride. Here black antiquity is set up
to rival such white institutional buildings as the National Bank of Commerce (A-30a), with its ancient Greek Doric columns. (We are grateful to
Eva Grudin for pointing out to us the interest of African Americans in
ancient Egypt.)

C-9   Mt. Olive C.M.E.Cathedral

(formerly First Baptist Church)
Linden Avenue and Lauderdale Street, northwest corner
1910

A domed structure with remarkable Ionic capitals that have ornaments
dangling from their volutes, like earrings from earlobes.

C-10   A.F.S.C.M.E. Local 1733,
Dr. Martin Luther King, Jr., Labor Center

485 Beale Street
Harold Thompson, architect, 1978

A very strong building that rises out of the green desert of eastern Beale
Street. It holds its corner site by thrusting diagonal steps out from a circular entrance pavilion of orange brick, into which a curved black strip window has been set above a white gash cut out for the door. The diagonal
black glass slice on the Beale Street side lights the staircase that ascends to

C-10

the second floor. On the Danny Thomas Boulevard side, the building steps back from the street as it moves south to create a series of sharply-cut black and orange angles. Behind the windows on the ground floor lies an ample corridor, whose inner wall is a series of complicated curves that are choreographed to respond to the angles of the outer wall. The contrast of these soft forms, painted a pale grey-blue, and the hard, brittle, outer skin produces quite a magical space.

C-11 Hunt-Phelan House

533 Beale Street
1830s, 1851

The original cubic block of this house, with its sheer brick walls, clearly was inspired by the Federalist architecture of the Eastern Seaboard from the earlier decades of the nineteenth century. The cube was softened only by a small one-story porch on the Beale Street facade. In 1855, the house was made much grander by a two-story addition to the rear and by the construction of a two-story Ionic portico across the Beale front. The columns were given particularly slender proportions in order to accommodate them to the tall shape of the existing house. The original porch was moved to the east, to make a new side entrance. Even though it is not all of a piece, the Hunt-Phelan House is probably the finest white-columned antebellum mansion to have survived in Memphis. It served as Gen. Ulysses S. Grant's headquarters in 1862. The chain-link fence that now protects it is palpable proof of the hard times on which the neighborhood has fallen.

C-11a

C-11b

C-11 (Lost Memphis) Robertson Topp House

565 Beale Street
P. Hammarskold, architect, 1841

Nearby was the even more elegant house of one of the developers of this part of Memphis, Robertson Topp, whose four-columned portico doubtless served as the inspiration for the added portico of the Hunt-Phelan House. In later years, the Topp House became part of Miss Higbee's School, an institution for the education of young women of the right sort, and then the headquarters of a labor union, which tore it down in the 1930s after claiming that the house was beyond repair. The house bore quite a resemblance to the Gayoso House (A-43 [Lost Memphis]), the hotel Topp built on Front Street the year after he built this house. One cannot help but wonder if the architect of the Gayoso House, the imminent James Dakin of New Orleans, may have made some suggestions about the design of the house as well.

C-12   Memphis Light, Gas and Water Division, Central Shops

703 Beale Street
1901

This flat facade with Ionic pilasters contains a wonderfully florid piece of Sullivanesque ornament in the identifying inscription that rests on the keystones of the pair of arched windows in the center of the building. The new sign that hides much of this ornament does the building a considerable disservice.

C-13   Memphis Publishing Company Building

495 Union Avenue
Walk Jones and Francis Mah, architects, 1977

The curved north wall that faces Union Avenue was designed to increase daylight in the newspaper offices of the *Commercial Appeal*, and also to increase the possibility for views to the exterior. Located on the north of the building, the glass wall conserves energy by avoiding the intense heat of the summer sun. The curvature is repeated, in a minor mode, on the east side of the rear of the building, where it backs up to Beale Street. Structurally, the building uses an open steel frame for its floors, to make the interior changes that will doubtless ensue over the years relatively easy to carry out. The large concrete hulk to the east is the printing plant, which predates the Jones and Mah offices.

C-13

C-14   Shelby State Community College

1256 Union Avenue
Walk Jones and Francis Mah, architects, 1974–78

This complex of seven severe brick boxes stretches south from Union to Linden. The exposed trusses of the gymnasium roof, visible from Linden, not only saved money (they didn't have to be enclosed in an exterior wall) but also give an appropriate sense of large scale to the whole. Rather forbidding of mien, Shelby State dates from that "hunker down in the bunker" period of campus design that followed the student uprisings of the late sixties and early seventies.

C-15   Scottish Rite Cathedral

825 Union Avenue
Jones and Furbringer, architects, 1909

Forrest Park, on which the Scottish Rite Cathedral fronts, was once surrounded by several such buildings of a classicizing nature. This is the only one left. Jones and Furbringer again focused their efforts on the center of the facade, which has a handsome overhanging balcony and a double-headed eagle at the top. The Scottish Rite Cathedral turned out to be a foretaste of what the same architects would do, even better, in 1914 for the Masonic Temple at Court and Fourth (A-95).

MEDICAL CENTER

The Memphis Medical Center, if it has a center, is focused on Forrest Park, named for Nathan Bedford Forrest, a Civil War general whose idea of winning battles was "to get there fuhstes' with the mostes'." The open land for the park was created in 1899, when the old City Hospital that stood on the block was torn down and a new hospital building erected on Madison northeast of Dunlap, on land previously occupied by St. Peter's Cemetery. From these first two hospitals grew the cacophonous complex that exists today, sprawling between Union and Poplar, with Dunlap as its main north-south axis. Many of the medical buildings are of little architectural interest, but some are among the best recent architecture in the city. Indeed, in this area one can experience the city's cautious flirtations with the modern style in the early fifties and some bravura performances of the seventies and eighties.

C-16 Forrest Park

George Kessler, Kansas City, landscape architect, 1915

In 1899 the city acquired this land, which had been the site of the old city hospital, and in 1915 opened it as a park designed by George Kessler, who had been responsible for Overton and Riverside Parks and for the Parkways. Forrest Park has lost most of Kessler's original romantic English garden design, which featured a lake surrounded by weeping willows. All that is left of the early-twentieth-century scheme is the statue of Forrest on horseback by Charles Henry Niehaus. The remains of the general and his wife were removed from Elmwood Cemetery and reinterred in front of the monument. Forrest is shown in the statue as the dashing cavalry officer he actually was. There were, however, less savory aspects of his career. He was a slave trader and an early member of the Ku Klux Klan. The whole ensemble is an example of the Civil War nostalgia that overtook the city's white citizens shortly after 1900, a period in which relations between blacks and whites were particularly strained. The architectural counterparts to this park are to be found in the great antebellum-revival houses, such as the Laurence House on Anderson (F-92) and the Crawford House (F-146) at the corner of Madison and East Parkway, of the same period. Magnificent as they are as architectural designs, they are nonetheless the architecture of white supremacy.

The buildings to the north of the park along Madison belong to the University of Tennessee Medical Center, as do the buildings to the east along Dunlap. A good place to begin a visit of the medical center is the model of the whole complex that is located in the lobby of the Randolph Student Alumni Center.

C-17 Wassell Randolph Student Alumni Center

800 Madison Avenue
Gassner, Nathan and Browne, architects, 1969

This bi-axial building with an "H" plan sits athwart what should be the eastern continuation of Court Avenue. Instead, there is a pleasant sunken garden in the center, reached by a pair of staircases (out of a sixteenth-century Italian garden) that descend from the central bar of the H. The residential tower that rises in front of the Madison Avenue facade, faced in the same smooth concrete, was designed at the same time by the same team of architects. Immediately to the northwest rises the dark brick mass of the Goodman House, formerly Forrest Park Apartments, a not very distinguished work of Hanker and Cairns of 1926.

C-18   Van Vleet Memorial Cancer Center and
Belz-Kriger Cancer Clinic

Madison Avenue and North Dunlap Street, northwest corner
Walk C. Jones, Walk C. Jones Jr., architects, 1951
Thorn, Howe, Stratton and Strong, architects, 1964

The original part of this structure, most of its southern half, was hidden in 1964 by the addition of a unifying reinforced-concrete screen that stretches across the Jones structure to link it to new additions to the north and south.

C-19   Cecil C. Humphreys General Education Building

8 South Dunlap Street
Roy P. Harrover and Associates, architects, 1977

Opening off the southeast corner of Madison and Dunlap is a wide flight of stairs that leads into the lobby of this building, which is cleverly shoehorned in among a number of buildings that were already there. The tall lobby, triangular in plan, occupies about a quarter of the large square that forms the plan of the classroom section of this building. A diagonal corridor slices through this large square. At either end of this diagonal, doors open into one-story corridors that lead to three large, pie-shaped lecture halls. These corridors are surrounded by benches set under depressed arches that conceal the sources of the daylight that falls on the benches. This theme of clever lighting from above is continued throughout the public spaces of the building.

From the lobby, the diagonal corridor leads south to the second part of the structure, the laboratory wing, which is laid out along a strong east-

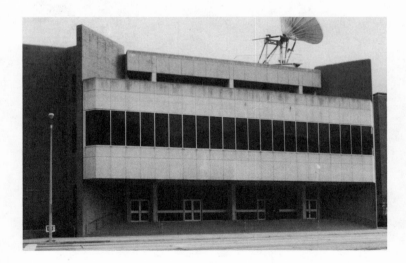

C-19

west axis. This wing terminates at the west in the most imposing space in the building, an enormous apse. Unexpectedly, you find yourself on the threshold of a three-story concrete half-cylinder, lit from above. Inside the threshold are semicircular theater seats. The whole seems a deserted anatomical theater of the kind that Jacques Gondouin designed in the 1760s for the College of Surgery in Paris. The top lighting of the cylinder, on the other hand, suggests the side chapels of Le Corbusier's pilgrimage church at Ronchamp of 1951–55. Windows in the walls of the half-cylinder allow people walking the corridors of the upper floors a peek-a-boo view of the theater seats below, which one suspects are never occupied by a theater crowd, or any crowd at all. The whole is a grand spatial gesture with little functional justification beyond giving surprise and pleasure. In a city where there are few interior spaces designed just to make us happy, this one stands out.

The laboratories that lie east of the apse are laid out in the manner of Louis Kahn's labs at the Salk Institute in La Jolla. Long, uninterrupted, flexible spaces are flanked by hallways, here interiors, that are broken on their peripheries with enclosed tower-like brick forms which alternate with open areas that, prosaically, contain lockers.

C-20

To the south of the Humphreys Building lie the older buildings of the UT Medical School campus. They all have a collegiate Gothic look, but none is a work of particular distinction.

C-20   Winfield Dunn Dental Clinical Building

Union Avenue and East Street, southeast corner
Gassner, Nathan and Browne, architects, 1977

Tooth Castle is a name one might give to this building, which can be taken for a giant molar. The corner towers hold the staircases, while the stumpy tower on the west face contains the elevators. Inside, rough concrete supports are paired to make handsome rhythms down long corridors. Their faces are curved into half circles, to give them a certain sculptural interest, and perhaps a certain toothsomeness. Is this *architecture parlante* of a particularly appropriate type?

C-21   University of Tennessee Single Student Housing

East Street and Linden Avenue, northwest corner
Robert Lee Browne, architect, 1986-88

A long building that breaks and snakes along the Linden Avenue side of the property. This housing group combines the sharply pointed blue-green metallic roof of Aldo Rossi's Modena Cemetery with a post-mod color scheme on the walls: two shades of red brick in stripes separated by single rows of glazed blue-green brick that match the roof. The colored bands make ingratiating what would have been, in Rossi's hands, truly stark. On the Linden Avenue side, the concrete balconies with curved ends, reached by daring cantilevered stairs, seem to have been taken from another architecture entirely—modern buildings of the 1930s, such as the Dixie Homes just a few blocks away or Pier Luigi Nervi's stadium in Florence.

C-22   University of Tennessee Medical Center
Library, Nursing, Biometry,
and Computer Science Building

877 Madison Avenue
Gassner, Nathan and Partners, architects, 1985–88

Giant reinforced-concrete pylons lift the bulk of this building high in the air, above a wide walkway that descends to a level below the street and ascends to the level of the hillside above. The pylons carry great beams that project into cantilevers on either side, so that the superstructure overhangs the spaces below dramatically. This is a cavernous entrance. The rear of the building, where the system breaks down to accommodate circulation, also packs a sculptural punch, this one reminiscent of Louis Kahn's service towers at the rear of his Richards Medical Research Center at the University of Pennsylvania.

C-23   Baptist Memorial Hospital
899 Madison Avenue

The Baptist Hospital first opened here in 1912, in a building designed by John Gaisford that is now largely buried in later construction. Since then, however, it has grown into the largest private hospital in the world. No small part of that size is due to the Madison East addition, by the Office of Walk C. Jones, Jr., Architects, 1956–60. This yellow building has two arms that reach out to embrace the street. In 1966–67 Walk Jones, Mah and Jones, the successor firm, doubled the size of this part of the hospital by adding a matching pair of wings on the Union Avenue face. Architecturally, however, the most interesting part of the Baptist Hospital complex is another block to the east.

C-24   Baptist Memorial Hospital School of Nursing
999 Monroe Avenue
Walk Jones and Francis Mah, architects, 1984

The problem was to provide an almost convent-like atmosphere for student nurses on a midtown site. The solution was to build a building that is almost completely closed to the outside, but open to light and air on the inside through tall indoor streets flanked by student rooms. From no room need one face the rudeness of the outside world. Where there are windows in the exterior walls, they light interior public spaces, such as corridors and bridges.

Inside, the pale yellow exterior gives way to sensuously pink walls (marked with gray stripes where the concrete has been left bare) that rise from red tile floors. Light floods the inner streets through high windows, and the students' rooms open onto those streets through balconies. The rooms themselves are a little claustrophobic; you have to open the balcony door to see much of the inside street. But the effect of the ensemble is remarkably serene, and even expansive.

C-25   BRZ Technology Innovation Center
(formerly University Interfaith Association Chapel)
740 Court Avenue
Gassner, Nathan and Browne, architects, 1969–70

A low wall, one of the most beautiful examples of rough concrete in these or any parts, surrounds this small building. The forms into which the concrete was poured were made of rough-sawn boards, set so that the sur-

C-24

faces of the boards were not all in the same plane. When the boards were taken off the poured concrete, the impressions of their surfaces were left in the wall. During the pour, the small stones of the aggregate oozed into the spaces between the misaligned boards, to make the warmly colored vertical lines that play off against the cool color of the concrete itself.

The entrance into the chapel was originally at a higher level than it is now (traces of the steps are visible in the side walls of the lobby), so that one was forced through a very low door into a room in which the ceiling got lower. All of this set you up for the experience of the chapel itself—a tall room, hexagonal in plan. The chief glory of the space is the light, provided by an almost-hidden triangular skylight, that falls in abundance onto the north wall of the chapel, opposite its entrances.

C-26   University of Tennessee Child Development Center

711 Court Avenue
Roy P. Harrover and Associates, architects, 1969
Bob Church, principal designer

The UT Child Development Center is Memphis' most brutal Brutalist structure. Brutalism is a style, or rather a constellation of styles, that developed after World War II. Generally, Brutalist buildings have masses that project boldly into space and are surfaced in rough concrete or other "tough" materials. The best Brutalist buildings have the kind of aggressive presence that this structure has. Harrover jokes that Francis Mah calls the building "Godzilla."

The building is best understood from the inside out. Its purpose was to house under one roof many disciplines, all interested in child development, so that each could inform the others. The plan organizes public spaces along a central north-south spine that rises six stories. In this central spine, particularly on the first and second floors, the designers managed to open up a number of surprisingly complex vertical paths of space through the building.

The public corridors in the centers of each floor are flanked by spaces that grow increasingly private as they reach the outer edges of the building. The idea behind this arrangement was to create a serene central area for visitors, who would not be aware of all the varied activities that take place simultaneously in the flanking spaces. On the second and third floors, the building expands laterally in groups of wings that house offices and rooms for clinical observation. These wings provide shelter for outdoor spaces that open off ground-level classrooms. In other words, the offices above make shelters for the children to play under.

The exterior reflects the play of solids and voids inside; the sides of the main mass of the building are marked by vertical voids that repeat, in their own way, those of the interior. The main six-story mass has its center marked by a clear frame of brick. From this center project the office wings, their concrete frames filled with dark panels of rough-surfaced slate. On both the Court and Jefferson sides (the Court side is even more dynamic,

C-26

because of its greater height), diagonal arms reach out to grab the visitor. A child might feel threatened by these entrances, for they suggest, at super-human scale, the grasping claws of a sci-fi robot—or maybe a child would feel elated at the prospect of entering a giant toy.

C-27 Southern Health Plan, Inc.

(formerly IBM Office Building)
600 Jefferson Avenue
Walk Jones and Francis Mah, architects, 1976

A no-frills office building that strove, with some success, to be high on dignity and low on cost. The horizontal and vertical structural members are clearly articulated, and a fairly grand entrance is achieved simply by opening up a large two-story space at the southeast corner.

C-28 Speech and Hearing Center

807 Jefferson Avenue
Roy Harrover and Associates, architects, 1960
Robert Emmet, principal designer

A broken-up two-story brick box with white concrete beams. The heaviness of the thick concrete members plays well against the seeming fragility of the brick walls under them. Abstract gargoyles on the upper beam suggest a certain romanticism of approach, while the deeply recessed windows in the second floor of the west wing cast an eye Kahn-ward.

C-29 Memphis and Shelby County Health Department

814 Jefferson Avenue
Office of Walk C. Jones, Jr., architects, 1957
Thorn, Howe, Stratton and Strong, architects, 1972

Directly on Jefferson rises the red brick mass of Memphis' own version of the Boston City Hall, one of the most influential buildings of the 1960s. This structure has been added onto an earlier building by Walk Jones, Jr., which contains a square two-story courtyard surrounded by a clearly expressed glass curtain wall. The floors are reinforced concrete slabs cantilevered from piers in the center. The steel frames of the glass walls are bolted to the edges of the concrete floors, so that the steel walls never actually touch the concrete. On the Jefferson Avenue side, the Jones building has a barrel-vaulted pavilion that breaks the strictly rectilinear character of the rest of the building, one of the first to introduce a modernist steel-and-glass vocabulary into a public structure in Memphis.

C-30a

C-30   The Med (Regional Medical Center)

Walk Jones and Francis Mah/Gassner,
Nathan and Partners, architects, 1983
Francis Mah, project architect
Clair Jones, Harold Thompson, associate architects

East of Dunlap, Jefferson is flanked by a heterogeneous group of buildings that form an almost indecipherable complex known as the Regional Medical Center, or The Med. On the northeast corner stands the former West Tennessee Tuberculosis Hospital, 1948, by Furbringer and Ehrman, in association with Everett Woods. On the southeast corner is the former E.H. Crump Memorial Hospital, 1955, by Eason, Anthony, McKinnie and Cox. This building, originally constructed for black patients, is now a maternity center. These and other earlier structures have been coerced rather than coaxed into one complex by Francis Mah's design, his spaciest ever.

The only way to understand The Med is to plunge in and experience it. From Jefferson, one sees glass-vaulted walkways with red undersides shooting across the street, beneath the hovering white bulk of a huge box held up on round piers that look like rockets or giant pencils. From here, you know at once that this building is all about moving around. A circular vestibule on the south side of the street puts you on an escalator beneath one of those round glass vaults. The escalator drops you one floor up, where you are confronted with too many choices of directions. Take them all, in whatever order you choose. One will lead you into a large cafeteria under a diagonal glass ceiling. Another will take you onto the walkway that leads across Jefferson. Another will take you south, under two more hovering white boxes. Still another will bring you to a corridor that has round windows that look down into the cafeteria, and then into another corridor that holds the great surprise of a triangular window looking out onto the street. The blood-red color of these circulation areas make you

C-30b

feel as if you have been miniaturized and thrust into the circulation system of the body—as if you were suddenly in the film *Fantastic Voyage*.

The white boxes, square in plan, have three floors. The bottom, with its louvered portholes, is for services, while the two on top house patients' rooms. The three squares suggest geometric vertebrae, cushioned by buff-colored discs that are actually circulation and service towers (Louis Kahn's served and servant spaces are never far from Mah's mind). Where the floor levels of the vertebrae have to be joined awkwardly to the floor levels of older buildings, the awkwardness is not all that well masked by stretching thin skins of black glass between old and new.

No structure in town, except the roller coaster at Libertyland, gives quite the kinetic thrill The Med produces.

C-30 (Lost Memphis) Memphis Steam Laundry
941 Jefferson Avenue
E.L. Harrison, architect, 1927
Nowland Van Powell, principal designer

Few cities are lucky enough to have a genuine Venetian palace in which the citizens can have their their shirts laundered. What connection Harrison and Powell saw between cleanliness and Ruskin's favored Venetian Gothic we shall probably never know. Perhaps they didn't see any connection at all. This may well have been the best piece of eclectic architecture the city ever had. Why it could not have found a place in the medical center many of us will never understand.

C-31   Le Bonheur Children's Hospital

Adams Avenue and Dunlap Street, northeast corner
J. Frazer Smith, architect, 1952
Eason, Anthony, McKinnie and Cox, architects for altera-
tions and additions, 1960-75
J. Wise Smith, architect for addition, 1976–80

Frazer Smith's original Le Bonheur and the Eason, Anthony, McKinnie and
Cox additions formed a graceful, intimately-scaled modern building that
threw out several wings around courtyards and varied its facades with
different window patterns. The newest part speaks a more monumental
rhetoric. The second Smith was not nearly as good at keeping a sense of
the scale of children as the first.

C-32   Memphis Mental Health Institute

(formerly Tennessee Psychiatric Hospital and Institute)
865 Poplar Avenue
A.L. Aydelott and Associates, architects, 1962

Despite the fact that this building won a *Progressive Architecture* award,
it represents the most depressing kind of modern design. The sight of it
could hardly improve a patient's mental health. Aydelott could be a lot
better. Extensive renovations were carried out in 1977, when the building
got its present name.

C-33   Memphis Towers

1080 Court Avenue
Walk Jones and Francis Mah, architects, 1978

A housing project for the elderly that organizes the units into three circular towers, connected by a common service and circulation core.

C-34   Southern College of Optometry

1245 Madison Avenue
Walk Jones and Francis Mah, architects, 1967–70

Many in Memphis consider this Jones and Mah's best building. The single
shaft of reinforced concrete and the accompanying one-story clinic, hidden
under a flat terrace to the south, contain within them all the functions of
the school. On the north face, large glass windows offer splendid views of
the city, while the other sides are blank, save for the one great circular eye
on the south that lights the student lounge on the fourth floor and the
library on the fifth. The eye is reminiscent of the four great circles Louis
Kahn cut into the interior walls of the central court of his library at Phil-

C-34

lips Exeter Academy in New Hampshire, a building designed in the same year as this one and completed a year later. The corners are cut away and filled with thin glass walls, set at right angles, to allow daylight into the edges of some of the interior spaces. This detail is also reminiscent of the Kahn library.

One great open interior space on the north, rising from the second to the fifth floors, produces a kind of vertical indoor campus, off of which open, through bridges that span the space, the classrooms, lounge, and library. The somewhat cramped entrance is to be expanded by an addition designed by Roy Harrover, who also plans to spread the name of the institution across the first big horizontal beam above the door. The only problem the building really has is one of visibility, because of the way it had to be shoehorned into a lot with little frontage on Madison and none on Union.

C-35 Med Express Building

> Union Avenue at Bellevue Boulevard, southwest corner
> Norman Hoover of 3D/International, Houston, architect,
> 1984

Here the architect of the Morgan-Keegan Tower downtown gives us a simpler but equally postmodern structure, with sheer red-brick walls, black glass, square windows, and a bit of frill up top—curved pediments that put a vaguely classical cap on the slickly grim building below. A bridge connects this building with the main bulk of the Methodist Hospital complex, of which it forms a part.

C-36   Wilson Hall, Dormitory for Methodist Hospital School of Nursing

251 South Claybrook Street
Yeates and Gaskill, architects, 1970

The concrete frame and brick curtain walls are artfully arranged so that the frame itself does double duty—as a clearly expressed structural system and also as the framing elements for the windows. The services are all put into the third floor, which is treated differently to express this fact.

POPLAR AVENUE

C-37   St. Mary's Episcopal Cathedral

692 Poplar Avenue
W. Halsey Wood, architect, 1895–97
L.M. Weathers, architect, 1897–1906
Hanker and Cairns, architects, 1922–26
Walk C. Jones and Walk C. Jones, Jr., architects, 1950–52

St. Mary's, built as the Episcopal Cathedral for the Diocese of Tennessee, has one of the most complex histories of any building in the city. The man who started to build the church, Bishop Thomas Gailor, sought a design from the New York architect Halsey Wood, who had been one of the four finalists in the competition to design the Cathedral of St. John the Divine in New York and who had also done a church in Chattanooga with which Gailor was familiar. Wood died in 1897, before he had started on the working drawings. All Gailor got from Wood was a set of perspective views. A local architect, L.M. Weathers, produced additional drawings that simplified Wood's sketches, and on that basis the first part of the church, that is, the steel frame of the nave and the stonework of the main facade, was erected and enclosed in temporary wooden walls.

In the 1920s, when there was a chance to raise the money needed to complete the building, and when a new dean, Israel Noe, got behind the project, the church was completed on the basis of designs worked up by Bayard Cairns, who claimed, when he took over, that he could find no working drawings for the project. Cairns reduced the bulk and height of the tower, eliminated the nave triforium, and cut out the sculptural decorations envisioned in Wood's project, all in order to reduce costs. He also switched to cheaper terra cotta for the facing of the tower.

The church presents an imposing mass to the street, although the narrow site between Poplar and Alabama did not allow the building to be given the length that one might expect in an Anglophilic cathedral. The Diocesan House at the west, originally built for the bishop's occupancy, dates from 1902 and presumably was designed by Weathers, since he was

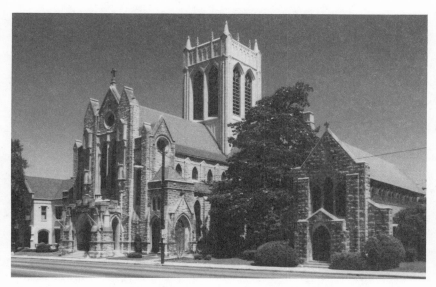

C-37

the cathedral architect at the time. The chapel to the east, which dates from the 1880s, was originally attached to St. Mary's School, an adjunct of the church for the education of young ladies. In the 1930s, the wood-and-brick structure was faced with stone to match the cathedral, under the direction and at the expense, of Bayard Cairns. Cairns connected the chapel to the cathedral with a stone arcade that was incorporated, in the 1950s, into the parish house designed by the Joneses, senior and junior.

Inside the cathedral, the vaults over the nave are supported by extraordinarily slender piers, which are actually steel posts faced with stone. The idea was to cut down pier bulk to increase visibility from every seat. The inner aisles, when observed from either end, have vaults that create an unexpected roller-coaster effect. The altar is from the earlier wooden church that stood on the site, while the reredos is a design of Bayard Cairns.

The earlier chapel, from the 1880s, has an interior of great warmth and charm. The hammer-beamed ceiling rises from a clerestory wall punctured by pairs of pointed arched windows and supported by wooden octagonal columns that rise from tall, square bases. This is one of the few wooden Gothic interiors from the late ninteenth century to survive in the city.

C-38   Dixie Homes Public Housing Project

940–990 Poplar Avenue
J. Frazer Smith, architect, 1935–38
Walk C. Jones, Sr.; Edwin B. Phillips; Everett Woods; R.J.
Regan; Anker F. Hansen; Dudley E. Jones; Louis Carlisle;
and Herbert M. Burnham, associate architects

The first two public housing projects built in Memphis, constructed simultaneously and designed by the same architect, were the Dixie Homes
and the Lauderdale Courts (A-72). The Lauderdale Courts, meant for
whites, were done in a reduced Georgian style, while the Dixie Homes, for
blacks, were in a very up-to-date modernist vein. Of the two, the Dixie
Homes are by far the more satisfying visually. Indeed, the Dixie Homes are
one of the high moments in the history of Memphis architecture.

The axis of Pauline Street enters the complex and then bends off to
either side to form the curve of Pauline Circle. The sense of the axis, but
not the ability to drive on it, continues from Pauline north to tie the
whole project together. From the geometrical center point of the circular
drive, walkways radiate outward to bisect two courtyards and to establish
the axes on which diagonally-placed buildings are set. All the two-story
apartment buildings are surrounded by wide lawns, to allow plenty of light
and air between them, and plenty of play areas for children.

These rather Baroque qualities in the plan (Louis XIV's palace at Ver-

C-38a

C-38b

sailles used the same tricks) are matched by the curvilinear vigor of the corners of some of the reinforced concrete balconies that are attached to many, but not all, of the apartment buildings. Here the designing is very bold. Indeed, the high quality of the design is rarely matched in public housing in this country or even in Europe, where more attention is generally paid to these kinds of architectural problems. Smith, through his close connections with the Federal Housing Authority in Washington, was obviously on top of the latest thinking in the field. It is a great tribute to his versatility as an architect, and to his mental agility, that he could, in roughly the same years, both write a history of the early nineteenth-century plantation architecture of the Middle South, *White Pillars*, and also plan a housing project this sensitive to recent international developments in housing design.

C-39   Patton-Bejach House

> 1085 Poplar Avenue
> 1884

The torch-holding columns along the side were added when a restaurant, aptly called the Flour Flames, occupied the house.

C-40   Greenstone Apartments

> 1116 Poplar Avenue and 200 North Waldran Boulevard
> Hubert T. McGee, architect, 1927

McGee got the chance to do the two buildings in Memphis that are identified by their color, the Pink Palace and the Greenstone Apartments. The stone, quarried in Ohio, had been used in a large house built on the

C-40

site in 1890. There was enough of this unusual material to cover the street facades of the new apartments. Also from the old house are the main stone door on the Poplar facade and the mahogany staircase in the hall behind it. The apartments themselves provided quite spacious living quarters with remarkably ample storage, in an area that had been dominated by large single-family houses, of which the Patton-Bejach House across the street is almost the only remaining nearby example. The insertion of I-240 took out several fine buildings here, including the garages of the Greenstone Apartments. The proposed widening of I-240 now threatens to take out the whole thing.

C-41   William R. Moore School of Technology

1200 Poplar Avenue
Walk C. Jones, Walk C. Jones, Jr., architects, 1938

The modernist wings of the shops, with their industrial sash windows, flank with classical symmetry the reduced classical portico of the central block. Here the Joneses, with considerable success, were trying to forge a union between traditional southern architectural forms and the steel-and-glass architecture of modern Europe. The central portico has a flat modern roof, instead of a triangular pediment, while the industrial wings still have a stone cornice with vestigial dentils inscribed on it. One might imagine this to be a building designed by Ashley Wilkes (the gentleman who failed to requite Scarlett O'Hara's love) after a period of study at the Bauhaus.

C-41

C-42 Maury Elementary School

272 North Bellevue Boulevard
B.C. Alsup, architect, 1908

Of the relatively elaborate school buildings that Memphis built in the early years of this century, this is one of the most lavish in its use of classical, and indeed unclassical, details on the centerpiece of the facade. The central doorway, framed by standard Ionic pilasters, is set into a three-story pavilion with very tricky edges. The heavy stone quoins at the corners suddenly, at the top, turn into pilasters carrying capitals that have bizarre cartouches stuck on them.

C-43 Chapel, Mid-America Baptist Theological Seminary

(formerly Temple Israel)
1255 Poplar Avenue
Jones and Furbringer, architects, 1915–16

Synagogues offer historicizing architects a peculiar problem, in that the standard Western styles used for Christian churches, the classical and the Gothic, don't always seem appropriate. Here Jones and Furbringer chose a mixture of Roman and Byzantine elements that they managed to link together in a powerful ensemble that makes clear the religious purpose of the building but sets it apart from the numerous Christian structures in the city. The strong twin towers, with a knowing play of horizontal and vertical planes in the brickwork, embrace a wide porch with three grand openings separated by pairs of columns that have spiral fluting—probably a

C-43

reference to the spiral columns of the Temple of Solomon. Above the porch rises a great round-arched window, also subdivided into three parts, that forces the pediment above it to repeat its curve, a curve that is then taken up by the small domes of the towers and the great dome over the sanctuary. The whole of the facade is embellished with highly sculptural terra cotta ornament and complex changes in the flat patterns of the brickwork. All of this adds up to a masterful exercise in theme and variation, climaxed by the unbroken curve of the dome.

The interior is one of the handsomes spaces in town. The general flatness and plainness of its walls contrast strongly with the relatively heavy relief and busyness of the brick walls outside. Over the space floats a dome of extreme flatness, covered by three rows of large coffers, reminiscent of those of the dome of the Pantheon in Rome. The dome is borne by four arches and four pendentives that rise from four diagonally-placed piers below. These piers separate the four arms of a cross that expands laterally into shallow bays and, front and back, into deeper arms. The space is both centralized under the dome and directional from front to back. It has been converted sensitively into a Baptist chapel by doing almost nothing to it. Only a couple of small wooden crosses have been hung on the wooden paneling to either side of the raised platform on the south side. One of the best details of the interior is the stained-glass window that lights the balcony. Here beautifully-drawn, slender vines, set with elegant restraint in a field of white light, form a graceful counterpoint to the weightier forms of the architecture itself. The notion that Israel is a vine is common in the Old Testament.

An education building, by Furbringer and Ehrman, was added to the south of the sanctuary in 1950–51.

C-44   Memphis Technical High School

1266 Poplar Avenue
Joe T. Wallace and Hanker and Cairns,
associated architects, 1928

The long three-story mass of Tech High is broken by a very shallow Corinthian portico in the center and by projecting pavilions at the ends, marked by Corinthian pilasters that carry vestigial entablatures, and by pediments so broken as almost not to be there at all.

C-45   Sacred Heart School

1317 Jefferson Avenue
Regan and Weller, architects, 1928–29

Sacred Heart Catholic Church

1324 Jefferson Avenue
Chighizola and Hanker, architects, 1900–1901

The school looks very much like its counterpart, by the same architects, to the east, Immaculate Conception (F-38), while the church is a severely reduced Gothic structure in the yellow brick that the Catholic Church in Memphis favored for a good part of this century.

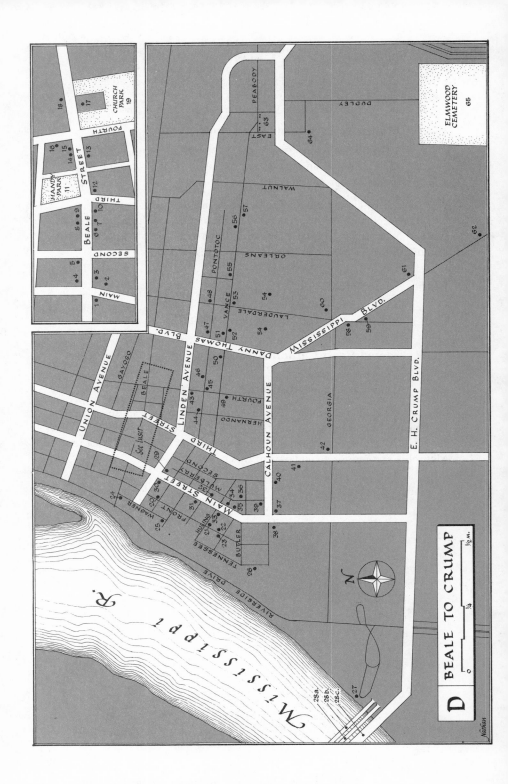

D BEALE TO CRUMP

D   Beale to Crump

The area south of downtown has had a checkered history, perhaps the most checkered in the city. Founded in competition with the original city as South Memphis, it was developed by shrewd real-estate speculators such as Robertson Topp, who built a great house in the 1840s on Beale Street, which is in many ways the main thoroughfare of this section. Beale itself devolved into the principal street of black Memphis, and one of the principal streets of black America, only to find itself, in the late 1960s, the devastated victim of an urban renewal program about which one cannot say enough bad things. To the south of Beale Street, Pontotoc and Vance avenues once were lined with large Victorian houses, of which only a very few remain, and those seem to be in full decay. Vance-Pontotoc was placed on the National Register of Historic Places as a historic district and then removed because of its continuing collapse. The destruction of the area directly south of Beale was at least partly to blame for the hard times Vance-Pontotoc has suffered.

Toward the river, South Main and Front streets responded to the coming of the railroads to that area in the late nineteenth and earlier twentieth centuries by becoming commercial and industrial areas. Front, originally called Shelby Street, had been residential. Crump Boulevard was built in the late 1940s in relation to the building of the Memphis and Arkansas Bridge, which was able to handle greatly increased automobile traffic across the Mississippi River.

BEALE STREET

Beale Street today is one of the saddest examples of what Urban Renewal did to American cities. It stands isolated in a green desert of grass that grows where once a thriving, or at least throbbing, black community lived and gave sustenance to one of the greatest centers of black culture in the United States. Beale Street's Urban Renewal blues go back at least to 1959, when Edmund Orgill, mayor of Memphis, announced his hope that it could be turned into an entertainment district along the lines of Bourbon Street in New Orleans. Orgill was a good man and surely never intended to reduce the street to its present straits. Indeed, following W.C. Handy's death in 1958, he organized the drive to raise funds for the statue of Handy that stands in Handy Park, not just as a monument to a great musician, but also to the black-white cooperation that erected it.

By 1964 the Memphis Housing Authority (MHA) had prepared a master-plan for the whole Beale Street area, which it announced in an eight-hundred-page report that suggested that Beale had to be destroyed to be

Fig. 3

saved. No one, of course, read the whole report. It was accompanied by a curious public relations brochure, short and easy to read, that illustrated all the street's great monuments, past and present, that were *not* black. Left out were pictures of the famous saloons, which the text did mention, and of the pawnshops that clogged the block between Main and Second, which the report did not mention. The brochure contained the ominous statement: "Beale Street has been permitted to deteriorate to a point where little remains, from a practical standpoint, of its lively past."

Consultants for the plan were Walter A.J. Ewald and Associates, who had submitted their report in 1963. They envisioned a Beale Street surrounded by new shopping malls. That is, they had decided, at the very beginning of the project, to tear down the surrounding community of houses and small businesses and replace them with a *cordon sanitaire* of shops, arranged like those in a suburban mall.

The project, of course, was sheer pie in the sky. There was no money to fund it, and there were no businesses lining up to open shops in those devoutly-dreamed surrounding malls. In 1964 the city told MHA to go ahead with an application for a federal grant, and in winter 1968 the project was still under not-very-urgent discussion. In April 1968, however, Martin Luther King, Jr., was murdered at the Lorraine Motel, just a few blocks from Beale. That assassination lead to the assassination of Beale Street. In November 1969, with almost miraculous alacrity, HUD set aside $11,000,000 to fund the Beale Street Urban Renewal Program, and in June 1970, a HUD undersecretary flew into town to announce another grant of $14,000,000 for renovation. The bulldozers were already at work. By the time they got through, all but about 65 of the 625 buildings that had stood on the 113 acres of the renewal area were gone. If decimation takes one in ten, what should we call an act that leaves one in ten? Fifteen hundred residents were displaced to other parts of the city.

Clearly, the city fathers had panicked. In the aftermath of the King shooting, they feared black uprisings; there had been a small-scale riot on Beale after the assassination, when the city was under martial law and tanks patroled the streets. Most particularly, they feared the black area, centered on Beale, that shouldered up to Main Street and appeared to threaten the downtown. Beale Street now had to be destroyed not only to save itself but also to save the center of the city. To the city fathers, it also seemed certain that Beale never could become the entertainment center they dreamed of if it were still in the heart of a black neighborhood.

Down came all the buildings, with the exception of a church or two, to the north, east, and south of Beale. Worse, even, the block of the street itself between Second and Main also was razed. Now Main Street would be forever insulated from Beale, whereas before they had joined seamlessly in a living urban fabric, even if the glue that held them together had been a row of pawnshops hanging their gilded balls out over the sidewalk.

After the swift destruction came a long languishing. In 1973 a contract was let to a private developer to do something with what still stood. Money was short, and the developer failed. Then came a non-profit group of well-meaning citizens, black and white, that also failed. In late 1975 the MHA was ready to let a contract to build a mall that would have put trees, benches, fountains, and cutsey lampests down the middle of the street, but the National Advisory Committee on Historic Preservation put a stop to the mall plan. Beale Street had been declared a National Historic Land-mark in 1966, and the advisory committee observed that the mall would turn the street, inappropriately, into a suburban shopping center.

It was not until winter 1980 that reconstruction work actually began on the street, and by that time some buildings that had stood abandoned for several years were so decayed that they were either falling down or could not be saved. The delay thus had meant further losses to the urban fabric. You sometimes hear it argued that all the buildings in the area were in such bad shape, even before the King assassination, that they had to be torn down. The fact is that ten years and more of abandonment turned many buildings from down-at-the-heels into down-on-the-ground.

By October 1983, when the first reconstructed section actually opened for business, all that was left of the original streetscape was a good chunk of the storefronts between Second and Third, the storefronts across from Handy Park in the next block east, the two Daisy Theaters and a couple of other buildings in the next block, and the Beale Street Baptist Church and Solvent Savings Bank Building, still farther east. Even the church, how-ever, had had to fight for its right to remain. At this writing, in summer 1988, the block between Second and Third still needs serious work.

In this dream to make Beale into a sanitized Bourbon North, no-one seems to have observed that Bourbon Street and the French Quarter are

Fig. 4

inseparable. Bourbon Street is part of a lively and whole district that includes any number of different commercial enterprises and types of residences. These all support each other. To put the issue simply, no-one, to my knowledge, has ever suggested saving Bourbon Street by tearing down the *Vieux Carré*. The cleaned-up Beale Street envisioned by the Memphis planners had as much chance of living without its neighborhood as an astronaut on the moon stripped of his spacesuit. The buildings of Bourbon Street are all more or less authentically old and thus more or less genuine. In Memphis, however, the planners seem to have thought that they could dupe tourists by substituting fake, if clean, new buildings for the actuality of the old ones. They wanted Main Street, Disneyland, instead of Beale Street, Memphis. They also wanted ample parking, which has been provided at the backs of the saved storefronts. From the vantage point of the parking lots, the present attractions of the street don't seem that attractive. A cigarette billboard that rose over the parking lot in summer 1988 (Fig. 3) contained the statement "Alive with Pleasure." The irony could well bring tears to the eyes.

What the street actually was, both in terms of architecture and of life, we now can know only through old views, particularly the splendid paintings that an Italian artist, Mario Bacchelli, made around 1950, when he was living and working in Memphis. Bacchelli recorded the rich irregularity of buildings such as the Panama Club at Beale and Fourth, which looked like a small brick replica of an Italian civic palace of the late Middle Ages, except that it housed all kinds of colorful day and night life (Fig. 4). We can also experience Beale as it once was in the description given in the late 1930s in the WPA guidebook to the state of Tennessee, quoted here at length because it is so evocative, even if some of the attitudes that lie behind it are not attitudes we might adopt today.

The blocks between Main and Third Streets are crowded with pawnshops, clothing stores, fruit stands, restaurants, doctors' offices, and photographic studios. Traders and merchants display goods on the sidewalks in front of stores. Smooth-tongued barkers entreat passersby to stop and inspect bargains.

On East Beale Street "conjure" doctors and medicine men still ply their trades. They offer luck bags to wear around the neck, containing strange mixtures to cure diseases and drive away trouble. Love powders, packets of "goobers" or graveyard dust, and black and white cat bones are among the charms offered for sale.

Of the famous old establishments still in operation under their original names are Peewee's Place, formerly owned and operated by Vigelio Maffi [sic] Peewee, Italian gambler, and now a favorite gathering place for musicians; the Panama Club; and Mannitt Ashford's Place.

On Saturday Beale Street is thronged with country Negroes from Arkansas, northern Mississippi, and western Tennessee, who arrive early and bargain for clothing, groceries, fish, and pork chops. Saturday night belongs to the cooks, maids, houseboys, and factory hands.

The "underworld" block, from Hernando Street to Fourth Street, is packed with social clubs, movie theaters, beauty parlors, and lunch rooms. Though quiet and peaceful in daytime, at night "we stomps the daylight into the flo." Street walkers and guitar players stroll up and down the avenue. Pickpockets and gamblers weave in and out of the crowd. The air is thick with the smell of fried fish, black mud from the levees and plantations, and whisky trucked in from the moonshine stills of swamps and hills. From the pianos in crowded honkytonks comes the slow, "hesitation" beat of the blues, or the furious stomp of swing music.

Things aren't quite the same.

D-1   Orpheum Theater

South Main Street
Rapp and Rapp, Chicago, architects, 1927
Awsumb and Williamson, architects for restoration, 1970s and 1980s

There has been a theater on this corner of downtown Memphis since the 1890s. The first, grandly called an opera house but often used for vaudeville, burned in 1923. The present, designed by Rapp and Rapp, a firm that specialized in building Orpheum movie houses around the country, has an ugly buff-brick exterior, but it is worth the effort to try to get in to to see the interior, which has been lovingly restored.

The lobby is rather bare for a great movie palace, but to the left is a glamorous new bar area installed by Carl Awsumb and Jim Williamson, the architects for the restoration. They caught the spirit of the movies here. The auditorium, however, is as glittery as you could want. Gilt and

D-1

velvet and plaster conspire to envelope the audience in a strange but evocative blend of baroque, rococo and Second Empire details, all of which bespeak luxury of the kind most people in America in the 1920s only experienced in Hollywood films or in the movie palaces in which they were shown. Downstairs, the bathrooms retain much of their original Art Deco furniture.

D-2   Memphis Light, Gas, and Water Division, Administration Building

220 South Main Street
Thorn, Howe, Stratton and Strong, architects, 1970

After the first wave of bulldozers, the city rushed in with a beachhead building to show its intention to win the Battle of Beale. This muscular structure not only pulled itself back from Main Street, to announce with its greensward the new suburban concept of downtown, but it also left ample room to the north for the insertion of Elvis Presley Plaza. The MLGWD Building replaced the Randolph Building, an all-masonry office structure of considerable size and presence and of arguably greater architectural interest.

D-3   Elvis Presley Plaza

Beale and Main, southeast corner
Eric Parks, sculptor, 1980

Because Elvis fused black and white music in his own work, there is justification for putting him at the entrance to a street that now seeks to bring together the blacks and whites of the city. Unfortunately, the sculptor didn't give Elvis vigor. It's hard to do public monuments today, and certainly Parks had no great tradition of bronze statues of rock stars to base his work on. Elvis holds his guitar in his left hand with apparent disinterest, while he lamely gestures us down Beale with his right. Why, we wonder, isn't he strumming his guitar, his mouth opened in song and his hips thrown into their famous gyrations? Elvis deserved a Bernini; he got a blah. Even his fringe is stiff.

D-4   Tri-State Bank Building

180 South Main Street
Walk Jones and Francis Mah, architects, 1975

This rough-cut concrete-block building gave a boost to the street during years when it needed a boost, but it also pulled itself diagonally back from Beale in an antiurban move to create a suburban parking lot.

D-5   Lansky's

126 Beale Street

To the east of the Tri-State Bank parking lot is a genuine old building, the home of Lansky's, a clothing store frequented by Elvis that still contains splendid Elvis memorabilia. Lansky's is one of two businesses on Beale to survive from the period B.B. (before bulldozers). Only court battles made this survival possible.

D-6   Police Museum

159 Beale Street

A one-story building, newly minted, that suffers from acute "cute-itis" in the wrought-iron shutters hung beside the windows.

D-7   A. Schwab

163 and 165 Beale Street
c. 1890 (?)

These buildings contain the other surviving retailer, A. Schwab, whose windows still display the kind of merchandise he has always carried. Both of the Schwab buildings are typical of the late-nineteenth-century commercial architecture that rose on both sides of the street. At ground level, cast-iron columns support a brick second floor that has little to do, visually, with what is beneath it. The bottom is for the display of merchandise and entrance to the store and the upper floor. The upper floor is the part of the building that most actively frames the street, because it has the weightiest architectural elements. In both buildings the segmental arches of the windows are emphasized by projecting brick courses that start about one-fourth of the way down the window, rise up to cross the window, and then go back down and across the facade to tie the windows together. Above the windows is an attic story with inset cast-iron grills that both ventilate the attics and offer an opportunity for a little fanciness. 163 Beale is still fancier in this zone, because it has pairs of squat pilasters that frame the grills and support the tall parapet that caps the facade.

D-8   162 Beale Street

1894

A more elaborate version of the standard commercial building, with particular attention focused on the central bay of the second story. There a round arch is surrounded by stone, and the keystone of the arch supports a round console. From there a flagpole rises through the cornice and beyond the rooftop, to be steadied by a decorative metal triangle. Few buildings give such importance to flagpoles.

D-7

D-9   164–82 Beale Street

The streetscape here is largely intact. The building at 174 was probably
built before 1865, while those at 176 and 178 are slightly later versions of
the same design. The corner building at 184 was built in 1925.

D-10   Gallina Building

177–181 Beale Street
B.C. Alsup, architect, 1891

This facade is tricky, if not downright mannerist. At ground level, the
building has five bays, created by cast-iron piers that carry steel I-beams all
the way across. Three of the bays are quite wide, while two are very narrow. These latter contained doors that led into the building.

Typical of these commercial buildings, the facade completely starts
over on the next level. Here four piers rise through the second floor to
carry great round arches that form the windows of the third floor. On the

D-10

faces of the two center piers heavy half-columns, held by round consoles, burst from the facade. These columns, the beefiest items in the facade, are poised, but not quite centered, over the narrow voids of the doorways below. Over this triply-divided part of the facade, arches a single curved pediment that spans the whole of the center bay and half of each side bay. The pediment rises just inside a clever arrangement of stones that carry the keystones of the arches vertically up into the sky. Over the central arch Alsup suddenly switched to a pair of small windows, and he also stuck in a band of terra-cotta ornament above the arches, to enliven even more the brick, stone, and cast iron of the rest of the wall.

An almost-all-purpose building, the Gallina was as lively in the functions it contained as in the rhythms and materials of the facade. Inside were a hotel, a saloon, and offices. Traveling opera troupes are said to have stayed there. It is lucky indeed that this, the best facade Beale Street had, is still with us, even if now it is just a facade, propped up like a stage flat.

D-11 Handy Park

Beale Street Between Second and Third Streets

The next block offers on the north Handy Park, with a statue of the great musician, made by an Italian artist, Leone Tomassi, and cast in Florence. The statue was dedicated on 1 May 1960. The park occupies the site of the Market House, a covered central market building erected in 1899 and razed in the 1920s to create Beale Street Square, now renamed to honor Handy. The renewal of the park in the 1980s included digging a large hole in its center to make an amphitheater for musical performances, and moving the statue closer to Beale. To the east, across Third Street, is a lifeless 1980s extension to Handy Park; you can often find musicians playing in its inhospitable wasteland. They, who give their talents to the public, deserve a happier environment.

D-12 197–209 Beale Street

Across the street from Handy Park is a row of old storefronts, preserved by new paint on their crumbling brick walls and by entirely new innards. None of the buildings is a great work of architecture, but as an ensemble they have a lot more to offer than the new buildings, trying to look like old, that one finds in the next block to the east. The pediment stuck on above the attic of 205, built in 1894, is a pleasant surprise, and the two-story pilasters on the building at 207–209, of the 1890s, give that building even a suggestion of monumentality.

D-12

D-13

D-13 (Old) Daisy Theater
329 Beale Street
1914

In the block between Third and Fourth, flanked by new buildings by Antonio Bologna, rises the old Daisy Theater, with a gaudy facade centered on a half dome that is one of the architectural high points of the street. The dome has very skinny ribs that promise something quite different at the top of the circle from the aggressively heavy garland that droops there. To each side rise piers with rounded tops that seem to come from no particular style at all, but the whole facade does suggest the possible confusion a movie mogul might have felt while trying to distinguish among the Byzantine, Renaissance, and California Mission architectural styles. Inside, the decoration is Neo-Regency, more or less. Patrons enter the theater alongside the screen, so that the moviegoers become part of the show. This must have been particularly jolly in the old days, when everybody on Beale knew everybody else.

D-14   New Daisy Theater

330 Beale Street
1942

Across the street is the New Daisy, less ornate but still no slouch. The Art Deco facade features an alternation of yellow-brick and grey-concrete vertical stripes. The concrete is incised with a diaper pattern in which sunbursts have been drawn. One wonders if the designer here may also have done the Luciann Theater on Summer Avenue (H-9). The New Daisy is flanked by two more survivors, both probably from the 1930s or early 1940s.

D-15   The Monarch Cafe

340 Beale Street
1923

Here is a typical commercial building—cast-iron piers below, masonry story above—that goes all out to be Venetian Renaissance. The two-tone brickwork features stripes and diaper patterns over the central stone window, which is carved as it might have been in the late fifteenth century.

D-16   W.C. Handy House

352 Beale Street
Early twentieth century

The street has endured the intrusion of the shotgun house Handy was born in, an import from Jennette Place on the southern fringes of the city. The house is set so far back from the corner of Beale and Fourth that, even though it was deliberately moved to Beale, it still has little physical relation to the street. The house suffered a fire a few years before it was moved, and so what you see is not necessarily original. Still, for many visitors, this will be the only view of a house type that was once, and still is, one of the most common in the city.

D-17 Beale Street Baptist Church

379 Beale Street
Edward Culliatt Jones and Mathias Harvey Baldwin,
architects, 1867–81

This church, said to be the first built in the South by blacks for blacks, was designed by two of the city's leading white architects. The stone exterior, painted white in 1964, has a tall basement from which the bulk of the church rises. The basement houses the Sunday school area. Twin towers flank a rose window with a central roundel surrounded by eight smaller roundels in a wheel pattern.

Of the twin towers, the one to the west once carried a tall steeple which, like most Memphis wooden steeples, eventually succumbed to termites. On the south tower stood a lead and bronze statue of Saint John the Baptist. According to an account in the *Commercial Appeal*, lightning struck the roof of the church in 1938, and workmen had to go up to make repairs. One of them bumped into the statue and knocked it to the ground.

D-17a

The bronze body shattered, but the lead head remained intact, to roll around the street. John the Baptist, it was noted, had lost his head again.

Steep steps, placed between the twin towers, lead from Beale Street into a narthex. From there double flights of stairs lead up to the sanctuary, a two-story space surrounded by galleries on three sides. The structure of the interior is wood, restored after a fire in the 1920s. Square wooden piers, beveled at the corners, separate the nave from the aisles and hold up the galleries. The piers continue upward to support wooden diaphragm arches that span the galleries and the nave and support the ceiling. The walls are composed of wide boards with wide battens tacked over the joints. The interior, filled with light from ample windows on two levels, has an airiness that makes it one of the most satisfying nineteenth-century interiors left in the city.

D-18   Solvent Savings Bank

386 Beale Street
Robert R. Church, designer, 1906

The designer was surely Robert R. Church, president of the bank. Church made millions in banking and real estate; indeed, he was the South's first black millionaire. He also usually designed the buildings he owned. The utilitarian character of this one, decorated with stamped metal pieces ordered from a catalogue, accords with other buildings by Church, such as the two-thousand-seat auditorium he built across the street in Church Park.

D-19   Robert Church Park

391 Beale Street
J. Ritchie Smith, landscape architect, 1986

You will never see anyone spending time in this park, because there is nothing to do or see. On this site in 1899, Robert R. Church laid out a park for the benefit of his fellow blacks, who had been given no public park by the city. He charged admission, however. The six-acre park included a playground, a bandstand, and gardens planned and planted by Mrs. Church. There was also an auditorium that held two thousand (D-19b). The building was just a utilitarian structure, but it did serve as a cultural and even a political center for the city's black population. A black historian of Memphis, G. P. Hamilton, tells us that Church had such a passion for architecture that by the time of his death in 1912, he had built over one hundred buildings, all of which he designed himself. As an architect, Church was self-taught.

The Church Park auditorium is memorialized today by two rows of concrete columns that stand forlornly in the grass just east of Beale Street

D-17b &
D-19a

D-19b

Baptist Church. They don't stand on the site of the original auditorium, which was placed back from the street. The columns take up an idea that Venturi, Rauch and Scott Brown had used in their reconstruction of Benjamin Franklin's House in Philadelphia in the 1970s—that is, the lost building is given to us only in skeletal form. But here the columns don't even begin to suggest what the actual auditorium looked like.

Church, at this end of Beale Street, like Elvis at the other, deserved better. The spaces dedicated to them, empty in the largest sense of the word, are the pair of vacuities that frame the picture of Beale Street as an urban tragedy.

D-20   John Alexander Austin House

290 South Front Street
c. 1875

Of the numerous townhouses that lined South Front Street in the late
nineteenth century, this is the only one largely intact (a fragment of another house still stands just to the north, at 278 South Front). All of the
others succumbed to the commercialization of the area that followed the
opening of the railroad bridge across the Mississippi in 1892. The Austin
house has Italianate detailing in its wooden brackets and window frames.
The original owner, a wholesale clothing merchant, was typical of the
people who lived in this area.

D-21   Paper Works Apartments

(formerly D. Canale and Co.)
408 South Front Street
1913
Antonio Bologna, architect for renovation, 1985

This industrial structure, once the home of a wholesale grocery business,
has a clearly expressed, well-proportioned concrete frame with brick and
glass infill. The restoration has preserved the straightforward clarity of the
original design.

D-22   Tayloe Paper Company

420 South Front Street
Jones and Furbringer, architects, 1912

An early-twentieth-century commercial building that could never quite
make up its mind what style it wanted to be. The five stories are separated
into three main horizontal divisions, each of which offers bits and pieces
of different architectural styles. Characteristic of Jones and Furbringer are
the textural effects achieved with the varied brickwork.

D-23   Barnes and Miller Hardware

427–435 South Front Street
B.C. Alsup or Neander M. Woods, Jr., architect (?), 1909

This handsome Beaux-Arts commercial structure has elegantly detailed
stone courses at the corners and handsome segmental arches tied together
across the top floor by a stone stringcourse. The similarities between this
building and the far more elaborate Joseph N. Oliver cold-storage building
(A-50) several blocks north on Front Street, designed by Alsup and Woods,

suggest that one of them designed this structure two years after their partnership broke up. This building served from 1920 to the mid 1930s as the headquarters building for Clarence Saunders' Piggly Wiggly stores.

D-24   Linden Station

245 Wagner Place
Chighizola, Hanker and Cairns, architects, 1905–1907

An industrial building that has undergone yuppification, Linden Station is particularly interesting for its very early use of a steel-and-glass curtain wall structure, long before that kind of system had become the cry in European avant-garde architectural circles. The idea may well have been brought back to Memphis by Bayard Cairns from his European studies.

D-25   Ballard and Ballard Obelisk Flour Co.

Wagner Place and Vance Avenue, northwest corner
1924

Undoubtedly the most imaginative Egyptian Revival building in Memphis. The corners of the dark red-brick structure are marked by stone obelisks that almost act as if they were pilasters, carrying the large cavetto cornice that crowns the whole. On each obelisk, the same hieroglyphs are repeated. According to experts from the distinguished institute for Egyptian studies at Memphis State University, the message of these hieroglyphs is (sadly) nonsense.

D-25

D-26

D-26   Tennessee Brewery

477 Tennessee Street
1890

The Tennessee Brewery is a collection of great castles for the production of beer, which nineteenth-century Memphians consumed in awesome quantities. The original one-story brewery structures stood on the vacant lot to the north of the present buildings. Between 1886 and 1890, the large northern section of the brewery seems to have been built as a storehouse for filled kegs, a function that its closely-packed, heavy masonry piers allowed it to continue to serve throughout the building's operation. In 1890, the other structures, beginning with the tower that bears the date, were added at the south, making use of a more elaborate architectural vocabulary. The architect of the 1890 addition sensitively fused his building with the warehouse that already stood, by reusing its ground-level door forms in the northernmost section of his building.

This second architect did not conceive the 1890 building as one piece, but as a combination of several parts. As the photograph from 1895 shows, the central facade of each section had a projecting signboard that announced its function: "Brewhouse," "Refrigerating Machine House," and "Boilerhouse." The whole building took on a picturesque irregularity of silhouette and mass that gives it much of its visual power. The irregularities, however, are held in check by consistent use of a heavy bottom story, broken by large round arches, that supports a second two-story section organized into narrower round-arched bays. Above these arches rises the third, frontispiece level. The tower building, in particular, is handsomely detailed, with round moldings set inside the window frames on the second and third floors, and round drip moldings, originally covered in copper, surrounding the arches. The brick arches themselves spray out into the wall dramatically. The steel roof trusses that cover the courtyard behind the main tower seem to have been inserted later, because they don't quite line up with any of the brick architecture to which they were applied.

As these words are written, the building is abandoned and subject to dangerous decay. Trees have taken root in its walls, just as you see them growing out of the ruins of ancient Rome in old paintings and drawings. The brewery is the finest industrial structure built in Memphis in the nineteenth century, and one hopes that a new use will be found for it before decay progresses to the point of no return. Had The Pyramid been built nearby, as was originally suggested, the brewery's future might be more secure.

D-27   First Unitarian Church/ The Church of the River

292 Virginia Avenue West
Roy P. Harrover and Associates, architects, 1976
Bob Church, principal designer

The point of this building is to give itself over to its spectacular site. Perhaps nowhere else in the city is the river seen to better advantage. The relatively anonymous white-brick, brown-roofed, ground-hugging structure is entered through a flat courtyard that leads into the sanctuary. The slope of the bluff provides a steep theater-seat configuration focused on the

D-27

D-28a

windows that open up to the river and all its life. The preacher gets to stand in front of a solid niche, but no matter how enthralling the sermon, the competition from the river view must be almost insurmountable. This church is a monument to a pantheistic view of the world, if ever there were one. From the bluff below the church, the trio of bridges that cross the Mississippi just to the south can be seen to particular advantage.

D-28a. Frisco Bridge

> George S. Morrison, Chicago, engineer, 1892

The Frisco Bridge was the first built across Mississippi after the construction of the Eads Bridge in St. Louis in the 1870s. It is a cantilever bridge that throws great steel trusses across the spaces between the piers. The longest distance between piers is 1,500 feet, spanned by two 750-foot sections that meet in the middle.

D-28b. Harahan Bridge

> Ralph Modjeski and K.G. Williams, engineers, 1916

D-28c. Memphis and Arkansas Bridge

> Modjeski and Masters, consulting engineers, 1945–49

SOUTH MAIN STREET

This area experienced rapid growth and change in the years following the opening of Union Station at Calhoun and Third in 1912 and Central Station at Calhoun and Main in 1914. Rooming houses, hotels, and restaurants served the railroads, while light industrial and commercial buildings housed enterprises that made use of the presence of the railroads in the area. The streetscape is largely intact, thanks in part to the fact that it never came under the baleful glance of the Memphis Housing Authority during the heyday of urban renewal in the city. The one great loss has been Union Station, the finest large Beaux-Arts building the city ever had. In general, the buildings follow the formula for commercial structures described above in the sections on Front and Beale streets. A cast-iron ground floor provides ample opening for doors and display windows, but does little to promote a sense of the building as monument. That task is left to the upper floor or floors, which are masonry, usually brick, with more or less elaborate ornament around the windows and at the cornice line. It is the job of these upper floors to define the edges of the street against the sky. We cite only a few buildings of particular interest here, but the whole street is worth exploring as an example of the variety that can be found in the commercial architecture of early-twentieth-century Memphis. The South Main Street Historic District was named to the National Register of Historic Places in 1982.

D-29   Headquarters, Church of God in Christ

(formerly Chisca Hotel)
262 South Main Street
Hanker and Cairns, architects, 1913

This, the largest hotel in the district, was a big hotel for Memphis in its day. But it was clearly built on the cheap; there is little here that is not strictly utilitarian.

D-30   The Adler

262–269 South Main Street
1908–1912

The south wing was built first, in 1908, followed by the north in 1912 . The latter imitated the former, but in slightly fancier terms. In between the two there is a glass insert that dates from the restoration of 1987.

D-31   361–365 South Main Street

c. 1930

The delight of this building is to be found in the three panels of glazed terra cotta in the attic story. Those to the sides are octagons, while the center features a larger rectangle. One might compare these panels to the decorative terra cotta ornament on the facade of Fairview Junior High School (J-1), built in 1930.

D-32   378–384 South Main Street
1905

These almost-matching buildings were built as two separate structures;
the masonry is not bonded together in the center. To give a bit of variety,
the designer made the center masonry pier wider in the building at 378
than in 384. Most unusual are the keystones in the tops of the round vents
in the attic. Circular openings like this rarely, if ever, have keystones.

D-33   The Puck Building
(formerly White, Wilson, Drew Manufacturing Co.)
409 South Main Street
Jones and Furbringer, architects, 1912

This warehouse for a wholesale grocery firm is presided over by a terra
cotta relief, in six panels, of the not-very-puckish figure of Puck that
graced the labels of the Puck Brand Food Products the firm produced.

D-34   Memphis Center for Contemporary Art
416–418 South Main Street
1912, renovated 1982

This building is of historical importance for at least two reasons. First, it
was from the bathroom window of 418 that James Earl Ray fired the shot
that killed Martin Luther King, Jr. Second, this was the first structure to

D-35

be renovated in this district, and thus it became the catalyst for the intense gentrification that is taking place in the late 1980s. Credit for the renewal of the area goes to Robert and Annie McGowan, who decided to turn 418 into their residence. The buildings themselves are fairly standard commercial architecture of the day. The north building has a wider facade, and its upper story contains three windows. The narrower facade to the south has only one fairly broad window above, but that is subdivided in three parts, to give it a relationship to the three windows to the north. The Memphis Center for Contemporary Art exhibits the work of local artists whose art is insufficiently commercial for most local galleries. 416 bears a 1980s inscription, "Nick's," that was put in when the building was used as Nick's China Shop.

D-35   Young and Morrow Building

(formerly Tri-Tone Drug Co. and Jopling Perfumery)
422 South Main Street
1910

This building is distinguished by the elaborate cast-stone ornament applied to the brick walls of the upper story. A lot goes on in the center here—the doorway, the richly foliated cartouche above it, and the small window above that to light the staircase leading to the two loft spaces. The original cornice and keystones of the arched windows have been ripped out and replaced by new bricks that make it easy to see where they once were.

D-36   Lorraine Motel

406 Mulberry Street
1925, 1955, 1964

The Lorraine Hotel and the motel added to it had a history of playing host to famous blacks visiting Memphis, including Cab Calloway, Count Basie, Nat King Cole, and Aretha Franklin. Its saddest moment came in April 1968, when the King assassination took place on its balcony. Plans are in the works to convert the motel into a National Civil Rights Museum, at the cost of some nine million dollars. There has been dissent, however, from those who insist, perhaps rightly, that King would have preferred that the money be spent on housing for the poor.

D-37a

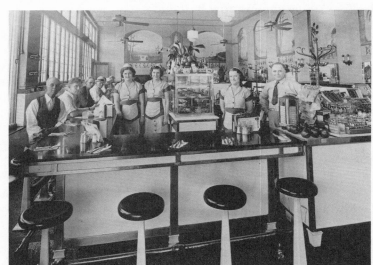

D-37b

D-37 Arcade Restaurant

540 South Main Street
1925, facade remodeled 1954

With little effort the original appearance of this restaurant, which is a land-mark in the district, can be reconstructed. The original neon sign that hung on the corner has been moved to the center of the Calhoun side, and the transom windows above the main plate-glass windows, open in 1925, were closed in during the 1954 remodeling. The interior has survived as a largely intact design of the 1950s. The original appearance is shown in the 1920s photograph of it reproduced here, complete with landscapes painted on the walls under round arches. For diner fans, the Arcade is a real winner.

D-38　Central Station

545 South Main Street
1913–4

When the Illinois Central Railroad refused to join the other railroads into the
city in building Union Station, it more or less committed itself to construct-
ing a competing station for its own use. The building is somewhat confused
as to type. The Main Street front, the principal facade, looks like a railroad
station for the first two stories. Giant cast-stone pilasters carry a broad entablature with the name of the station carved in bold Roman capitals. Between
the pilasters, the openings are filled with cast-iron grills that hold the windows in place and also give the whole a strongly classical air. Above this base,
however, the building turns into a five-story office tower that seems to have
nothing to do with the station below.

Even as a station, the building was somewhat less than adequate. The
tracks run high above street level, so that departing passengers were forced to
climb a lot of stairs to catch their trains. The station itself does not enclose
the tracks, but rather sits awkwardly alongside them, so that arriving passengers felt that they were being dumped on a wooden platform alongside an
office building. This was hardly a celebration of arrival in a great city. (Actually, the trackage is a bit unusual, in that some trains passed directly by the
station, while others backed in in the standard terminal configuration.) Inside, however, there was a capacious waiting room surrounded by four rows
of square columns supporting a clerestory that filled the station with light.

D-39

D-39   Arcade Hotel

(formerly Winona Hotel)
108–110 Calhoun Avenue
1914

One of the best buildings in the district, the Arcade Hotel has a ground floor topped by a horizontal tin garland held up by huge brackets. Above the garland, the pilasters have frames that stop just under the arches on top to do a little geometric jig. Under the splendid tin arches, complete with egg-and-dart moldings, are roundels, made of red and white brick, that come straight from fifteenth-century Italian architecture. There's a lot of joy in this facade.

D-40   United States Post Office

161 East Calhoun Avenue
James A. Wetmore, Acting Supervising Architect of the
Treasury, 1928

This is a smaller but perhaps even more elegant version of the classical, columniated architecture Wetmore provided in the Front Street facade of the Customs House downtown (A-64). The Calhoun post office, in its wide intervals between columns and its flat roof, suggests something of the late-seventeenth-century Grand Trianon in the gardens of Versailles. The recent walling up of the window openings between the columns may have been functionally appropriate, but it did a considerable disservice to the aesthetics of the facade.

D-41   United States Postal Service
Automated Handling Facility

555 South Third Street
Walk Jones and Francis Mah, architects, 1970–71
Mel O'Brien and Associates, associate architects

Between Wetmore's elegant facade on Calhoun and the corner of Third Street stretches a large parking lot backed up by loading docks. The largest building in this complex faces on Third. It is a long, low, bushhammered concrete structure that is probably Jones and Mah's most serious attempt to do a rough-textured Brutalist structure, with boldly-scaled projections thrusting into the surrounding space. That this just wasn't their style seems perfectly clear. The textures are not sufficiently rough and irregular, and the projections aren't convincingly bold. They were thinking, perhaps, of Paul Rudolph's Endo Labs on Long Island, but as designers they are too restrained to indulge in the abandon the Rudolph brand of Brutalism requires.

D-41a

D-41 (Lost Memphis) Union Station

199 East Calhoun Avenue
J.A. Galvin, architect, 1912
Walter F. Schultz, engineer

The Jones and Mah facility took the place of the finest big Beaux-Arts structure ever built in Memphis. Many reasons were doubtless advanced to explain the impossibility of converting it to a postal handling facility. One wonders, however, if a more serious effort toward adaptive reuse might not have been made, had it survived to the present day.

This monumental building, with a grandeur learned from nineteenth-century French architects, who knew what grandeur was all about, made arrivals and departures the exciting events they were supposed to be in the great days of the railroads. Union Station was approached by whites up the grand staircase in the center, while blacks used the smaller staircase to the east. Behind the massive, heavily rusticated stone terminal were cast-iron train sheds.

D-41b

D-42   GMC Building

660 South Third
1947–48

The unfortunate yellow paint job cannot hide the fine Art Deco detailing of this round-cornered building, which is very much like a building at 670 Huron (B-13).

D-43   St. Patrick's Catholic Church

(originally Church of the Incarnation)
277 South Fourth Street
Hanker and Cairns, architects, 1904
Claude Braganza, architect for remodeling of apse, 1968

The street view presents us with a facade straight out of late-sixteenth- or early-seventeenth-century Rome, a two-story elevation with pilasters on both levels, with the narrower upper level connected to the lower by means of elaborate volutes. To the southeast rises a bell tower that also looks as if it had been built in Rome, but during the late Middle Ages. Inside, the church is basilican in plan, with a wide nave separated from the aisles by plaster columns, painted to resemble marble, that carry gilded capitals from which arches spring. Light enters through square windows in the clerestory that carries a flat wooden ceiling with deeply recessed panels. The interior looks as if it might be an Early Christian church in Rome remodeled in the sixteenth or seventeenth century, or one of those

D-43

churches built in seventeenth-century Rome in imitation of Early Christian models. What Cairns did here was create a church with a fictitious history: an Early Christian basilica to which a bell tower was added in the Middle Ages and a new facade in the sixteenth or seventeenth century, when the nave got a facelift and a new ceiling. The paintings in the apse, of the Incarnation flanked by Saint Patrick and perhaps Saint Monica, also look vaguely early baroque, and they are surrounded by stucco frames that would have been current in Rome around 1600 or a little later. The white paint that now covers the whole interior masks the darker colors and gilding the building originally had.

The church fell on hard times (it sits on the edge of the Beale Street desert), and an easy-to-heat chapel was tucked into the apse in 1968 by Claude Braganza. The chapel interferes with the space of the nave, but it is so eminently practical a solution to a serious economic problem that one finds it hard to quibble. The nave is now called a "multi-purpose" space. The early Christians would not have used this term, but they would have understood putting the big space of a church to many uses. They did the same thing themselves.

D-44   Clayborn Temple

(formerly Second Presbyterian Church)
280 Hernando Street
Long and Keys, Minneapolis, and Edward Culliatt Jones, architects, 1891–92

This building, with its tall, sheer walls of ashlar masonry, is one of the most imposing churches in the city. The great stone tower, which occupies the corner of Hernando, is embraced by two projecting arms of what appears to be a Greek Cross plan. Inside, however, the sanctuary is on the diagonal, with the pulpit opposite the corner tower. Balconies, hung off the surrounding walls, turn the space into an irregular octagon, with the result that you lose any sense of the cruciform shape of the exterior. A neat trick. In this building Martin Luther King, Jr., gave his "I Have Been to the Mountaintop" speech the night before he was assassinated.

VANCE-PONTOTOC DISTRICT

This area of grandiose late-nineteenth-century houses is in a state of almost complete decay. Home to wealthy blacks and whites alike in the 1880s and 1890s, Vance-Pontotoc was once one of the richest parts of the city in handsome domestic architecture. Such proximity of blacks and whites in southern cities was not uncommon in the decades following the Civil War. Before the war, black and white had lived close to each other, and those patterns continued until a younger generation of whites decided

D-44

to break them. After 1900 the wealthy whites began to move out into the Central Gardens, and then farther east. Whites tended to live on Vance and Pontotoc, blacks on St. Paul and Georgia. On Cynthia lived the first black woman doctor in the city. The final blow to the neighborhood seems to have been the destruction of the Beale Street area immediately to the north; that manufactured wasteland encouraged the growth of a wasteland here. In the late 1980s a series of fires took out many of the abandoned houses that time had not already destroyed in other ways.

Old houses remain at the addresses that follow. The neighborhood is in such decline, however, that we cannot guarantee that any of them will be standing when you go to look at them. Indeed, as this book was being written, the Mrs. Collin Adams House at 634 Pontotoc, a splendid Victorian cottage of 1892,with a mansard roof and square turret, disappeared, as did the A.J. Hayes, Jr., House, a brick Italianate structure of 1874 at 564 Vance.

D-45   Commercial Building

Pontotoc Avenue and South Fourth Street, southeast corner
Robert R. Church, designer, c. 1890?

Of the more than one hundred buildings Church designed and built in his lifetime, this is one of the two or three commercial structures that still stand. This building is documented as his through mention in his will.

D-46   Double Cottages

378–380 and 382–384 Pontotoc Avenue
Robert R. Church, designer, early 1890s

One of the primary sources of Church's fortune was real estate. He built a considerable amount of rental housing, of which these two frame double cottages are among the few remaining examples.

D-46

D-47

D-47 C.D. Smith and W.B. Gates Houses

492–494 Pontotoc Avenue
1904–1905

A double Romanesque house, one all pointy, the other all rounded. 492 has a steep gable over the entrance, a gabled dormer, a three-sided bay window, and even some curves in the Doric columns of the porch. The entrance at 494 is under a low Richardsonian arch, the dormer above the arch has a curved pediment, and the bay window is a nice round bulge capped by a roof with a conical shape. An imaginative and even powerful pair of houses. The proximity of this relatively pretentious double house to the wooden double cottages that Robert Church rented to blacks (D-46) makes clear how close well-to-do whites and not-so-well-to-do blacks lived to each other around the turn of the century.

D-48 West J. Crawford House

290 South Lauderdale Street
1878

A red-brick townhouse with a one-story porch. The two bays to the south project and have their own gable in the roof, while the bay to the north recedes and contains the door. The windows on the front have heavy carved stone cornices, while those on the sides content themselves with simple projecting brick drip moldings. The richly-carved cornice brackets, which are very close to those on the more pretentious Busby house at 678 Vance (D-56), are perhaps the finest part of the ornamental scheme.

D-49 William A. Mode House

355 South Fourth Street
1905–1906

Steamboat Italian with a garnish of orientalia in the horseshoe arches of the ground-floor bay window, all somewhat retarded in date (one would expect such a house to have been built in the 1880s). Above the bay window, a freestanding wooden arch acts as a screen in front of the wall behind it. The only connection the arch seems to have with the body of the house is at the eaves. The carpenters had a field-day here, in the ornate porch and even in the way they laid the clapboards, horizontal above and below but with a band of vertical boards that act as stretchers in between. The owner, appropriately named William Mode, had his ladies' tailoring establishment on the premises.

D-49

D-50

D-50   The Rev. George White House

448 Vance Avenue
1885

The best surviving Jacobean townhouse in Memphis. The narrow front
pavilion rises from a high basement through two stories to the crown of its
elaborate ogee-arched gable. The verticality of this block is accentuated by
the quoins at the corners that seem to wedge the windows in between
them. On the east side is a companion gable, but less elaborate, with three

angular steps instead of the curves of the arch in front. This gable rises from a roof slightly lower than that of the main pavilion, so that it and the mass under it act almost like a dwarf transept. A cleverly designed house to be treasured.

D-51   510 Vance Avenue
1871

A two-story Italianate brick house with frilly terra-cotta medallions over the door and the window above it, and just enough pressed-tin ornament left to make one aware of what has been lost.

D-52   Dr. William Voorheis House
519 Vance Avenue
1893

This monster of a turreted and gabled house may well have been the biggest Queen Anne pile in town. It now has piles of junk in the front yard.

D-53   Mount Nebo Baptist Church
(formerly Grace Episcopal Church)
555 Vance Avenue
James B. Cook, architect, designed 1894

A stone Gothic church with transepts and side aisles. Cook's design for the facade, with a great tower placed asymmetrically to the west, was one of his very best. Unfortunately, the facade was never finished, and a less-than-wonderful facing has been put on to preserve the north wall.

D-54   Foote Homes
J. Frazer Smith, Max Furbringer, Dudley E. Jones, architects, 1938–41
Harland Bartholomew and Associates, St. Louis, landscape architects

The Lauderdale Courts and the Dixie Homes were so successful that almost immediately the city embarked on another pair of public housing projects, the Foote Homes for blacks and Lamar Terrace for whites. The extraordinary architectural qualities of the Dixie Homes, however, do not quite reappear here, because the budget was severely limited. Smith tried to achieve a certain visual pleasure through the irregular placement of some of the buildings on the site and through the landscaping, which has largely disappeared. An addition to the Foote Homes was built in 1953–54 on the south side of South Lauderdale Street. This extension caused the destruction of the Robert R. Church House.

D-53. Drawing by James B. Cook, 1894.

D-54 (Lost Memphis) Robert R. Church House
384 South Lauderdale Street
Robert R. Church, designer, 1884

Here the first black millionaire in Memphis, and perhaps in the nation, built the house to which he brought his bride in 1885. Placed on a corner lot 55 feet wide and 309 feet deep, the three-story Queen Anne house had fourteen rooms, some frescoed by Italian artists. The neighborhood in those days was a mixed one, a fact not widely recognized even today. Next door to the Churches lived the Memphis postmaster, and in the same block could be found a Main Street merchant and a wholesale grocer from Front Street. All were well-to-do whites. A block farther south on Lauderdale lived Kenneth D. McKellar, who became U.S. Senator from Tennessee for six terms. Almost immediately to the north was Grace Church, which housed an Episcopal congregation composed of the city's white upper class.

Downstairs the Church house had a central hall, ten by thirty-six feet, flanked right and left by pairs of rooms, each sixteen feet by eighteen feet

D-54

that together formed a length equal to that of the hall. On one side was a double parlor, and on the other a reception room and the dining room. On the second and third floors, the central hall running all the way through was repeated, with bedrooms to either side. The plan was simple, something a devoted amateur of architecture like Church well could have worked out for himself. Although the plan originated in the Georgian architecture of the eighteenth century, it was common in large houses in the Middle South in the years prior to the Civil War. Almost every antebellum house in Natchez, for instance, has precisely this arrangement.

The exterior showed the flair for massing and the knowing used of textures and wooden details the Queen Anne style required. Church here proved to be a designer of some talent. When the house was destroyed in 1953 to make way for the extension of the Foote Homes that now stands on the site, the Memphis Fire Department set the house ablaze for practice. The act was reported, with pictures, on the front page of the *Commercial Appeal*.

D-55 J.J. Thornton House

578 Vance Avenue
c. 1875?

A pleasant Italianate carpenter house.

D-56

D-56   J.J. Busby House

678 Vance Avenue
Edward Culliatt Jones, architect, 1882

A huge, elegant, brick Victorian house with large brackets and a big bulging cornice that turns into a fancy baroque pediment. Under the cornice is a triple window, the center of which has been stre-e-e-tched to fit the aspiring curved gable above. Cornices of equally baroque complexity decorate the tops of the windows on the street side, but on the east and west the plain round arch windows are left alone. The chimneys even get into the bulging act; they suggest ladies in tight corsets. The superstructure signals the hand of Edward Culliatt Jones, that master of the overweight upstairs. Had the Busby House had been built in the 600 block of Adams, where its closest standing relatives reside, it might have come through to us in better shape.

D-57   H.B. Hart House

733 Vance Avenue
1907

A two-story clapboard house that looks as if it had been designed by a committee. The jutting polygonal porch has square columns with excess entasis. On one side of the porch, a steep triangular pediment says "Enter Here"—but you can't, because the steps and the door are somewhere else. A huge Palladian window to the west is hardly balanced by the window to the east that is drastically stretched vertically to fit a staircase behind it. The designer tried to apply the classical forms of the Colonial Revival to an uncooperative recipient, an irregularly massed Queen Anne house. The attempt didn't quite work.

D-58 Booker T. Washington High School

709 South Lauderdale Street
Regan and Weller, architects, 1926

Booker T. Washington High School for many years was the only high school in the city for blacks. Regan and Weller provided a typically competent, if dry, design that achieves a certain grandeur of scale through the largeness of the building itself rather than through any application of ornament. The building is very bare and flat.

D-59 Giannini Building

577–579 Mississippi Boulevard
1932

A little bit of Italy on the boulevard called Mississippi, this building proudly proclaims not only the name of its owner but also his ethnic origin. The trapezoidal building fits its trapezoidal lot at the intersection of Mississippi and Danny Thomas (formerly Wellington Street). Over the intersection looks the terrace of the family apartment on the second floor (how Italianate can you get?), while below are the shops. The two-story part carries a red tile roof, and the yellow-brick walls, a substitute for yellow stucco, are decorated with an Art Deco version of North Italian mannerist ornament, particularly the little pilasters with a reverse taper that carry pseudo-capitals with flat volutes and palmettes. A wavy frieze ties the whole building together.

D-60 Georgia Avenue Elementary School

690 Mississippi Boulevard
Office of Walk C. Jones, Jr., architects, 1960–61

The architects used standard elements of the modernist architectural vocabulary—a concrete structural frame and a glass curtain wall—to create a school that was to symbolize the promise of a new world to the kids who studied in it. The spans of the concrete frame are wide and filled with

D-60

horizontal steel sash that reinforces the horizontality of the whole design. The doors, on the other hand, are colored vertical planes that read, a bit confusingly, as stronger than the structure. The school sits on a lot that slopes, and the architects made use of the site to construct two-story buildings on the lower level and connect them to the one-story front part with concrete bridges that form handsome links across space. The Memphis Board of Education had broken the modern architecture barrier with Richland Elementary School (I-48) a few years earlier and was, by 1960, willing to build schools of this kind of uncompromising modernism.

D-61　Formerly Fire Station #8

832 Mississippi Boulevard
Regan and Weller, architects, 1929

It was the policy of the Memphis Fire Department to build fire stations in residential neighborhoods that might be compatible in some way with the houses around them. Regan and Weller did a Tudor station here, while in another part of town they did one, now destroyed, that looked like a bungalow.

D-62　Praise of Zion Missionary Baptist Church

(formerly Mississippi Boulevard Christian Church)
974 Mississippi Boulevard
McKissick and McKissick, Nashville, architects, 1938

Everything in the facade of this bold building builds to the pyramid atop the central tower. The flanks step up to the irregular octagon of the base of the tower, which in turn supports the square base from which the metal pyramid rises. The main masses, of yellow brick, are topped with a thick gray stone coping with channels cut into it to make it seem weightier. The triple opening of the porch is created by two piers faced with three sides of engaged octagonal columns. These carry block capitals like those of the ancient Egyptian Temple of Queen Hatshepsut at Deir-el-Bhari. The same firm did a more elaborately Egyptoid building for Universal Life on Linden Avenue. This was a church that dared to be different, to adopt an architectural style not sanctioned by tradition, whereas most Memphis churches opted for the classical or the Gothic, or at least some recognizable historical style. Here the architects opted for something probably inspired by one of the great masters of early-twentieth-century American architecture, Bertram Grosvenor Goodhue. They also opted for a style that celebrated black pride (see C-8 above).

D-63   Estival Park Houses

First R. Brinkley Snowden House, 927 Peabody Avenue, 1894
P.A. Shepherd House, 933 Peabody Avenue, 1902
M.E. Denie House, 937 Peabody Avenue, 1902
Newton Copeland Richards House, 975 Peabody Avenue, 1889–90

Estival Park was a new residential development opened in 1888 by the George Peabody Real Estate Company of Massachusetts, hence the name given to one of its principal streets. Directing the enterprise locally, and prophetically, was real-estate developer and amateur architect Brinkley Snowden, who was to become the prime mover in the expansion eastward of the city's upper-class residential quarters during the early years of the twentieth century. His own house at 927 is modesty itself in comparison to the castellated fantasy, Ashlar Hall, he was soon to design for himself at Central and Lamar (F-23).

Estival Avenue, the title street, is now bereft of original houses in good condition, but the first block of Peabody still is amply endowed with characteristic houses of the period. 933 has a remarkably placed diagonal entrance porch attached to a polygonal tower. 937 is a particularly fine Queen Anne house—indeed, a better example of that richly textured and gabled genre than the Newton Copeland Richards House (1889–90) at 975, which alone among these buildings has been placed on the National Register of Historic Places. It was suggested in the nomination of this house that Snowden may have been its designer, but there is no hard evidence to back up this hypothesis.

D-64   Coward Place

(formerly H.M. Grosvenor House)
919 Coward Place
1843–56

An Italianate house of a decidedly urban character in its flat facade and blocky massing, even though it was built to command a large agricultural operation far from the center of the city. The flat facade seems to belong to a Federal style house of thirty or forty years earlier. Probably this is the result of the fact that the original house of 1843, a time in which Federal buildings were still being built in Memphis, was enlarged in 1856. Only the terra cotta overwindows and the rather timid brackets under the roofline suggest the later Italian Villa style of the 1850s. The portal also mixes periods. The channeled Doric pilasters carry an Ionic entablature with a detail most entablatures don't have, a keystone. Over this classical portal, which also may date from the 1840s, the designer of the 1850s layered an Italianate terra cotta topping.

D-64

D-65   Elmwood Cemetery
      South End of Dudley Street
      Founded 1852

Elmwood Cemetery is entered from the north over a one-hundred-foot
bridge designed by J. A. Omberg, the city engineer, in 1903. The bridge
spans the railroad tracks that had been built along a city right-of-way
called Broadway. Just inside the cemetery is the office, a Gothic cottage
(D-65a) built around 1880, that is probably the best domestic-scale building in this style left in Memphis. There is a porch with three pointed
wooden arches in the front. Under the eaves of the steeply pitched metal
roof are elaborately carved barge boards that end in pendant bosses under
the peaks. A five-sided bay to the south was added in 1900 to provide a
waiting room, and in the same year a one-story brick vault was added to
the north, to provide space for the storage of documents. Immediately
across the road from the office is the large Crump obelisk, marking the
burial place of "Boss" Crump himself.

Elmwood is laid out like an English garden, with winding roads meandering through gently rolling land. The layout of the roads and the large
specimen trees, particularly oaks, elms, and magnolias, make the cemetery
one of the most beautiful examples of landscape design in the city. One
would like to know who laid Elmwood out and designed the original plantings.

D-65a

Here is buried a diverse group of Memphians, ranging from 1,400 anonymous victims of the yellow-fever epidemics of the 1870s, to the nuns and prostitutes who died helping them, to some of the city's most illustrious citizens. The monuments will repay a leisurely visit, particularly for those who find pleasure in the conceits of death displayed in nineteenth-century memorial structures. You will find here many of the names you have come to know from the streets you use while touring the city, or from paying attention to the movers and shakers in Memphis real estate or Memphis history. We are going to single out a few monuments that you should try not to miss, but our list in no way includes everything worth seeing.

Bear left after the office to the corner of Grand Tour and Central. There on the right is the monument to S.B. Williamson, d. 1869, and Mary E. Williamson, d. 1877. Williamson himself appears at eye level in a relief portrait. Above him rises an octagonal, draped obelisk with Gabriel, trumpet in hand, prepared to blow the Williamsons into heaven.

Follow Central and come, on your right, to the monument of J. Oliver Greenlaw, d. 1864, who laid out the Greenlaw subdivision north of the center of the city (D-65b). The monument is Masonic. A broken column shaft presents a book open to a Masonic symbol on its slanted center. An unfurled scroll, attached we know not how to the column, proclaims the name of the deceased. Even more miraculously, the toppled top of the column is frozen, upended on its capital, in its fall onto the steps of the base. Sarah Elizabeth, Greenlaw's wife, is memorialized next door by a pile of carved fieldstones with lilies and fern leaves and a name scroll.

A bit farther on the right is the twenty-ton, fifty-five-foot brown marble obelisk of the William Green Thomas monument, 1926. It is said that two hundred men and twenty mules were required to set it up. This is not a standard obelisk, but one that has taken on Art Deco qualities, particularly in the reveals at the edges and the engaged colonnettes at the top.

D-65b

D-65c

Continuing on Central, as it approaches the corner of Hill, you have a view of a most impressive erection of obelisks (D-65c). (There being in English no standard accepted collective noun for a group of obelisks, we herewith supply one.) Among these verticals is the horizontal monument of Napoleon Hill, whose six Ionic columns rising from a flat slab are the prototype for the Harahan Monument in Forest Hill Cemetery. Beyond Hill is the statue of Henry A. Montgomery, who is shown in the pose of an orator. Montgomery dropped dead just as he began a welcoming address at a convention. On the base is the inscription: "God's finger touched him and he slept."

Central ends at the intersection of Gardiner and Valley. There, on the corner, stands the granite mausoleum of Robert R. Church, at the head of the black section of Elmwood. This building with four Ionic columns is the only classical mausoleum in the cemetery. Church, who died in 1912, probably designed the building himself and had it erected before his death. On the bronze doors are reproduced quotations from the editorials that appeared in the *Commercial Appeal* on the occasions of the death of Church and of his son, a figure equally important in Memphis history.

Another group of interesting monuments is found at or near the intersection of Byrd and Porter. On the angle proper stands the Snowden monument, with a life-sized bronze angel holding an upended torch and mourning over a sarcophagus. Robert Bogardus Snowden and Annie Overton Brinkley Snowden, owners of Annesdale, are here, as is their son Brinkley Snowden, who built Ashlar Hall and was responsible for much of the growth of Memphis around 1900. Just beyond the Snowdens, on Byrd, is T.O. Vinton, who joined Snowden in the development of Annesdale Park. The Vinton monument is a stubby obelisk topped with acanthus leaves. On the opposite side of the street and a few paces farther on, is the monument to Dr. D.T. Porter, whose heirs purchased Memphis' first skyscraper as a memorial to him. His monument here shows him standing, life size, on a stone mountain adorned with various Masonic devices, including the broken column, ferns, a lily, ivy, and climbing roses. Under his left hand is a stack of books, and attached to the mountain is an opened book that bears, among others, the inscription: "He bore the cross in life to wear the crown in heaven."

E   Evergreen

This large and primarily residential section of midtown is bounded on the west by Cleveland, on the South by Poplar Avenue, on the east by East Parkway and Trezevant, and on the north by Vollintine. Within this area are several distinct neighborhoods, as well as Overton Park, the largest open space in the city, and Rhodes College, Memphis' most impressive college campus.

This part of town began to be developed in the last years of the first decade of this century, but the majority of the houses and other structures here date from the 1920s, when residential expansion on a large scale began, through the 1940s. The laying out of North Parkway at the turn of the century provided a direction for future residential growth, although at the time of its opening, the section from McLean to East Parkway was used more often as a horse-racing track than as a motorway. Until 1910, in fact, it was called the Speedway. As part of the group of boulevards which were laid out to ring the city, North Parkway was intended to provide Memphis residents with a pleasant area for automotive diversions as well as to serve as a sort of "beltway" around the municipal borders.

The first organized residential development in this part of town was the Stonewall Place subdivision of Robert Brinkley Snowden and his partners, which was opened in 1909 as an attempt to repeat—on a grander scale—the successes of the Annesdale Park (1903) and Annesdale-Snowden (1906) areas to the south. Building had already been occurring sporadically further to the east, between Stonewall and Overton Park, as the four-squares marched north from the Central Gardens. The teens and twenties saw the development of the streets immediately to the west of Overton Park.

The real catalyst for expansion north of the Parkway came in the early twenties, when Southwestern Presbyterian University, as it was then known, decided to relocate to Memphis from Clarksville, Tennessee, and change its name to Southwestern at Memphis. One hundred acres, fronting on North Parkway just across from Overton Park, were obtained, and a Nashville architect, Henry Hibbs, was hired to create a Gothic Revival campus, in the manner of Oxford and Princeton, on the banks of the Mississippi. Before the college even opened its doors in 1925, a new subdivision, Hein Park, had been started immediately to the east of the college property, extending to Trezevant, the northward extension of East Parkway. Through the boom years of the 1920s the area to the west of Rhodes College (since 1984 the new name for Southwestern at Memphis) was built up, with what is probably the largest collection of bungalows in the city.

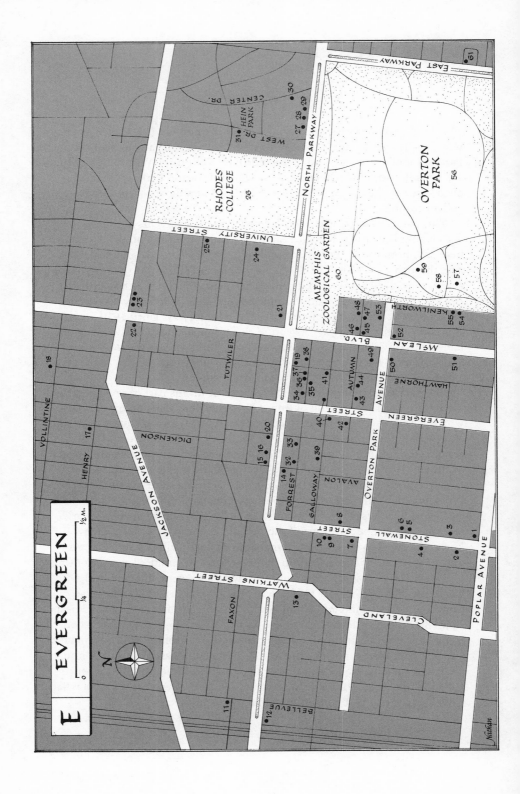

E EVERGREEN

N

0   ¼   ½ M.

Nathan

RHODES COLLEGE
26

HEIN PARK
31

CENTER DR.

WEST DR.

UNIVERSITY STREET

NORTH PARKWAY

EAST PARKWAY

OVERTON PARK
56

MEMPHIS
ZOOLOGICAL GARDEN
60

KENILWORTH

McLEAN
BLVD.

HAWTHORNE

AVENUE

EVERGREEN

OVERTON PARK

AVALON

STONEWALL
STREET

GALLOWAY

FORREST

STREET

AUTUMN

TUTWILER

JACKSON AVENUE

DICKINSON

VOLLINTINE

HENRY

FAXON

WATKINS STREET

BELLEVUE

CLEVELAND

POPLAR AVENUE

30
27 28 29
25
24
23
22
21
18
17
16 15
20
14
32
33
39
40
42
12
11
13
10
9
8
7
6
5
4
3
2
1
34 36 37 19
35 38
41
43 44
45 46 47 48
49
50
51
52
53
54 55
57 58 59
61

STONEWALL PLACE

The remarkable size of this street (it is one of the widest two-lane streets in the city) and the grandness of some of its houses make it clear that the developers had high hopes for this new subdivision. If these hopes were not all realized, this is still one of the more memorable residential streets in midtown.

E-1   Duplex

200 Stonewall Place
Hanker and Cairns, architects (?), 1917–18

The first house on the east side of the intersection of Stonewall and Poplar is a smooth stone Beaux-Arts number. Its Stonewall facade is elegant in a restrained way, and there are recognizable proportional relationships with the facade of the Newburger house (corner of Union Avenue and East Parkway South) by Hanker and Cairns (F-154). Cairns was a cousin of the developer, Robert Brinkley Snowden. The designer, whoever he was, put everything into the front of the house; the two long flanks are quite dull.

E-2   R.T. Cooper House

227 Stonewall Street
1910

One of the first houses on the street, this must have been a model for what the developers hoped would happen in the area. R.T. Cooper was the president of the Stonewall Place Co. and one of R.B. Snowden's partners in the venture. The buff-brick house exudes expansiveness, with the wide doorway echoing the remarkable width of the facade.

E-3   M.H. Hunt House

244 Stonewall Street
1913

Although the architect of this stucco house is unknown, its similarity to the Joyner House at 790 East Snowden Circle in the Annesdale-Snowden development (F-21) is immediately seen in the use of the great porch piers that stick up through the roof.

E-4 Robert C. Clinton House

291 Stonewall Street
1910

R.C. Clinton advertised himself as an "architect and builder," and we may assume that he was responsible for his own house. That he was more of a builder than an architect is readily apparent, but his free use of all sorts of motives makes for a charmingly eclectic effect.

E-5 W.R. Harrison House

312 Stonewall Street
Mahan and Broadwell, architects, 1914

Some of the earliest houses of this prolific architectural duo can be found on Stonewall. Since they returned about a decade later to do another pair of houses a block or two farther north, one can get a vivid picture of the development of a single architectural firm as one moves along the street.

This house is essentially a standard four-square, but already Mahan and Broadwell were showing their ability to do unconventional things with conventional forms. They put a Colonial, Doric porch all the way across the front of the house and extended it visually by adding a porte-cochere to the south. Underneath this porch, the standard doorway and large window have been replaced by three sets of French doors facing the street and one pair under the porte-cochere. The severity and harshness so common in four-squares have been relieved by putting a bend into the driveway, so that it meets the street in the middle of the lot.

E-6 A.B. Knipmeyer House

326 Stonewall Street
1913

The random stonework of the ground floor, the diagonal porte-cochere, and the gambrel roofline, as well as the date, make it likely that this is another house built by R.C. Clinton for the new neighborhood.

E-7 August Longinotti House

395 Stonewall Street
Mahan and Broadwell, architects, 1914

Another very early house by Mahan and Broadwell, but this one lacks the inventiveness of the four-square at 312. It is a plain brick box, marked only by a pair of severe gables on the front.

E-8 Edward C. Gause House

420 Stonewall Street
Mahan and Broadwell, architects, 1921–23

This clapboard cottage shows how far Mahan and Broadwell had progressed as domestic architects by the early 1920s. The elegant triple window on the right, surmounted by a blind fan, is countered by a very large
and deep porch on the left. The triple columns supporting the corners of
the porch, almost too thin for their load, are echoed by pilaster strips
where the porch meets the body of the house. For a later example of this
asymmetrical play with classical elements, see Mahan's McElroy House at
2240 North Parkway (E-28).

E-9 Herbert H. Samuels House

449 Stonewall Street
Mahan and Broadwell, architects, 1922–23

The house that has been called "the best little bungalow in Memphis" is
certainly an architectural delight. Serious architects could and did easily
overlook the possibilities in the bungalow form, but Mahan and Broadwell
here have taken every opportunity to do something fun rather than something boring, not just in the massing but also in the rich detailing. The
house is a standard airplane bungalow, but scarcely noticeable as such
under its mountain of a roof. There are five different rooflines, mounting
to the "tail" of the airplane. The house is asymmetrical, but nicely balanced, and the central entrance with its twisted columns juts out towards
the street. The ensemble produces a Sino-Hispanic effect, the former in the
roofs, the latter in the columns with spiral channeling. There is a remarkably similar bungalow at 1259 Castalia Street.

E-9

E-10

E-10 Eugene Woods House
457 Stonewall Street
1920

Another beautiful bungalow, this one suffers only by being next door to 449. What this house lacks in the adventurousness of its neighbor it makes up for in straightforward elegance. It is worthwhile comparing the "tails" of these side-by-side "airplanes." The architect of this house has created a frank and open second story by placing a long string of windows in the street facade. On the other hand, the retiring "tail" of the Mahan and Broadwell bungalow next door plays peek-a-boo with the street. There is something reminiscent of Frank Lloyd Wright's early houses in the clean horizontality of this bungalow.

NORTH PARKWAY

The old name for this stretch of road—the Speedway—has remained particularly apt, and it is downright dangerous to attempt to drive at much less than the general flow of traffic while gawking at the houses. Most of the houses are of average quality, and even the good ones suffer from the cramped scale of the lots. The Parkway itself is a very grand boulevard, and the narrow, shallow lots here do not contribute the same effect of grace and space as the big lots of East Parkway. On North Parkway, however, the bungalow found an expansive, tree-filled setting appropriate to its rustic nature that it seldom found in other parts of the city, or even in other parts of the country. North Parkway must have been one of the great bungalow streets.

E-11

E-11 Speedway Terrace Baptist Church

601 North Bellevue Boulevard
Nowland Van Powell, architect, 1952, 1954, 1965

Not many churches get named for streets that have become race courses, but this one staunchly maintains a local tradition of naming churches for the streets on which they stand. The steeple, in which Powell plays around with early-nineteenth-century English architectural ideas in his own inimitable way, lines up with a street called Faxon that does not run directly into the church facade. The effect is to make the rest of the building seem a bit lopsided, when you come upon it from the North Parkway angle. No-one could get more for less money out of the classical style than Powell did in churches like Speedway Baptist. Indeed, his churches are testaments to what a shrewd architect can do with a limited budget.

E-12 Harry Blockman House

1155 North Parkway
Mahan and Broadwell, architects, 1921

E-13 Sears, Roebuck Warehouse

495 North Watkins Street
1927

Designed as a suburban store to serve newly-automobiled Memphians, the Sears warehouse shows some restrained but very up-to-date Art Deco design, expecially around the great tower that marks the entrance. This was the biggest building in Memphis when it was built, and after the additions of 1929 and 1937, Sears proudly claimed that it covered more ground than the great pyramid in Egypt. Most warehouses are eminently forgettable structures. The back of this building fits that category, but the street fa-cade, with its wonderful tower, makes a real architectural statement.

E-14   Harry C. Yerkes House

1597 North Parkway
Mahan and Broadwell, architects, 1915

Another early house by Mahan and Broadwell, but one showing them beginning to branch out a little. The plain but elegant entrance porch is echoed on the left by an open porch, and the triple window above the main doorway lends a touch of class to the whole facade.

E-15   Hiram D. Jordan House

1614 North Parkway
Mahan and Broadwell, architects, 1922

E-16   W.G. Cavett House

1630 North Parkway
1918

A marvelously inventive airplane bungalow, this one built of smoothly-cut ashlar. What one notices immediately is the octagonal wooden pilot house contraption sticking out of the "tail." Because the "airplane" looks like a pilot house, maybe we should call this a steamboat bungalow. Whatever the rooftop projection may refer to, it is still the ubiquitous Memphis sleeping porch—an absolute necessity in pre–air conditioning days, and still a pleasant feature of many of the city's houses.

E-16

E-18

E-17 David Cummins House

865 Dickenson Street
George Mahan, Jr., architect, 1925–26

Here, Mahan, working without Broadwell, does yet another turn on the bungalow. The house has the requisite porch, but this time it is the typical porch stretched across the entire front that one find on small rural houses, even sharecropper cabins, all over the South. The large eyebrow window in the roof, however, reminds us that we are still in bungalow-land.

E-18 Baron Hirsch Synagogue

1740 Vollintine Avenue
George Awsumb, architect, 1947
Educational building 1952, dedication 1957

Awsumb's powerful gray mass for the synagogue, at least in the central block, looks back fondly to Eliel Saarinen's entrance to the museum at Cranbrook. This building once served the large community of Orthodox Jews who lived around it, but now that community has moved east, to be served by a new Baron Hirsch that was under construction as this book was being written.

E-19 B.W. Hale House

540 North Hawthorne Street (originally 1793 North Parkway)
1923

This is a curious house: very large, although it looks small because its siting below street level hides most of the ground floor. Its main doorway, on Hawthorne, opens into the second floor. The large fireplace is in the center of the house, and the whole central section surrounding it is raised above the general roof level to create a clerestory with hints of Frank Lloyd Wright.

E-20   Judge Frank M. Gutherie House

1650 North Parkway
Mahan and Broadwell, architects, 1920

The judge evidently was a man of very austere taste, and it would be difficult to find another house so devoid of ornament anywhere this side of an Adolf Loos house in Vienna.

E-21   Snowden Junior High School

1870 North Parkway
Jones and Furbringer, architects, 1909

The oldest part of this school is the block at the corner of Parkway and McLean. This again shows Jones and Furbringer's penchant for putting all of their architectural eggs in the central entrance basket. As the neighborhood expanded in the 1920s, so did the school: eastward, like so much of Memphis. The gymnasium and the three-story addition strung out along the Parkway are from 1924; later accretions date from 1939 and 1979.

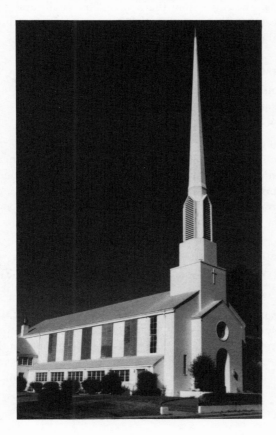

E-22

E-22　McLean Baptist Church

815 North McLean Boulevard
Edwin A. Keeble and Associates, Nashville, architects, 1953

One of Keeble's few works in Memphis. A stripped-down Colonial style church, this one works much better than the common run of this genre, largely because the proportions are right even though ornamental detailing has been left off. The giant rolling barn-door shutters for the upper windows serve both as functional shutters and as necessary visual breaks in the long flanks of the building. The shutters demonstrate that doing something cheaply doesn't always mean doing it badly. Keeble's churches in Nashville are famous for the prodigious heights reached by his spires. They don't just aspire to be tall, they do something about it. The spire here, while tall for Memphis and visible from miles away, is modesty itself in comparison.

E-23　Samuel A. Thompson House

1865 Jackson Avenue

Dr. Thomas A. Ingram House

1875 Jackson Avenue

Edward B. LeMaster House

1895 Jackson Avenue
Mahan and Broadwell, architects, 1922–24

LeMaster built a cozy English cottage by Mahan and Broadwell for himself. At the same time he housed his two daughters and their husbands next door in equally cozy cottages designed by the same architects.

E-24　Evergreen Presbyterian Church

613 University Street
Office of Walk C. Jones, Walk C. Jones, Jr., architects, 1951

Another example of the Colonial revival that swept Memphis in the postwar years, this handsome church with white columns and tall steeple sits far enough back from the street so that it can be seen the way it ought to be seen. It is very similar to the Church of the Holy Communion on Walnut Grove Road (I-43), which the same architects had designed in 1949.

E-25

E-25 "House of Happiness"
705 North University Street
E.L. Harrison, architect, 1935

To encourage people to borrow money, insured by the FHA, to build houses, and thereby to encourage the construction industry in a Depression-struck Memphis, the morning newspaper, the *Commercial Appeal*, and its radio station WMC sponsored this model house. The chief architectural feature, beyond the general "Colonial" character, was the New England front door, which was reported at the time to be derived from a house either in Salem or in Marblehead, Massachusetts. This seems to be one of the earliest examples of the developer Colonial style that was to be the hallmark of Memphis domestic architecture for the next fifty years.

E-26 Rhodes College
2000 North Parkway

Rhodes College (the name was changed from Southwestern at Memphis in 1984) is one of the real architectural surprises in Memphis. It is probably the only college campus in the whole country that has maintained the continuity of its Gothic Revival style of architecture, and much of that architecture is of high quality indeed.

The campus (E-26a) is located on a one-hundred-acre tract north of North Parkway and west of University Street that was offered to the college in the early 1920s, when it was contemplating a move from Clarksville, Tennessee, where it had been known as Southwestern Presbyterian University. The president of the College, Dr. Charles Diehl, saw more of a future in Memphis than in Clarksville, and in 1924 the college changed its name to Southwestern at Memphis and began the relocation.

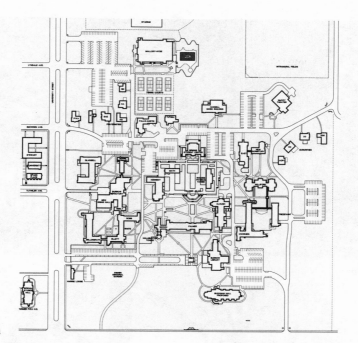

E-26a

Dr. Diehl was a man who knew what he wanted, and he wanted Charles Z. Klauder, who was one of the best Gothic Revival architects in the country. But Klauder was already booked up. Klauder's name is associated with the college in a vague way as a consulting architect, but his real contribution was to recommend Henry C. Hibbs of Nashville, and it was Hibbs who did the actual design work. It was a good recommendation. Even if the campus was not built completely according to Hibbs' plans (how rarely that happens), parts of it reflect beautifully the architectural and social ideals that lay behind the Gothic Revival style of building for American college campuses in the early part of this century.

Almost all of the best Rhodes buildings are the earliest ones, but there is such a remarkable consistency and coherence to the architecture that even the less successful buildings seem better than they really are because of the success of the ensemble. There is much talk of the importance of "contextualism" in architectural circles these days, and Rhodes College is as good an example as you might hope to find of what contextualism really is. The college even owned its own stone quarry in Arkansas for many years, in order to insure the consistency of its building material.

Southwestern opened its Memphis doors for the 1925 academic year. At that time Palmer Hall (Henry Hibbs, 1923–25), the main College Hall, the Kennedy Science Building (Hibbs, 1924), and the early dormitories—Neely, Robb and White (all Hibbs, all 1924)—were standing.

E-26b

E-26c

Palmer (E-26b) originally didn't look quite as it does now, since the Halliburton Tower at the west end of the building was added later, a fact that most people need to be told, since the match is such a good one. The tower was erected in 1961 to designs by Clinton Parrent. Parrent for many years was the chief draftsman in Hibbs' Nashville office, and at the death of Hibbs, the college hired him as its architect. This was a good move, since Parrent was a man who knew what a Rhodes College building should be. Halliburton Tower (it was named after the American adventurer and arch-Romantic Richard Halliburton) provides a soaring piece of lively Presbyterian Gothic to play off against the strong horizontality of Palmer Hall.

Palmer itself is a relatively plain and simple building, its angular austerity relieved only by the pointed arches of the main entrances in the centers of the long sides. Inside those entrances is a very handsome vaulted central hall.

Palmer originally was supposed to be the first side of a collegiate quadrangle, one of several that made up Hibbs' campus plan. The "quad" is a fundamental part of the idea of Collegiate Gothic architecture as practiced in America. Ironically, when it came right down to it, American colleges have never much liked quadrangles, and very few of them have been finished. Rhodes is no exception to this general principle, and Palmer Hall remains unquadrangled.

The early dormitories, to the west of Palmer, come closer to achieving this elusive collegiate ideal, however, and in so doing they form one of the prettiest corners of a pretty campus. Robb (Hibbs, 1924), White (Hibbs, 1924), Ellett (Hibbs, 1946 [E-26c]), and Bellingrath (Parrent, 1960) Halls are some of the nicest dormitories to look at anywhere. Hibbs' general inspiration came from the slightly earlier work of Cope and Stewardson at Princeton (it was natural for a small Presbyterian college to emulate the architecture of that faith's pre-eminent American institution of higher learning), but the sense of completeness is more vivid here, and the scale is a little more intimate. The irregularity of windows, rooflines, and doorways is more apparent than actual, but the marvelous collegiate feeling is very real, especially in the fall when the leaves are coming down, or during a rare Memphis snow. Then the only things seemingly missing are spires and crockets. There is also a funny little chapel stuck onto the northwest corner of Bellingrath Hall that, despite the linoleum on the floor, is probably the most authentically "Gothic" space on campus—very narrow and high, with long, skinny windows.

The other side of the campus may not have anything that quite matches this group of dormitories, but East and New Halls (Taylor and Crump, 1985 and 1986 respectively) make a very fine pair of buildings on the northeast corner of the campus, just before things straggle off to Sorority Row and Hein Park. Other than using the same building stone and the same slate roofs, these dorms don't have much to do with the kind of buildings that Hibbs and Parrent designed. Nevertheless, their architects have succeeded in creating the sort of irregular massing and carefully manufactured feeling of *ad hoc* growth that has always been a basic part of the collegiate Gothic style of architecture. The essentially square block of New Dorm is joined to the longer East by a sort of cloister walk. East is a more-or-less "normal" Rhodes College dorm on the north, with a huge Norman-like square keep stuck on behind the entrance at the southwest part of the building. Behind this, in a pleasant little quasi-quad (reached through a Gothic arch which never got the wall you think it ought to have been built into), the building descends in a great swoopy roof that is almost too dramatic. The brick chimneys on the south end of East provide some of the boldest Elizabethan detailing on any recent building in the city.

E-27 Henry C. Nall, Jr., House

2230 North Parkway
George Mahan, architect, 1927–28
Everett Woods, associate architect

E-28 Dr. James B. McElroy House

2240 North Parkway
George Mahan, Jr., architect, 1925–26

Mahan liked to do houses with strong classical elements arranged asymmetrically, and thus unclassically. The McElroy House shows him playing this game particularly well, by balancing the strong doorway off against an almost equally strong window element.

E-29 William A. Hein House

2250 North Parkway
Jones and Furbringer, architects, 1926

Hein was the man who developed the subdivision called Hein Park that stretches to the north of this rather conservative Jones and Furbringer house.

E-30 J.H. Van Natta House

607 Center Drive
J. Frazer Smith and Herbert Burnham, architects, 1926

E-31 George C. Wallace, Jr., House

671 West Drive
J. Frazer Smith and Herbert Burnham, architects, 1926

This handsome stone and timber Tudor building was constructed to house an automobile dealer. It now houses the presidents of Rhodes College.

E-32 C.A. White House

1618 Forrest Avenue
1914

A curious house, part cottage and part bungalow. The modesty inherent in both these types of house is compromised by the large porte-cochere angling off the front. This house, more plainly than any other, shows that the porte-cochere had come to be seen as the symbol of a really elegant house in Memphis around the time of the First World War.

E-29

E-31

E-33

E-33 Henry Gluck House

1640 Forrest Avenue
1907

The cottage still reigned supreme in 1907 as the preferred building type for less pretentious Memphians. This very carefully designed cottage is endowed, unexpectedly, with the elegance of a Palladian window in the living room wall. That window is then echoed in the upstairs gable. This judicious use of architectural elements gives this good solid house quite a bit of class.

E-34 Max Furbringer House

1734 Forrest Avenue
Max Furbringer, architect, 1907

A surprisingly modest house for one of Memphis' most prominent architects in the early years of this century. This small, shingled, two-story structure clearly reveals an architect's hand in the well-wrought detail of the projecting windows which box in the chimney on the west side.

E-35 Arthur C. Bruce House

1751 Forrest Avenue
Mahan and Broadwell, architects, 1921

E-36 M.E. Clark House

1766 Forrest Avenue
1924

A stucco house that could be termed "carpenter Wedgwood" for its lavish use of molded relief decoration. A curious feature of this house is the way the architect insisted on treating each story as if the other did not exist. There is no vertical correlation between what happens downstairs and what goes on above.

E-37 Winfield S. Myrick house

1772 Forrest Avenue
Mahan and Broadwell, architects, 1924–25

Myrick was the department superintendent for the Memphis Power and Light Company when he had this twin-gabled Spanish Mission bungalow (or maybe cottage) built. This is yet another of Mahan and Broadwell's clever variations on the theme of bungalow.

E-34

E-39

E-38　Hiram B. Jacobson House

1796 Forrest Avenue
Mahan and Broadwell, architects, designed 1921, built 1924

E-39　Luther H. Graves House

1620 Galloway Avenue
Mahan and Broadwell, architects, 1922

Every bungalow that Mahan and Broadwell did was different. This one is a half-timbered Tudor version, and it is probably the only one in that style in town. This is a very subtle house that at first glance looks a lot like hundreds of other bungalows all over town. A second look might start with the three-sided entrance bay under the porch. In this same year, Mahan and Broadwell designed their own houses at Autumn and McLean in a Spanish vein (E-45).

E-40   Trinity United Methodist Church

1738 Galloway Avenue
Hubert T. McGee, architect, 1924–25
Education Building (across street)
Lucian Minor Dent, architect, 1960–61

A rambling American Gothic design, perhaps to match the "rambling American Romanesque" of McGee's Pink Palace (I-1) of a couple of years earlier.

E-41   W.E. Howard House

1780 Galloway Avenue
Jones and Furbringer, architects, 1913

The Tuscan Doric doorway on this house is one of Jones and Furbringer's finest sixteenth-century Italian Renaissance details. For the porch on the east, the architects conceived a curious mix of inset, freestanding columns with sloping walls that seem to act as buttresses.

E-42   L.M. Weathers House

1694 Autumn Avenue
L.M. Weathers, architect, 1906

Weathers was an architect prominent enough to have been given the commission for St. Mary's Episcopal Cathedral (C-37) on Poplar after W. Halsey Wood of New York, the original architect, died. Perhaps the fact that he was pouring all his creative energies into that job explains why this is such a dull house. It is a four-square—big, but otherwise very average. Maybe he didn't even design it.

E-43   Henry L. Taylor House

1731 Autumn Avenue
1907

This big Victorian two-story is a throwback to an earlier architectural style. But it is done with verve and style. The turret to the left is balanced by the polygonal bay to the right, and the attic window is crowned by an exclamation point keystone (of wood). There is a house very much like this one at 1731 Glenwood Place (F-93), also built in 1907.

E-44

E-44   Miss L. Bergner House

1741 Autumn Avenue
1907

No guidebook would be complete without mention of one of the town's pre-eminent architectural nightmares. L.M. Weathers' four-square down the street may be dull, but this one is wild. A postmodern critic might call it an ironic Ionic four-square. But the architect, builder, and owner responsible for this had no such excuse. The combination of clapboards and shingles is dubious enough, but the addition of huge, overscaled Ionic pilasters, which vary in width but not height, on the porch and at the corners of the house makes this a textbook example of how the orders can be used to create disorder.

E-45a   (Lost Memphis) George Mahan, Jr., House

434 North McLean Boulevard
Mahan and Broadwell, architects, 1922

E-45b   James J. Broadwell House

410 North McLean Boulevard
Mahan and Broadwell, architects, 1922

E-45a

E-45c (Lost Memphis) Levy-Block Duplex

1853 Galloway Avenue
Mahan and Broadwell, architects, 1922

In 1922 the partners George Mahan and James Broadwell built for themselves not-quite-twin houses on the east side of McLean at the corner of
Autumn. At the same time, they built a duplex north of the Mahan house,
at the corner of McLean and Galloway, in the same Spanish style they had
chosen for their own dwellings. Of these, only the Broadwell House remains. The others succumbed to the misguided intention, fortunately
stopped, of bringing I-40 right through Overton Park and this part of the
city. The bulldozer path that now runs through the entire Evergreen area
did no greater architectural damage than the destruction of these two
buildings, which formed part of a coherently and elegantly designed residential quarter.

The land on which the three Spanish houses were built belonged to Ike
Block, who had acquired the entire block of Autumn between McLean and
Overton Park, as well as the frontage on McLean. The owner of one of the
city's major department stores, Block was one of Mahan's principal clients
for many years. He built his own house directly east of Mahan's, and he
sold lots along Autumn to friends and associates, two of whom also hired
Mahan and Broadwell to do Spanish fantasies. Unfortunately, the rest of
the people to whom Block sold lots didn't build houses by the same team.

The Broadwell House, surrounded by a wall that is not original, shows
to perfection the Mahan and Broadwell trick of doing a house in telescoping sections pulled out toward a street corner. The biggest block of the
telescope is graced by a triple-arcaded opening, now glassed in, that
brought the outside into the mass of the building, while a piece of relief

E-45b

E-45c

sculpture, of indeterminable subject, is used to emphasize the second section.

The Mahan house telescoped in the opposite direction, so that the pair shot smaller masses from the largest masses toward the street in between. Together, they formed a gateway to the Block block of Autumn behind them. The duplex to the north did the same for the next street, Galloway, at least on one side.

Because the character of the neighborhood was so strongly created by these three Spanish houses, and by two more by Mahan and Broadwell to the east, we feel it should be known as Spanish Autumn.

E-46   Ike D. Block House

1856 Autumn Avenue
Mahan and Broadwell, architects, 1921

Ike Block, whose money made all of this possible, chose to house himself
Anglophilic rather than Hispanophilic, probably for reasons of personal
taste. Mahan and Broadwell always asked their clients what style they
wanted for themselves. (One client reportedly said she didn't much care
what the style was, so long as it was fancy.) Block got one of the earliest
and best of Mahan and Broadwell's symmetrical dark-red-brick houses,
with a great white English Baroque doorway in the center. Others are
found at 2285 Washington (F-134) and at 604 South Belvedere (F-63).

E-47   Nathan H. Wellman House

1883 Autumn Avenue
Mahan and Broadwell, architects, 1921

Of the Mahan and Broadwell houses here, this is the least satisfactory,
because it is the least imaginative. The disappearing chimney, however,
provides some delight.

E-48   Leo Goodman House

1886 Autumn Avenue
Mahan and Broadwell, architects, 1922–24

Lurking behind a massive recent wall is one of Mahan and Broadwell's
finest Italo-Hispanic creations, broad of facade, carefully massed, and elegantly detailed. The rear, visible from Galloway, is not nearly so refined an
architectural composition, but it makes up for that lack of refinement in a
joyously bumptious play of asymmetrical forms.

E-48

E-49   Robert Galloway House (Paisley Hall)

1822 Overton Park Avenue
1908–10

Robert Galloway was the chairman of the Memphis Park Commission when Overton and Riverside Parks, and the Parkways, were laid out. Galloway had a special love for Overton Park, which he continued to embellish from time to time with such conceits as a pseudo-Persian gazebo that contained two stone fragments from the Temple of Ptah erected in the original Memphis around 550 B.C. The gazebo has long since disappeared, and the temple fragments are now on display in the Egyptian collection of Memphis State University. Galloway bought a whole block of land near Overton Park to erect this very pretentious house, impressive more for its size than its relatively crude and unimaginative architectural detailing. The name of the architect so far has not surfaced, which may suggest that it was designed by someone from out of town.

E-50   O.P. Bailey House

1835 Overton Park Avenue
1915

A brick and stone building with a lot going on, shape-wise. The sharp gable on the west is balanced by a round turret on the east which has a dinner-bell roof and a curved porch underneath. This house has a lot more life than the stolid Galloway pile across the street.

E-51   First Dr. Harry Schmeisser House

279 North McLean Boulevard
Mahan and Broadwell, architects, 1922

South of Spanish Autumn, the same architects, in the same years, put the Schmeissers into a Tudor cottage that is as convincing, in its own way, as the Spanish fantasies of Autumn are in theirs. Particularly fine here is the combination of materials and patterns that the Tudor style allowed. For the same couple, in the late thirties Mahan, helped considerably by Nowland Van Powell, designed probably the biggest and best Tudor house in town (I-36), out on Walnut Grove Road.

E-52   Herbert P. Jordan House

1857 Overton Park Avenue
1924

A handsome Colonial Revival structure with an inset two-story porch in the middle of the facade, this house begins the block between McLean and Overton Park proper very well.

E-53　John C. Norfleet, Jr., House

1896 Overton Park Avenue
Mahan and Broadwell, architects, 1923–24

Another of their big Spanish houses. A comparison of this and the relatively inept Spanish-style house across the street, with the rounded corner, makes clear how much better Mahan and Broadwell were at this genre than most of their local competitors.

E-54　William A. Gage House

259 Kenilworth Place
Jones and Furbringer, architects, 1920

E-55　Herman M. Rhodes House

269 Kenilworth Place
Jones and Furbringer, architects, 1923

Jones and Furbringer's houses of the twenties can often be quite conservative, if not sometimes downright stodgy. This one, however, is just the opposite. The center of the facade looks like three bays of an ordinary two-story house of a generally Colonial persuasion. To the left, however, the one-story sunporch fairly flaunts its Ionic order. On the right, the whole facade steps forward in a vertical mass that is bordered by two extremely skinny stone pilasters that have urns perched precariously on top of them. The contest among the three parts for our attention makes this facade one of the liveliest Jones and Furbringer ever designed.

E-55

E-56   Overton Park

George Kessler, Kansas City, landscape architect, 1905

The decision to lay out Overton and Riverside Parks and to connect them with a series of roads was one of the most important in the urban history of Memphis. The land was acquired in 1902, and construction began in 1905, on the basis of designs submitted by the Kansas City landscape architect George Kessler, who had already begun to turn his home city into something of a garden spot. Kessler created a series of roads that wound through the old farmland to make as picturesque a use of the flat landscape as he could. In the northeast corner, he left standing a primeval forest that provided the title and a location for Peter Taylor's short story, "The Old Forest." (Recently it has been argued that the forest is not primeval, but rather new growth after a total destruction caused by the great earthquake of 1811.) Inside the park are a public golf course, a shallow pond for sailing boats, some sculpture of no particular artistic merit, and some buildings of considerable interest.

E-57   Memphis Brooks Museum

(formerly Brooks Memorial Art Gallery)
James Gamble Rogers, New York, architect, 1916
Walk Jones and Francis Mah, architects for the addition, 1970–73
Skidmore Owings and Merrill, Houston, Rick Keating and Craig Taylor, designers, architects for the addition, designed 1987
Askew, Nixon, Ferguson and Wolfe, associate architects

Rogers' elegant white-marble garden pavilion, inspired in part by McKim, Meade and White's Morgan Library in New York and in part by the sixteenth-century Villa Giulia in Rome, has a perfectly scaled entrance arch flanked by reliefs of an almost rococo delicacy that show that this is the realm of the Arts. To the sides, herms, a favored device of sixteenth-century garden designers, act like pilasters on the upper story.

Jones and Mah, in their Brutalist addition, acknowledged the fact that in 1970 one could no longer do the same kinds of things Rogers had been able to do in 1916. Instead, they designed a large-scale, roughly-textured series of spaces to accommodate the art of our day. The structure makes use of the Mah-LeMessurier system they used on such apartment buildings as the Luther Towers on Highland near Central (I-13). Square concrete piers form the vertical supports. On these are hung concrete beams that support the floors and the roofs. At the sides of the galleries, between the piers, barrel-vaulted skylights let natural light flood the walls on which

E-57

E-59

pictures are hung. The light naturally attracts the eye of the museum-goer to the paintings. Many parts of the scheme, however, are based on an early project of Louis Kahn for the Yale Center for British Art in New Haven.

As this book is being written, work has begun on a second large addition that replaces a small wing designed by Everett Woods in the 1950s. Rising east of the Rogers building, the new wing will have a south-facing, convexly-curved entrance flanked by the Rogers wing and by a new structure that will match the Rogers wing in size and proportions but not in material. In this way, the architects associated with Skidmore Owings and Merrill hope to integrate the old and new buildings happily. From the curved entrance a strong diagonal will thrust forward to make a comment on the fact that the facade of the museum is not parallel to Poplar Avenue to the south.

E-58   Raoul Wallenberg Memorial Shell

(formerly Overton Park Shell)
Max Furbringer, architect, 1936
M.G. Ehrman, associate architect

The concentric half-circles of the backdrop to the stage create good acoustics for the audience as well as a pleasing shape. For many years, the shell housed the Memphis Open Air Theater (MOAT), which did summer productions of operettas.

E-59   Memphis Academy of Arts

Mann and Harrover, architects, 1956

To get the commission for this building, the architects won a competition juried by Philip Johnson and Paul Rudolph. Once finished, the building got an award from *Progressive Architecture*, a blessing few other buildings in the city have received. The original program called for an art school and a performing arts center. Mann and Harrover's idea was to put both parts, separated by a space, on one podium, so that the whole would be a unified building. The art-school wing was built first, on the north end of the platform. Around 1970 the performing arts center was dropped, and the academy expanded into a new wing built to the south, with the originally conceived space in the center still there. The building has a grace and an openness that fit it well into the large trees that rise around it.

E-60   Memphis Zoological Garden

Founded 1905

Going to the Zoo is a favorite Memphis pastime. The stone lions, from a house belonging to the Van Vleet family, were placed at the entrance in 1935. Inside, almost dead ahead, is the Carnivora Building, designed by

E-60

L.M. Weathers in 1909, which features putti cavorting on the cornice with altogether-too-docile lions. The old Pachyderm Building (see photo), also designed by Weathers in 1909, is a wonderful piece of packaging. It seems shaped to the dimensions and proportions of the elephants it housed.

The zoo was considerably enlarged by the WPA. From 1935 comes the graceful metal flight cage, and from the following years of the same decade come the Monkey Island (1936), the Sea Lion and Swan Pool (1936), the great concrete caves for bear and other large beasts (1938), as well as the Ibex Mountain. All of these structures were in line with the most advanced ideas about zoo design, in which the animals were made to appear to be free and to occupy the same space as the humans looking at them. Only deep moats protected one from the other. Nowland Van Powell designed the Aquarium in 1958, and possibly the Aviary as well. The new Pachyderm House, c. 1972, Bologna and Hamilton, architects, has concrete surfaces even rougher than the skins of the elephants and rhinos housed within.

E-61   First Clyde L. Van Fossen House

292 East Parkway North
Mahan and Broadwell, architects, 1922

Spanish-style houses on corners by this pair almost invariably have a telescoping mass, with the smallest part pointed to the corner. This handsomely-detailed house also has another mass pulled through the central block and out the back, a detail that can be observed from the Strathmore Circle side.

F Central Gardens

The Central Gardens area contains one of the city's two primary collections of early-twentieth-century houses. In the 1850s large landowners who farmed the area built houses here, and a few of these still remain. The landowners were followed early in this century by a few adventurous rich who began to construct large residences along Central Avenue, the head of which was marked in 1896 by the great Gothic pile of Ashlar Hall. Two subdivisions led the way in the thicker settlement of the area—Annesdale Park, 1903, and Annesdale-Snowden, 1906. Both were made possible by the opening of trolley lines that allowed residents to commute to work in downtown offices, and both were the brainchildren of Robert Brinkley Snowden, amateur architect and builder of Ashlar Hall. It was on his family land that the subdivisions were erected.

Development of big houses spread rapidly eastward from Bellevue to South McLean. Belvedere Boulevard, the most ambitious street in the area, was opened in 1906, and the first houses were standing on it in 1907. The eastern edge of this area, marked by East Parkway, began to be built up in the teens, when its most picturesque adjunct, Morningside Park, was also opened. Finally, in the twenties, a small enclave of equally elegant houses appeared on Washington, Jefferson, and Court in the angle created by Poplar and East Parkway North. Mixed in with these pretentious buildings were first modest wooden cottages. Then came the ubiquitous foursquares and bungalows, which sometimes take up whole streets by themselves and sometimes mingle in easy cohabitation. South of Central, in the neighborhood known as Cooper-Young, is a particularly well-preserved and consistent streetscape of this holy trinity of Memphis middle-class housing.

There are also later residential enclaves. Kimbrough, which grew up in the twenties and thirties, lies between Peabody and Union on the south and north, and Kimbrough and Rozelle on the west and east. It is dominated by one of Memphis' finest Art Deco building, the Kimbrough Towers apartments. North of Central, the Rosemary Lane subdivision, of the late thirties, ushered in the Williamsburg fever that has infected much of Memphis residential architecture for the last fifty years.

Union Avenue, which has suffered intense commercialization since World War II, also was once a major residential street. Almost none of the great houses that stood there remain. Poplar Avenue, the northern boundary of the area, has suffered a similar fate. Madison Avenue has maintained its residential character only between Cooper and East Parkway.

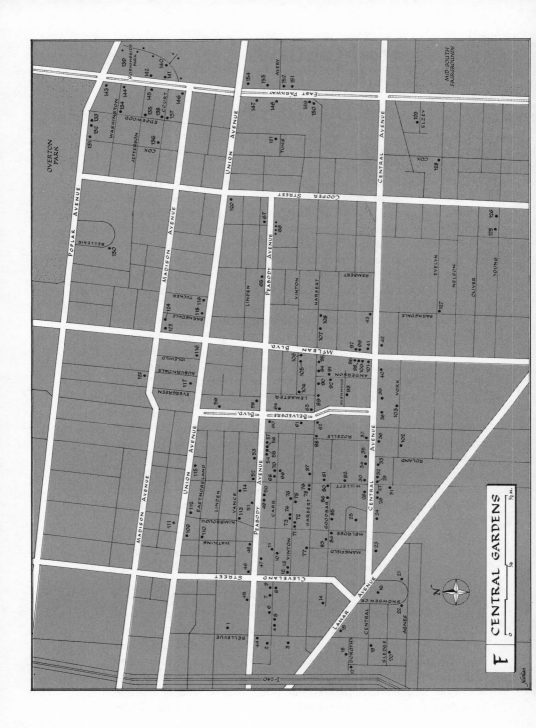

CENTRAL GARDENS

F

F-1   Central High School

306 South Bellevue Boulevard
B.C. Alsup, architect, 1911

F-2   Bruce Elementary School

1206 Carr Avenue
B.C. Alsup, architect, 1908

F-3   Bellevue Junior High School

575 South Bellevue Boulevard
Jones and Furbringer, architects, 1927

These three schools were built to serve the area that grew rapidly after the opening of Annesdale Park in 1903.

ANNESDALE PARK, 1903

The first independent suburban real-estate venture of Robert Brinkley Snowden, one of the most important of the early-twentieth-century Memphis developers (he also had been involved in the development of Estival Park in the last years of the previous century). The original boundaries of Annesdale Park were Bellevue, Peabody, Cleveland (including the first lots east of Cleveland), and Lamar. Carr was the first street developed, and it has the grandest houses, marked by an eclectic abandon that delves particularly into medieval sources. The other three streets in the neighborhood, Vinton, Harbert, and Goodbar, have houses of more modest character.

F-4   J.H. Taylor House

1247 Carr Avenue
1909

A prepossessing Jacobean gable as the centerpiece gives this house distinction.

F-5   Edgar D. Williamson House

1273 Carr Avenue
1905

Mix-and-match eclecticism. There are an Ionic porch, a Doric door, tall chimneys, assorted gables, Adamesque swags, stone walls below, and shingles above.

F-6   H.B. Hull House

1290 Carr Avenue
1907

A powerful cylinder marks the east corner.

F-7   M.R. Patterson House

1306 Carr Avenue
1905

The handsome Doric porch at ground level is marked by double columns in the central bay to indicate the front door behind. Unfortunately, a second story has been glopped onto this porch, and the whole house has succumbed to asbestoscide.

F-8   Simeon Hill House

1333 Carr Avenue
1907

A grand Norman baronial front shields a folksier shingled behind.

F-9   A.S. Buchanan House

1336 Carr Avenue
1905

A great, rough depressed stone arch addresses the street. Over the arch rises a shingled wall with a Palladian window, whose central arch is marked by exaggerated wooden voussoirs. The heavy stone tower to the right features a surprisingly delicate Adamesque swag in the frieze around its top. This mix-and-match attitude toward elements taken from medieval and classical architecture is almost exactly duplicated, doubtless by the same architect, down the street in the facade of 1387 Carr (F-10). He also may have designed 1273 Carr (F-5) and 1475 Central (F-24).

F-10   W.G. Patteson House

1387 Carr Avenue
1911

This house differs from 1336 Carr (F-9) in that it has a flat architrave, supported by inset Doric columns, instead of a stone arch, over its large porch opening. Other differences are the delicate wreath in the arch of the Palladian window and the even more miniscule wreaths in the frieze of the western tower.

F-9 F-10

F-11   C.P. Cooper House

1396 Carr Avenue
Augustine Chighizola, architect, 1909

There are so many similarities to Chighizola's own house at 1379 Peabody (F-47) that he must be the architect of this as well.

F-12   First Walk C. Jones, Sr., House

1346 Vinton Avenue
Walk C. Jones, Sr., architect, 1907–1908

This, the first house Walk Jones, Sr., designed for himself, has been particularly badly treated. Its front porch has been knocked off, aluminum siding has been applied, and other indignities also have been inflicted. Jones and his partner, Max Furbringer, had a thriving practice that lasted from the early years of the century to 1935, and Jones founded a three-generation dynasty of architects, all of whom bore, or bear, the same name.

F-13   T.O. Vinton House

1354 Vinton Avenue
1909

Vinton, for whom the street is named, was one of Brinkley Snowden's partners in the development of Annesdale Park. His house has a splendidly-decorated gable with a socko bull's-eye window.

F-14   Haynes Barnwell, Jr., House
1308 Goodbar Avenue
1922

An airplane bungalow with particularly fine Craftsman details in the clearly-applied, cleanly-cut wooden ornaments.

ANNESDALE–SNOWDEN
1906

This subdivision spread the Snowden real-estate developments south across Lamar into the land that directly surrounds one of the city's greatest nineteenth-century houses, Annesdale, where the Snowdens lived and continue to live. The streets in the neighborhood, Minna, Dorothy, and Agnes, were named for Robert Brinkley Snowden's children, as was the street between Dorothy and Sledge that first was known as Bayard, but had its name changed to Central in 1913. This is a well-preserved early-twentieth-century neighborhood, with only a handful of later interpola-

F-16

tions. Here you can still get a very good feeling of what a turn-of-the-century middle-class residential district in Memphis was like.

Snowden seems originally to have envisioned Annesdale-Snowden as a more modest adjunct to the slightly earlier development in Annesdale Park, and the earliest houses, in the southwest corner of the neighborhood (Agnes Place and Sledge, west of Bellevue), are cottages. Within a couple of years, however, the development pitch moved upscale, and doctors, lawyers, and planters began to build larger houses. The early cottages gave way to four-squares, which make up the majority of the houses in the area.

While Annesdale-Snowden is valuable chiefly for its consistency as a neighborhood, there exists a handful of individual houses worthy of note.

F-15   Daniel C. Newton House

1247 Lamar Avenue
Mahan and Broadwell, architects, 1920

A bungalow, built for the city building inspector, fancied up by a Palladian window in its gable.

F-16   Annesdale (Snowden House)

(formerly Dr. Samuel Mansfield House)
1325 Lamar Avenue
c. 1855

This Italian Villa mansion was built by a Dr. Samuel Mansfield, a wholesale druggist, probably as a wedding present for the wife he married in 1855. In 1869 Robert Brinkley bought it as a wedding gift for his daughter, Annie Overton Brinkley, who married Col. Robert Bogardus Snowden. The two-hundred-acre estate was named Annesdale, pronounced "Annie's Dale," in her honor.

Architecturally, the house, with its square tower, bracketed cornice, round-arched porch, and asymmetrical plan, was absolutely up-to-date for the mid-1850s. Although the name of its designer is unknown, details of the exterior and elements of the plan quite possibly were derived from a "Norman Villa" designed by the Philadelphia architect Samuel Sloane and published in his book, *The Model Architect*, in 1852. Sloane designed one of the South's great houses, the Arabian-Nights fantasy of Longwood, at Natchez, in 1859, which was based on "An Oriental Villa" in *The Model Architect*.

Set in the center of the remains of the Snowden estate, the house is difficult to see, but tantalizing glimpses are available from various spots on Snowden Circle.

F-17   William J. Hanker House

1159 Dorothy Place
William J. Hanker, architect, 1906

Hanker was one of the leading architects of the city at the turn of the century. He was in partnership with Augustine Chighizola in 1902, when they
designed the Scimitar Building at Main and Monroe (A-103). Shortly there-
after, Bayard Snowden Cairns joined the firm, and after Chighizola's death
in 1911, he and Hanker formed a partnership that produced some of the
city's finest buildings. Because of its lack of architectural verve, this house
suggests that Cairns was the better designer of the two.

F-18   Duplex Bungalow

1182–1184 East Dorothy Place
1929

Duplex bungalows may not be as rare as two-headed snakes, but they can
be just as surprising.

F-19   Bayard Cairns House

1207 Central Avenue
Bayard Cairns, architect, 1912

In a neighborhood of few houses of architectural distinction, the powerful
two-columned porch of the Cairns House stands out with force. The
enormous rough-stuccoed shafts emerge baseless from the wall below and

F-19

submerge themselves, capital-less, into the wall above. They support, over a vast span, a startlingly thin and low pediment. Inside the porch, Cairns flanked the door with two great glass ears. Although documentation for much of Cairns' career has yet to surface, his taste for hefty columns appears in other documented works and probably can be used as a device for attributing some buildings in the city to him.

F-20   W.K. Pickett House

> 1183 Sledge Avenue
> 1911

A house undergoing a metamorphosis from the traditional wooden cottage into the newly-arrived type of the bungalow.

F-21   Emmett E. Joyner House

> 786 East Snowden Circle
> Bayard Cairns, architect (?), 1911

The powerful stucco-covered piers that mark the central door and side porch of this otherwise rather standard Dutch Colonial house may signal the presence of the hand of Bayard Cairns. The fact that his mother was a Snowden certainly makes it likely that he designed a house on this street.

F-22   J. Alma Goodman House

> 789 West Snowden Circle
> Mahan and Broadwell, architects, 1912

This carefully detailed box of a house, with a large brick porch on the front, is one of the earliest independent works of George Mahan, an architect who, with various partners, would play a dominant role in domestic architecture in Memphis for the next thirty years or more. The present pink color of the upper story is not a blush applied by the original designer.

CENTRAL AVENUE

F-23   R. Brinkley Snowden House (Ashlar Hall)

> 1397 Central Avenue
> R. Brinkley Snowden, architect, 1896

Ashlar Hall was the castle of one of the city's greatest real-estate barons. In 1899, the *Evening Scimitar* noted that he had "built more houses than perhaps any other" in Memphis. An 1890 graduate of Princeton, where he studied architecture, Snowden built this house at the triangular intersection of Lamar and Central almost as a beacon for the subsequent expan-

F-23

sion of Memphis around it. The undulating west facade, with a convex
porch flanked by round towers, is particularly strong; this facade faced
toward the city from which Snowden's clients came out to buy his lands.
Unfortunately, the development he started has now closed in so tightly—
Ashlar Hall's towers are oversoared by huge (for Memphis) high-rise apartments—that the felicity of the original siting has been lost. Not lost, however, is the lowering stonework of the crenellations. One wonders what
books about medieval castles Snowden brought back with him from Princeton, or if perhaps the whole may have been influenced by a too-early
reading of *Ivanhoe*.

F-24 J.S. White House

1475 Central Avenue
1902

This somewhat incoherent house—the swoopy roof and the chateau tower
fail to meet in a reasonable way—betrays a sensibility that enjoys mixing
heavy elements from the Romanesque and French-chateau traditions with
delicate detailing derived from the work of the eighteenth-century English
architect Robert Adam. Such mixings of the same elements were not unknown in other American cities at this time. There also are a few touches
of the Gothic, such as the window on the west side that rises up under the
steep gable of the roof. What this house shows is that architects of the day

did not much care for stylistic purity. Rather, the overall effect was what mattered. Architects were happy to employ whatever would work, no matter what the source. The same designer may have done two or three similar houses on Carr Avenue (F-5, F-9, F-10) in subsequent years.

F-25 Rosemary Lane/Park Lane Subdivision
J. Frazer Smith, architect, 1938

Smith skillfully subdivided a large plot of ground in this territory of the old rich to produce thirty-three reasonably-priced houses for the middle to lower-middle class. Park Lane, which runs off Melrose, bears a grand name, but it is really only an alley leading to the garages of the houses on the south side of Rosemary. By putting the garages in the back, Smith could give the Rosemary lots smaller frontages, and thus increase the density, without giving up the amenity of housing for the family car. Rosemary itself turns twice, so that the street always seems short and intimate in scale. The Wiliamsburg-style houses are slightly smaller versions of Smith's contemporary houses in The Village (J-14), on Poplar just east of Goodlett.

Smith's interest in small, well-designed, well-made houses was not accidental. He got into the problem at the request of the head of the Federal Housing Authority for the state of Tennessee. The purpose of the FHA, founded during the Depression, was not just to make it possible for people to borrow money to pay for better housing, but also to provide jobs by encouraging home building. The FHA director began to worry, however, about having to guarantee twenty–year loans on badly-built houses. He called on Smith, one of five architects nationally serving on the housing committee of the AIA, for help. At first Smith disclaimed interest in small

F-25a

F-25b

houses, but with typical flexibility he changed his mind. In 1937 Smith founded the Memphis Small House Construction Bureau, a consortium of architects, contractors, developers, and realtors, quite probably modeled on the Architect's Small House Service Bureau founded in Minneapolis in 1921. According to Smith, the bureau was founded "to stop Memphis from building what is known as the carpenter bungalow, most of which were badly financed and eventually foreclosed, shoddily constructed, and not, by any stretch of the imagination, well designed."

The bureau produced a group of over one hundred house plans that could be built for prices ranging from $2,500 to $8,000. The buyer would be assured of a house designed by an architect, built of good materials, and supervised by an architect during construction. Within a year, apparently, 95 percent of the houses in Memphis submitted to the FHA were architect designed. The program attracted national attention and was copied in a number of cities. A group of architects in California, however, attacked the program on two counts: as a tacit admission that architectural services were too costly for the average person to afford and as a way of foisting off assembly-line plans on the public. In Smith's case, however, the latter criticism was hardly justified. His small-house plans were remarkably personal.

F-26   Robert Mann Duplex

> 1505 Central Avenue
> Estes Mann, architect, 1927

F-27　Robert Ruffin House

1511 Central Avenue
Jones and Furbringer, architects, 1916

F-28　Walter Lane Smith House

1520 Central Avenue
Charles Oscar Pfeil, architect, 1908–1909

The first steel-frame and reinforced-concrete structural system in a Memphis house is said to lie behind these boxy, dark-red-brick walls. The structural system was adapted from the skyscrapers Pfeil and his partner, G.M. Shaw, had recently built downtown, such as the Tennessee Trust Building (A-21) and the Business Men's Club (A-29).

F-29　J.B. Goodbar House

1557 Central Avenue
1906

Goodbar was one of the local tycoons for whom the streets in Annesdale Park were named. Like Brinkley Snowden, he opted to house himself castellated.

F-30　C. Hunter Raine House

1560 Central Avenue
W.J. Dodd, Louisville, architect, 1904–1906
Jones and Furbringer, associate architects

The first major example of the Colonial Revival in Memphis, the Raine house is also one of the grandest of that genre. The establishment occupies its entire lot, beginning at a handsome brick wall pierced by an elegant wrought iron gate. The house itself is in splendid condition, but the upper part of the sunporch to the west was added later, slightly upsetting the

F-30

ruling symmetry. It turned out that Raine, a banker, had embezzled a good bit of money, possibly including some that went into this house, and he ended up in jail.

F-31 Jefferson Ward Crosier House

755 South Willett Street
Mahan and Broadwell, architects, 1917

Mahan and Broadwell's bungalow has been "modernized" with startling lack of sympathy, turning it into what one might call a *bungalow rovinato* (or "bungled bungalow"). This should be viewed as a cautionary tale.

F-32 J.C. Sutton House

1565 Central Avenue
Regan and Weller, architects, 1929

A modest and relatively late entry in the Colonial Revival sweepstakes.

F-33 J.C. Norfleet House

1585 Central Avenue
1911

One of the most original and imposing of the houses on Central, the Norfleet house falls into a stylistic category known as Mission, in honor of the California missions it imitates. The scrolled gables on top are the crucial detail in this regard. The narrow arches in the diagonally projecting porches, however, suggest Moorish delights, while the central porch is dominated by standard Tuscan columns out of the architectural vocabulary of ancient Rome. Particularly strong here is the big third story, with a ballroom inside, that dominates all the architectural activity below. Guests arriving for balls were accommodated two carriages at a time at the entrance porch. Each end of the porch has built-in stone steps to receive, at proper height, the alighting feet of the carriage-borne.

F-34 Fred Montesi House

1592 Central Avenue
Regan and Weller, architects, 1937

When Regan and Weller did a Spanish house, they did it in a more sober way than the style favored by George Mahan. Here they combined traditional stucco walls and tile roofs with metal-sash windows, a new kind of material more generally found in factory architecture, but one that was making its way into domestic structures in the thirties.

F-33

F-35

F-35   Clanlo

1600 Central Avenue
1850s?

One of the finest surviving nineteenth-century houses in Memphis, Clanlo once dominated a plantation that occupied much of the ground between the Snowden property centered on Annesdale and the Rozelle place to the northeast, now at 1737 Harbert (F-89). Like the Pillow-McIntyre (C-6) and the Rayner Houses (G-13), Clanlo has a four-columned portico with slender proportions and flattened acanthus leaves on its Corinthian capitals, two details which seem to recur frequently in Memphis plantation houses.

F-36 Rhea P. Cary House

1649 Central Avenue
Jones and Furbringer, architects, 1905

A cool Colonial Revival nicely sited to dominate the end of Rozelle Street, which intersects Central across the way.

F-37 G.F. Fitzhugh House

1656 Central Avenue
Jones and Furbringer, architects, 1905

A tall box, made physically taller by a lofty mansard roof and visually taller by the giant order of pilasters applied around the walls. Seventeenth-century chateaux in France, such as the wings of Vaux-le-Vicomte, are recalled here.

F-38 Immaculate Conception Cathedral

1695 Central Avenue
Regan and Weller, architects, 1927–38

Regan and Weller were the preferred architects for Catholic buildings in Memphis in the first half of this century. The twin-towered facade of Im-

F-38

F-39

maculate Conception, with its play of varied stone textures and classical orders, is undoubtedly the best thing they ever did. It has been suggested that James J. Broadwell may have been taken on by the firm to help with the design of the church. The interior has a low plaster vault that spans a wide, well-lit space focused on the windowless apse. The two boxy Italianate buildings to the west of the church also are by Regan and Weller.

F-39   Immaculate Conception High School

1725 Central Avenue
A.L. Aydelott and Associates, architects, 1952–56
Joseph Barnett of Allen and Hoshall Architects, architect for addition, 1974

The high school to the east of the cathedral echoes both Mies van der Rohe's campus at the Illinois Institute of Technology in Chicago and Eero Saarinen's General Motors Technical Center at Warren, Michigan. It is one of the best essays in that 1950s modern style in town and one of Aydelott's most pleasing works.

F-40   James Edward Stark House

1779 Central Avenue
George Mahan, Jr., architect, 1927–30
Everett D. Woods, associate architect

F-40   Joseph D. Fly House

1828 Central Avenue
J. Frazer Smith and Herbert M. Burnham, architects, 1926

Smith had visited Italy in the twenties, and the Fly house shows that he had studied sixteenth-century-Italian architecture, particularly the work of Vignola, carefully. This house is as stiff and tight in design as his own Italianate house of the same time, at Walnut Grove Road and Waring Road (I-38), is relaxed and expansive.

F-42 C.W. Metcalf, Jr., House

1833 Central Avenue
1905

The slender proportions of the columns and the treatment of the main door are both drawn directly from antebellum houses, for which the Metcalf house could pass itself off with surprising ease. This is one of the early-twentieth-century houses in the city which are likely to be tagged with the label Colonial Revival, but actually they are direct revivals of the domestic architecture of this region from the first half of the nineteenth century.

F-43 A.L. Foster House

1900 Central Avenue
1912

The asymmetrical massing of this two-story house and the variety of surface patterns achieved in its wooden skin are typical of the Queen Anne style, which flourished in this country some decades before this house first appears in the city directory. Either it is an earlier building moved here from another spot, or it is a deliberate throwback to an earlier time. Such stylistically retarded buildings are not unknown elsewhere in the city. The Mode House at 355 South Fourth (D-49) appears to be another example.

F-46

This area, whose name, of relatively recent coinage, is meant to invoke the splendors of nineteenth-century New Orleans, represents the eastward continuation of Annesdale Park from Cleveland to South McLean. Most streets run east-west, but the three major cross streets—South Willett, Belvedere, and South McLean—make architecturally important interruptions in this pattern.

F-44   St. John's Methodist Church

1207 Peabody Avenue
B.C. Alsup, architect, 1907–1908

St. John's Methodist was one of the first churches to move into the eastern suburbs from a location close to downtown. Alsup gave the congregation a handsome, straightforward, classical building that lacked the quirkiness he sometimes summoned up for his clients.

F-45   Daniel Greif House

1324 Peabody Avenue
Regan and Weller, architects, 1914–15

F-46   Dr. Henry Posert House

1350 Peabody Avenue
1909

A stone Beaux-Arts house that clearly marks the entrance to this part of town from the downtown area. The six densely-packed columns carry elaborate Corinthian capitals. They emphasize the corners of the porch with an intensity similar to that found in a house of a similarly classical bent at 643 Anderson (F-92). In both of these houses one may see the Beaux-Arts-trained hand of Bayard Cairns.

F-47   Augustine Chighizola House

1379 Peabody Avenue
Augustine Chighizola, architect, 1909

Chighizola, who was born in Memphis, was one of the most successful architects of the period around 1900. This half-timbered house rising from a stone ground floor has a flatness of surface typical in his buildings. There is a house very much like this at 1396 Carr Avenue (F-11), which must be by Chighizola as well. Unfortunately, he died only two years after his house was built.

F-47

F-48   Nathan Karnowsky House

1412 Peabody Avenue
Mahan and Broadwell, architects, 1921–23

A rigidly symmetrical stone house of Italianate character. The client must have insisted on the symmetry, for it is not typical of Mahan and Broadwell when they worked with Mediterranean styles.

F-50a

F-49   First Neander M. Woods, Jr., House

1509 Peabody Avenue
Alsup and Woods, architects, 1907

Neander Woods occupied this newly-built house for only one year before
he sold it and moved to the second house he designed for himself at 1475
Vinton (F-73). That home, in turn, he sold a year later. The two quick
moves in a row probably indicate that this house and the one on Vinton
were speculative ventures. The wall that now obscures the house from the
street is not original. Behind that wall you can make out a carefully-detailed, boxy house with a deeply overhanging roof typical of the Prairie
School houses that had been built in the Chicago area earlier in the decade. While this house was up-to-date, it was quite conservative in contrast
to what Woods was to build next door at 1521 Peabody two years later.
That conservatism may be explained by the fact that in 1907 Woods was
still in partnership with B.C. Alsup, whereas in 1908 he opened his own
practice in offices in the new Goodwyn Institute Building that he and
Alsup had designed. After 1908 his architecture took off into flights of
great originality.

F-50   Third Neander M. Woods, Jr., House

1521 Peabody Avenue
Neander M. Woods, Jr., architect, 1909

Neander Woods moved into this house in 1909, only a year or so after he
had sold the house next door and moved to 1475 Vinton (F-73). He stayed
in this one for several years.
    The brick body of the building (now unfortunately painted white) is
broken by the jagged irregularity of the stone window surrounds, and it is

F-50b

topped by a deeply overhanging tile roof supported on wooden brackets of considerable heft. Most exciting is the diagonal porte-cochere that swings out from the main block of the house to thrust itself into the front yard. Woods had used this same device at the house on Vinton, but there the porte-cochere is only one story tall, so that it appears tacked on, rather than the organic part of the building it is here. In both houses, the porte-cochere extends beyond the driveway to form an outdoor room that joins house and yard in a particularly happy manner. One of the best views of the house is from the east side, where the bulging roofs of the main block and the porte-cochere, both pierced by arrow-like dormer windows, form a particularly powerful ensemble.

The third Woods house is one of his very best. As a group, his houses are probably the most original buildings built in Memphis in the early part of this century. They even stand up well alongside the inventive domestic architecture of the Midwest and the West Coast from the same years. Part of Woods' inspiration, including the diagonal projection and the rich mixing of materials and textures, came from Shingle Style houses of the 1880s, but the ensemble makes a very individual statement.

F-51   R.E. Hunter House
> 1510 Peabody Avenue
> Estes Mann, architect, 1927

F-52   Mrs. Walter Goodman and Mrs. J.M. Richardson House
> 1554 Peabody Avenue
> Jones and Furbringer, architects, 1907

F-53   F.L. Lang House
> 1600 Peabody Avenue
> 1909

The orange brick with a cobalt-blue aggregate, also used in two other houses in the city, came from Atlanta. The curved walls at the sides of the projecting west bay are quite powerful.

F-54   William J. Hardin House
> 1613 Peabody Avenue
> Jones and Furbringer, architects, 1910–11

A stone house with a strong centerpiece (the eagle is not original), the Hardin House, even with its complex porte-cochere on the west, seems quite restrained in comparison with the two houses just to the east of it, which we attribute to Neander Woods.

F-55 Frederick W. Reisinger House

1625 Peabody
Neander M. Woods, Jr., architect, 1910

Although the Reisinger House lacks Woods' characteristic diagonal porte-cochere, it does have his characteristic stonework with curvy mortar beds.

F-56 J.A. Ely House

1631 Peabody Avenue
Neander M. Woods, Jr., architect, 1909–11

Only slightly less assertive than the third Woods house to the west (F-50), the Ely House is particularly strong in the variety of its roof shapes.

F-57 Second J. Frazer Smith House

1635 Peabody Avenue
J. Frazer Smith, architect, 1937

Frazer Smith adopted a thoroughly southern mode in this modest house with a row of white columns across the front. The whole is reminiscent of,

F-56

F-57

although certainly larger and more pretentious than, traditional sharecropper cabins of the rural Middle South. The end bays of the colonnade are filled with shutters, which provide privacy for porch sitters but seem a bit incongruous on the north side of a house. In the thirties, Smith developed a passionate interest in the architecture of the Middle South. This resulted in the publication in 1941 of his book, *White Pillars*, one of the first serious studies of the pre–Civil War houses of the area.

F-58   Grace-St. Luke's Episcopal Church
1720 Peabody Avenue
Hanker and Cairns, architects, 1912–13

Here the Beaux-Arts trained Cairns tried his hand at the Gothic, with which he proved not as comfortable as with the classical. The interior, with its steep, open, timber roof rising from white walls, is reminiscent of Calvary Church downtown, but the transepts with twin gables strike a rather unorthodox note. Three windows by Louis Comfort Tiffany—the Ascension over the choir loft and the two single angels that flank the chancel—make a visit to the church essential. The stained-glass sunsets in the Ascension window and in the angel window in the west wall of the chancel are glorious.

SOUTH BELVEDERE BOULEVARD

One of the most impressive residential streets in the city, South Belvedere was laid out between Union and Central in 1906, and the first houses, at 186, 205, and 206, were occupied in 1907. The street is lined with man-

F-60

sions built by some of the city's wealthiest businessmen and professionals. Most of the houses are grand rather than great, so that the ensemble is stronger than most of its parts. Of note, however, are several structures:

F-59   Harry A. Darnell House

> 216 South Belvedere Boulevard
> Mahan and Broadwell, architects, 1918

A simplified French Provincial house with large French doors in front and a curved wall at the north side that, in typical Mahan and Broadwell fashion, betrays the presence of a staircase behind it. The house was sold in 1922 to Abe Plough, founder of Plough, Inc., a drug firm that became one of the city's largest businesses.

F-60   J.G. Falls House

> 529 South Belvedere Boulevard
> Hanker and Cairns, architects, 1910–12

The diagonal porte-cochere thoughtfully addresses the corner of Peabody and Belvedere, while the Mission-style scrolled centerpiece gives the facade coherence and the long Belvedere side is terminated by an ample porch with beveled corners that echo the diagonal of the porte-cochere. Inside, a centrally-placed entrance hall, with columns at each of the four corners, opens amply to either side into a spacious living room and dining room, so that the entire Belvedere front is essentially one room subdivided into three parts. This is one of Hanker and Cairns' finest houses, almost up to the level of the Newburger House at Union and East Parkway South (F-154).

F-61   A.R. Strong House

> 581 South Belvedere Boulevard
> 1923

A low, delicately-detailed, classical pavilion that offers a welcome respite from the ponderous rhythms of the houses that surround it.

F-62   W.P. Halliday House

> 619 South Belvedere Boulevard
> Charles Oscar Pfeil, architect, 1911–12

The dark mass of the brick has a power comparable to that of the Walter Lane Smith House at 1520 Central (F-28), designed by the same architect two or three years earlier.

F-63   Benjamin B. Harvey House

604 South Belvedere Boulevard
Mahan and Broadwell, architects, 1923

In the twenties, Mahan and Broadwell did several large symmetrical brick houses with flat wall planes from which massive white doorframes, ultimately English baroque in origin, project. Others in this group are the Block House at 1856 Autumn (E-46) and the Thornton House at 2285 Washington (F-134).

F-64   Henry Solomon House

532 South Belvedere Boulevard
Mahan and Broadwell, architects, 1922–23

F-65   E.H. Crump House
1962 Peabody Avenue
1909–10

Crump, newly elected as reform mayor of Memphis when he began this house, became the chief figure in the city's politics until his death in the 1950s. The house plays an interesting game with the Doric order. Doric columns support a porch which essentially lacks an entablature. The brackets that hold up the roof, however, are turned into the triglyphs that should have been part of the entablature that the porch, by rights, ought to have.

F-65

F-66 Shotgun Houses

2065, 2071, 2073, and 2075 Peabody Avenue
c. 1906

The character of neighborhoods in Memphis can change with a rapidity that makes some urban planners groan but fills others with delight, because of the rich mix of housing types, and therefore of economic levels, that can occur in a fairly small area. 2065 Peabody is an odd mix of house types: a bungalow shotgun.

F-67 Office of A.L. Aydelott (formerly)

2080 Peabody Avenue
A.L. Aydelott, architect, 1952

It is said that Aydelott had sufficient pull in City Hall to get a zoning variance to allow him to build his office in a residential neighborhood. It is also said that when the building was finished, E.H. Crump walked down the street from his house to look it over and just shook his head. The Aydelott office was one of the earliest truly modern buildings in the city, a fitting fact, given that Aydelott was largely responsible for introducing modern design into Memphis architecture. He acted as a kind of godfather to the young architects who came to Memphis in the fifties and who have since designed many of its most important structures in a modern mode.

The office itself is surrounded by a serpentine brick wall, which traditionalists could enjoy as an echo of Thomas Jefferson's walls at the University of Virginia, but which others could read as a surrealist-inspired, biomorphic form typical of the fifties. Of course it's both. The wall provides privacy for the glass-walled offices of the building proper, which has a particularly airy drafting room on the north side. The architectural firm of Yeates, Gaskill, and Rhodes acquired the building from Aydelott and occupied it until they merged with Jones and Mah. The building was too small to house their combined forces.

F-68 H.H. Crosby House

1566 Carr Avenue
1909–1910

A large two-story brick house with powerful, curved walls in the central projection that rises over the stone front porch.

F-69   Percy L. Mannen House

1583 Carr Avenue
Neander M. Woods, Jr., architect, 1910

Neander Woods gave this house a sense of delicious eccentricity. He
mixed stones and shingles on the ground floor. He put a polygonal turret
on the east corner of the second floor, a deeply recessed window over the
entrance arch, and then above that a huge gable, flanked by a tiny gable
that mediates between the turret and the great gable. This may well be
the wackiest house in the neighborhood. In 1988 the house received much-
needed repairs, but the pink paint job on the stone was not a happy idea.

F-69

F-71a

F-70　Frank J. Rice House

1584 Carr Avenue
1909

A handsomely-detailed, symmetrical house that one might term Prairie Beaux-Arts. Its no-nonsense character is made all the more evident by comparing it with the Mannen House by Neander Woods across the street.

F-71　H.J. Parrish House

1461 Vinton Avenue
Neander M. Woods, Jr., architect, 1909–11

Woods took full advantage of the corner lot site to design a house of great sculptural vigor that works from any direction of approach. Woods' trademark diagonal porte-cochere splits the two-story, circular bulge on the east from the elaborate play of planes and roof levels on the west. The mixture of materials and the wavy joints of the stonework are particularly marvelous here. One would dearly like to know the name of the extraordinarily talented mason. The Parrish House is one of Woods' finest efforts.

F-72　Second Neander M. Woods, Jr., House

1475 Vinton Avenue
Neander M. Woods, Jr., architect, 1908

From the tall, rectangular two-story main block of this house projects a shallow two-story bay, placed almost in the middle. To the east, a one-story porte-cochere advances diagonally into the garden. Beyond the driveway it continues into a kind of open living room that extends the space of

F-71b

F-72

the house into its yard. Here the whole porte-cochere appears tacked on, whereas a year later he pulled off the same trick at 1521 Peabody (F-50) with much greater finesse.

This appears to be the first house on which Woods tried out the masonry that was to become one of his trademarks. Here it seems a little tentative, especially when one compares it with the fluidity of the curved joints in the Parrish House next door to the west. The stone lintels and the voussoirs over the triple window on the ground floor are still quite traditional and carefully cut. In the Parrish House, and in all the later houses, the simple lintels disappear, and the voussoirs become as curvaceous as the rest of the masonry. Woods lived here only one year before moving into one of his masterpieces, at 1521 Peabody.

F-73   Robert Cohn House

> 1480 Vinton Avenue
> Jones and Furbringer, architects, 1910

F-74   Henry Daspit House

> 1488 Vinton Avenue
> Neander M. Woods, Jr., architect, 1909

In a rather standard large box of a house, Woods applied his favored trefoil arched dormers and his typical curvy masonry to the porch. The house has lost its original tile roof. In the 1950s, its walls, whatever they may have been originally, were sheathed in asbestos siding, and "picture" windows replaced the original ground-floor windows.

F-75 W.A. Waddington House

1511 Vinton Avenue
1911

A house delightful for its mixture of rough brick, stucco, and half timbering, and for the two very fancy dormers over the windows upstairs.

F-76 John Ellett House

1516 Vinton Avenue
Jones and Furbringer, architects, 1911

The Ellett House is one of this firm's best, largely because of the elegant organization of the center of the house into three superimposed groups of triple openings which focus on the lavish display of fruit, symbolic of hospitality, or of fecundity, in a carved panel on the second floor.

F-77 John T. Fisher House

1412 Harbert Avenue
Neander M. Woods, Jr., architect, 1910

Here Woods sided the house with clapboards instead of stone, but he varied the texture by using wide boards on an extended ground floor and narrow boards above. The central gable contains a deeply-recessed window, similar to the one at 1583 Carr (F-69). Only the diagonal porte-cochere has Woods' random ashlar masonry.

F-76

F-79

F-78   Mrs. G.F. Devon House

1530 Harbert Avenue
Neander M. Woods, Jr., architect, 1911

Woods employed almost classical restraint on this relatively small house
that is sided in wood, like the Fisher house to the west on the same street.
The excitement comes from the dormers that break into the roof and from
the diagonal porch (no porte-cochere on this narrow lot).

F-79   R. Walker Balch House

1542 Harbert Avenue
Neander M. Woods, Jr., architect, 1909–10

Here Woods put the diagonal on the back, in a porch (enclosed later) that
projects from the northwest corner. The restrained massing, however,
seems to have allowed him the freedom to indulge in an orgy of texture
and pattern. The flat stone arches over the triple windows have wiggly
keystones, and the upper floor is given a half-timber pattern that knits the
whole together magically. The central mass that projects into a curved
gable competes successfully with the heavy dormers with trefoil arches
that poke boldly up into the roof. Downstairs there are only three rooms
across the front; the entrance hall at the east side, a small living room, and
an unusually long dining room to the west.

F-80   A.D. Armstrong House

635 South Willett Street
1910

A fairly close copy of nearby Clanlo (F-35) with, however, setback wings and one-story side porches that suggest that the designer may have looked at Thomas Jefferson's buildings around the lawn at Charlottesville.

F-81   Robert M. Carrier House

642 South Willett Street
Bryant Fleming, Ithaca, New York, architect, 1926

Carrier was a native of New York State, and it must have been there that he came in contact with Fleming, who was a professor of landscape architecture at Cornell. The house, which is difficult to see from the street because of the surrounding wall and the thick plantings, is composed of elements of Jacobean, Elizabethan, and Tudor buildings collected by Fleming in England and then reassembled as the centerpiece of the handsome gardens that he laid out for the Carriers. Because so many of the interior details are authentic, the house has a remarkable presence.

F-82   J.O.E. Beck House

684 South Willett Street
J.O.E. Beck, designer, 1982

Although Beck is not a registered architect, he is a designer of considerable gifts. This strong, clean piece of abstract sculpture, minimalist in its reticence, is set down uncompromisingly in the midst of one of the most impressive eclectic streetscapes in the city, with the classical Raine House to the south on the corner of Central, the Tudorbethean Carrier House to the north, and the quirky Balch House by Neander Woods on the northwest corner of Willett and Harbert.

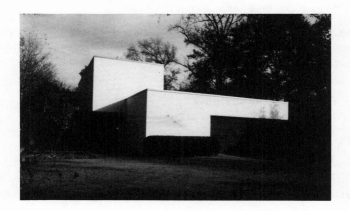

F-82

F-83   Edward C. Klaiber House

1430 Goodbar Avenue
Mahan and Broadwell, architects, 1913

An early Mahan and Broadwell house, on which they used orange brick with cobalt blue aggregate, the same brick from Atlanta that had been used on the Lang House at 1600 Peabody in 1909 (F-53).

F-84   George C. Kaucher House

1447 Goodbar Avenue
Mahan and Broadwell, architects, 1921

F-85   Pope M. Farrington House

1473 Goodbar Avenue
1924

A large, handsome English cottage, with a particularly strong triple chimney.

F-86   W.P. Maury House

1508 Goodbar Avenue
Jones and Furbringer, architects, 1913

This is one of the earliest Italo-Iberian houses in town. Jones and Furbringer did it fairly straight, in comparison to what Mahan and Broadwell would do a decade later. The new wall around the house hides many of its charms, such as the arcade on the east side, from the street, but the handsome door beside the driveway is still visible.

F-87   John O. Bomer, Jr., House

1574 Harbert Avenue
Mahan and Broadwell, architects, 1918

Mahan and Broadwell experimented with designing classicizing bungalows in all price ranges. This is one on the modest end of the scale, inserted into a lot that must have been carved from that of one of the houses next door.

F-88   First Peter Grant House

1655 Harbert Avenue
1908

The slender proportions of the four columns of the portico and the flat leaves of the capitals are so close to the proportions and capitals of Clanlo (F-35) and the Pillow-McIntyre House (C-6) that one wonders if these may not have been saved from a destroyed antebellum structure. The same question might be asked of the round window in the tympanum. Here we may have a classical revival house with actual antebellum elements.

F-89 Rozelle House
1737 Harbert Avenue
Mid-1850s

This clapboard cottage with six gables and delicate architectural orna-ments was the plantation house for much of the area of the Central Gar-dens. Not as pretentious as nearby Clanlo, it may be, because of its inti-mate scale, more charming. It apparently was built, toward the end of his life, by Solomon Rozelle, who settled in the area in 1815, before the city was founded, and died in 1856.

F-90 Francis Gassner House
1749 Harbert Avenue
Francis Gassner, architect, 1967

It is a tribute to Gassner's skills as a designer that he could insert so un-compromisingly modern a house into a neighborhood of such different character without making the insertion an intrusion. The secret is in the heavy plantings in front of the house, which make the low blank white wall the house presents to the street appear to be a garden backdrop rather than a house. The large yellow numbers, a bit on the Pop Art side, give away the 1960s date and also tell us that the house is not entirely self effacing. The clearly planned interior opens up through large glass walls to the private walled garden that occupies the entire back of the lot.

F-89

F-91 Hubert F. Fisher House

640 Anderson Street
Mahan and Broadwell, architects, 1919

F-92 Adolph A. Laurence House

643 Anderson Street
1910–12

One of the most powerful Colonial Revival houses in town. The triple
Ionic columns at the corners of the portico give the whole house a most
impressive sense of strength and massiveness, while the balustraded terrace anchors the house firmly to the ground. Flat arches with strong voussoirs surmount triple windows that form bold frames for the porch. The
most likely designer seems to be Bayard Cairns.

F-93 J.M. McCandless House

1731 Glenwood Place
1907

The style of this house, more Victorian than anything else, is a bit retarded
for the date, but that fact is irrelevant in the face of one splendid touch,
the exclamation point voussoir that pops up out of the attic dormer. There
is another such exclamation point on a house at 1731 Autumn (E-43), built
in the same year.

F-94 Donald P. Mann House

1785 Harbert Avenue
1911

The finest true Colonial Revival structure in the city, the Mann House is a
close imitation of the eighteenth-century John Hancock House in Boston,
not as it actually had been, but as the Boston architectural firm of Peabody
and Stearns had reconstructed (and redesigned) it to serve as the Massachusetts Pavilion at the World's Columbian Exposition in Chicago in
1893. In 1917, the house was sold to Peter Grant, who sold it in 1925 to
L.K. Thompson, by whose name the house is now generally known.

F-95 Second Peter Grant House

1803 Harbert Avenue
1912

Four years after he built the traditional columned house at 1655 Harbert
(F-88), Peter Grant built the closest thing Memphis has to a house by
Frank Lloyd Wright. The deep overhangs of the roof that parallel the hori-

F-92

F-94

F-95

zontal line of the ground make this a fine example of the Prairie Style that Wright had invented in the previous decade. Grant, however, was a restless man. In 1917 he bought the Mann House next door at 1785 Harbert, and then in 1925 he moved to Germantown, into a very large house designed by George Mahan, Jr., in the Mount Vernon manner. Unfortunately, that house was destroyed by fire.

F-96   Shelby Gabbert House

> 687 South McLean Boulevard
> Mahan and Broadwell, architects, 1922–23

In the early twenties Mahan and Broadwell mined the Italo-Hispanic vein assiduously. The large Gabbert House is distinguished by the curved walls of the projecting pavilion on the right and by the heavy rinceaux frieze under the roof.

F-97   W.W. Robinson House

> 688 South McLean Boulevard
> 1922, columns added 1960s

This large brick four-square gained in pretension, if not in grace, when four columns from the facade of Alsup and Woods' now-destroyed Goodwyn Institute Building (A-101 [Lost Memphis]) at Madison and Third were applied to its facade. Because of the height of the columns, an overweening pediment had to be added awkwardly to the roof. It's good, of course, that the columns were not thrown away.

F-102

F-98 Dr. Robert E. Baldwin House

695 South McLean Boulevard
Mahan and Broadwell, architects, 1922

A fairly sober Tudor house with half timbering, a stone chimney, and a
projecting entrance vestibule.

F-99 Joseph Maury House

696 South McLean Boulevard
Mahan and Broadwell, architects, 1921

A Tudor cottage graced by a lion's head in the flat niche inserted in the
stone chimney. Flat niches in chimneys were favored devices of this pair
of architects.

F-100 V.E. Schevenall House

705 South McLean Boulevard
1926

A sophisticated variation on the bungalow, this one is a symmetrical little
stone house with clearly Mediterranean ancestry.

F-101 Giles B. Bond House

717 South McLean Boulevard
Mahan and Broadwell, architects, 1921

A house calculated for its corner site, so that it looks good both from Central and from McLean, the Bond House brings to a close our journey down
a street which might, for this stretch, be renamed McMahan. On the Central Avenue side, the curved wall with one large window tells us that there
is a staircase behind. This is Mahan and Broadwell at their most relaxed,
and the house makes a nice contrast with the tensely symmetrical Fly
House (F-41) by Frazer Smith and Herbert Burnham on the opposite corner.

F-102 First George C. Bowen House

1637 York Avenue
1904–1905

George Bowen was one of those enterprising building entrepreneurs who
build houses and live in them until they are sold, at which time he builds
another one and moves into it. He was also the man who introduced the
bungalow to Memphis (F-108), something for which he deserves to be
remembered forever. This is an inventive Queen Anne cottage of the pre-
bungalow era, with varied textures and a cylindrical tower rising unexpectedly over the entrance porch.

F-103 Charles E. Chapleau House

1718 York Avenue
Mahan and Broadwell, architects, 1913

An early bungalow by Mahan and Broadwell. The main interest of the house is that its ordinariness makes clear what extraordinary things they were to do with the genre in the next few years. Behind the bungalow rises the enormous, uninterrupted yellow-brick mass of the apse of Immaculate Conception Cathedral (F-38).

F-104 E.C. Cook House

1741 Vinton Avenue
1916

The bungalow, as a house type, was intended to brings its owners closer to nature, or at least to suggest a kind of sylvan retreat to which the man of the house could retire after a hard day downtown at the office. In pursuit of such rusticity, the architect of the Cook bungalow gave it a porch that pretends to grow out of living rock, and piers with jagged tops that suggest nature untamed.

F-105 R.S. Mason House

1801 Vinton Avenue
1916–17

Here the typical rectangular volume of the second floor of an airplane bungalow has been twisted around so it is parallel to the street and close to it. This maneuver gave the house a much grander facade on Vinton, while it also allowed room for what must be one of the earliest built-in garages in the city.

F-104

F-106   O.S. Warr House

> 583 South McLean Boulevard
> 1921

Just to the east of 1801 Vinton is a bungalow of traditional form but untraditional largeness. The roofscape that results from the great size of the house is dazzlingly complex.

F-107   Roy H. McKay House

> 1875 Harbert Avenue
> George Mahan, Jr., architect, 1926–28

A cottage in which the doorway and chimney have been fused into one element.

F-108   Second George C. Bowen House

> 1901 Harbert Avenue
> George C. Bowen, developer, 1908–1909

Probably this is the first bungalow built in Memphis, and so it is of considerable historical significance in a city that bristles with bungalows. The ship-bottom roof over the east porch is unusual, if not unique. Unfortunately, the Bowen bungalow has received a not-very-sympathetic modernization on its northeast corner. Earlier, Bowen had built and lived in a splendid Queen Anne cottage at 1637 York (F-102).

F-108

F-109 Nineteenth Century Club

(formerly Rowland J. Darnell House)
1433 Union Avenue
1909

In 1926 this grand house, the last remaining of the great houses that once lined Union Avenue, was bought by the Nineteenth Century Club, a philanthropic and cultural women's organization. A number of additions were made to the house, including a swimming pool by George Mahan, but they have all disappeared. The Colonial Revival house is one of the few in Memphis actually to have stone columns. The well-preserved interior is dominated by a central hall, off of which the major rooms open. The intricate leaded glass on the stair landing is particularly fine.

F-110 First Congregational Church

234 South Watkins Street
Jones and Furbringer, architects, 1909–10

The handsomest detail here is the pediment window, surrounded by a lavish frame in the shape of a shield from which swags are draped.

F-110

F-111   Julius Lewis Store

1460 Union Avenue
Hanker and Heyer, architects, 1950

As the population of Memphis moved inexorably east after World War II,
Union Avenue became increasingly commercialized in this midtown area.
The Julius Lewis Store replaced three large houses that stood on this
block, facing Union, and several more houses on Monroe to the north gave
way to the store's parking lot. Even if the store seems unable to make up
its mind between a kind of Wrightian rusticity and classical symmetry, it
has considerably more architectural verve than the fast-food restaurants
that moved in *en masse* in the 1980s. The Julius Lewis Store is prime
evidence of the difficulty classically-trained architects such as Hanker had
in adapting themselves to the modern style, which had become *de rigueur*
for commercial buildings in Memphis by the 1950s.

F-112   Kimbrough Towers

172 Kimbrough Place, corner of Union Avenue
Herbert M. Burnham, architect, 1939

The Kimbrough Towers apartment building is one of the finest Art Deco
structures in the city. Particularly strong are the vertical projections that
articulate each side of the asymmetrically planned mass. Originally it was
a monochromatic building. The recent paint job has rendered a bit obvious
the architect's carefully-crafted, subtle play of light and shade on the sur-

F-112

F-113

F-116

face, created only by the variety of relief on the walls. The stores to the east along Union also are part of Herbert Burnham's scheme, and they present us with a particularly good Art Deco commercial strip development.

F-113   Herbert M. Burnham House

1467 Vance Avenue
J. Frazer Smith and Herbert M. Burnham, architects, 1927

A chunky French chateau is here reduced to suburban size; its very big chimney anchors the house to a corner lot in the Kimbrough subdivision, which was developed by the same family that developed Kimbrough Towers. To the chateau, a carefully-rendered sixteenth-century Italian doorway is applied. Burnham was Frazer Smith's architectural partner in these years, and he designed the Art Deco Kimbrough Towers twelve years later on his own.

F-114   J.F. Kimbrough, Jr., House

> 1521 Vance Avenue
> J. Frazer Smith and Herbert M. Burnham, architects, 1927

A downward-swooping roof that projects out to cover a front porch is a
distinguishing characteristic of at least three houses by Smith and
Burnham. The others are the J. Hunter Van Natta House, 607 Center Drive
in Hein Park, of 1926 (E-30), and the J. Stalley Wellford House, 35 Belleair
Woods, of 1930. Of the three, this, designed for the developer of the subdivision in which it stands, may be the best.

F-115   Rainbow Studio

> (formerly Pig 'n Whistle)
> 1579 Union Avenue
> Estes Mann, architect, 1931

Under later layers lies the first drive-in restaurant in the city, with the
remarkable name of "Pig 'n Whistle." For reasons which are not totally
clear, Mann made this restaurant into a Tudorbethean country house.
Were the customers, as they sat in their cars sipping malts, to imagine
themselves about to join in a fox hunt? Or did the ersatz exterior attempt
to disguise the up-to-date eatery as a jolly Olde English Inne?

F-116   Helen of Memphis

> 1808 Union Avenue
> Nowland Van Powell, architect, 1950, 1958

Under Powell's new skin lurk, to the west, a building by George Mahan for
a women's club and, to the east, the small chapel of an Episcopal mission,
sent out east by Grace Church. The buildings were brought together to
form the Helen Shop a number of years before Powell was asked to give
the ensemble an almost-impossible-to-achieve coherence. His solution
was to encase all the disparate elements in a sheer wall brought right out
to the sidewalk. He decorated the wall with classical motifs so shallow
that they seem to flatten themselves to its surface in fear of Union Avenue
traffic.

F-117   Idlewild Presbyterian Church

> 1750 Union Avenue
> George Awsumb, architect, 1926–27

Looking like a part of Rhodes College that has strayed off campus, this
enormous church complex is George Awsumb's contribution to the mild
Gothic fever that hit Memphis after Southwestern (now Rhodes College)
moved to Memphis from Clarksville, Tennessee, in 1925. An accom-

plished master of this revival style, Awsumb used stone from the same Arkansas quarries that still supply Rhodes to create the "chapel" that that college has never had. More than one president of Rhodes has been heard to wish for a skyhook big enough to transport this church a couple of miles to his campus.

This is a Presbyterian monastery, complete with cloister walks, chapter house, and what is probably the tallest tower between downtown and east Memphis. Inside the church itself, a convincing French Gothic nave arcade and triforium hold up a good English Gothic painted timber roof. The large wooden transverse beams are supported on very un-Presbyterian carved stone corbels. Indeed, the church is remarkable both for the amount and the high quality of the carving in it. The traditional cross plan of the sanctuary is disguised by running the pews almost up to the chancel steps.

Although the style is medieval, the construction of Idlewild is very definitely twentieth-century. The office and classroom buildings are of reinforced concrete underneath all the stone and dark oak and tracery. It is difficult to disguise a hefty reinforced concrete building, but Awsumb has done it. You must look long and hard to see that the massive oak beams exposed on the ground floor are really made of concrete, chamfered and painted to look like hand-hewn wood.

F-118   Hinds-Smythe Cosmopolitan Funeral Home

1900 Union Avenue
George Awsumb and Sons, architects, 1938

The great portico of white columns suggests a grand domestic establishment, something like the Darnell House (F-109) down the street that became the Nineteenth Century Club, rather than a funeral home. There also may be a certain amount of Scarlett O'Hara sentiment in this porch.

F-119   Union Avenue Church of Christ

1930 Union Avenue
1945–46

A domed church with a classical portico, but not as vigorous as the red-brick Union Avenue United Methodist Church a few blocks to the east.

F-120   Union Avenue United Methodist Church

2117 Union Avenue, at Cooper
Hubert T. McGhee, architect, 1923

The main cube of the building is articulated on the street sides by groups of four pilasters, suggesting that here we are dealing with a kind of Villa Rotunda that has scrunched in its symmetrical, columned porches to fit itself to its restricted site. Thus is created a tension between the implied

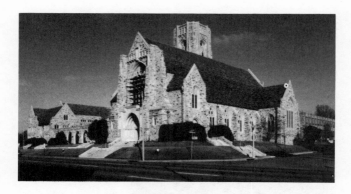

F-117

F-120

extension of the building and the reality of the corner site. The only room for the Sunday school was in a raised basement that jacked the domed sanctuary up so high that it could be reached only by a precipitous flight of steps.

F-121   Lenox School

519 South Edgewood Street
John Gaisford, architect, 1909
Jack Tucker, architect for remodeling and additions, 1983

The chief glory of this building is the main entrance on the east facade. Two octagonal columns with quasi-Romanesque capitals support an arch with three outlandishly overscaled voussoirs that, with a joyous sunburst effect, tie the arch to the gable above. Over this great eagles preside. This entrance is so extravagant that it must have been fun to go in, even when

F-121

it was a school. Jack Tucker has now made the school buildings part of a skillfully-worked-out condominium complex, which includes the school proper, a c. 1920 building to the southwest, and a group of cozily domestic wooden buildings that form a forecourt for the school building on the west.

F-122   Madison Professional Building

1750 Madison Avenue
Roy P. Harrover and Associates, architects, 1975

F-123   Gilmore Apartments

6 South McLean Boulevard
William Lester, architect, 1929–30

Tall apartment buildings never became common in Memphis. The Gilmore Apartments were an early attempt to introduce the type to the city, and the building is more interesting for this historical fact than for its rather lackluster Art Deco design.

F-124   La Vogue Beauty Salon

1873 Madison Avenue
William Lester, architect, 1940–41

This facade luckily retains its original glass tile and glass brick, as well as its original neon sign. Clearly it was designed to harmonize with the Gilmore apartments next door.

COOPER-YOUNG NEIGHBORHOOD

The southeast corner of the Central Gardens area is formed by the Cooper-Young neighborhood, so named for the intersection which almost exactly marks the center of the area. Here is a remarkably well-preserved group of wooden cottages, bungalows, and four-squares. It is one of the best examples of a middle- to lower-middle-class suburban neighborhood of the early twentieth century in the whole city. The effect of the ensemble is what is important, rather than individual buildings, an effect created and sustained by modest but pleasant houses on small lots. Within the neighborhood, however, a few buildings deserve to be singled out.

F-125 Peabody Elementary School

2086 Young Avenue
Jones and Furbringer, architects, 1910–12

One of eight public schools designed by this firm between 1902 and 1915, Peabody boasts a particularly splendid main doorway, surrounded by a rich terra-cotta border of rosettes. When they set their minds to it, Jones and Furbringer could whip up architectural textures with great skill. This door almost comes up to the level of their Masonic Temple downtown on Court Avenue (A-95).

F-126 Captain Harris House

2106 Young Avenue
Before 1898

The most ambitious house in the neighborhood, set on the largest lot. In 1925 the Queen Anne house was turned from its original west-facing position to face south. The lively south facade shows what fun one can have

F-126

with wood architecture in terms of varied shapes and surface textures. The severe east side, with its symmetrically-arranged windows, seems completely out of character with the surface delights, push-pull volumes, and asymmetry of the south. One wonders if the Queen Anne elements may have been added to an earlier and far simpler structure, the remains of which are still visible on the east.

F-127   Charles L. Tucker House

1915 Evelyn Avenue
Mahan and Broadwell, architects, 1921–23

Tucker was a business associate of Peter Grant, who built the Prairie Style house at 1803 Harbert (F-95).

F-128   M.O. Davidson House

2216 Evelyn Avenue
1925

One of the delights of Memphis architecture is the surprising discovery of still another variation on the bungalow. Here is a Moorish one, complete with a porch of horseshoe arches set under a roof pierced by an eyebrow ventilator, a form more at home in the Richardsonian Romanesque of the 1880s. The house fits its corner lot particularly well.

F-129   Elzey Avenue Bungalows

2280 to 2301 Elzey Avenue
William Chandler, developer, 1928

Chandler was one of the most important real estate developers in the city. Clutches of his bungalows are found all over town. These on Elzey, from the late twenties, seem to have reached an almost decadent stage. 2280 Elzey (F-129a) is a transitional bungalow metamorphosing into one of the house types that supplanted it: the Cotswold Cottage, identified by the roof swooping groundward. As Elzey moves east, the bungalows pair off across it to form an unusually coherent yet varied streetscape. Most of the bungalows that Chandler built, such as those of the Shadowlawn development of South Parkway or those to the immediate west of the Sears Building on Cleveland, are not nearly so imaginative in design or layout. Chandler had a particularly talented designer here.

F-128

F-129a

F-129b

F-130 G.I. Frazier House

25 Belleair Woods
1928

Almost all the great Spanish-style houses of the city are by Mahan and Broadwell. This is one of the few that apparently isn't. Whoever the architect may have been, he handled the style with considerable flair, particularly in the way he played with twisted columns.

F-131 Max Heilbronner House

2221 Poplar Avenue
Jones and Furbringer, architects, 1915

F-132 David Sternberg House

2245 Poplar Avenue
Jones and Furbringer, architects, 1915

F-133 Second John Sneed Williams, Sr., House

2269 Poplar Avenue
George Mahan, Jr., architect, 1929
Everett D. Woods, associate architect

F-134 Leslie A. Thornton House

2285 Washington Avenue
George Mahan, Jr., architect, 1924–26

Again Mahan poses a richly three dimensional baroque doorframe against a pure, flat wall that was originally dark red brick. Above the door is a Palladian window with a difference. The pilasters carry through above the arch instead of supporting it, and the window under the arch has an elegant flower-petal fanlight.

F-134

F-135 Henry T. Stratton House

72 North Edgewood Street
1979

The midtown area has so few houses in a contemporary architectural mode that when you run across one, you may well get excited. The Jefferson Avenue facade is the best part, particularly the treatment of the skylit two-story space, which allows not only the space of the exterior, but also the gaze of the onlooker, to pierce the interior, in which a jungle of plants thrives.

F-136 Charles Galloway Morris House

2238 Court Avenue
Mahan and Broadwell, architects, 1921–23

F-137 Lawrence S. Vaccaro House

2281 Court Avenue
Mahan and Broadwell, architects, 1918

F-138 John R. Flippin House

2284 Court Avenue
Jones and Furbringer, architects, 1917

An insensitive paint job has done little to compromise the strong architectural effects of this house, which plays numerous skilful variations on the number three. The whole facade is divided into three parts. In turn, those parts are also subject to triple subdivisions, such as the triple arcade of the central porch, or the triple windows in the side bays.

F-138

F-139   Morningside Park

The first two houses in Morningside Park were built in 1916, and others quickly followed. One of the first is number 12, the Charles G. Smith House (1916), by Mahan and Broadwell, with an elegant doorway and slender windows reminiscent of Back Bay Boston in the early nineteenth century. Number 36, the Augusta C. Semmes House (1929), is a handsome neoclassical block that almost looks as if it could have come from late-eighteenth-century France, while number 46, the William B. Chapman House (1926), is a severe Tudor with only a touch of half-timbering to pick out the entrance. The J.S. Speed House, number 100, is an English cottage designed by George Mahan and Everett Woods in 1936. Number 135, by Lucian Minor Dent, was built by Mrs. Bryan Eagle in 1940. Number 103, the Leonard P. Janes House, 1928, tries for a Jacobean grandeur that it never quite attains, partly because the treatment of the door seems anticlimactically flat. Number 79, the Elizabeth H. Polk House (1929), has an unclassical use of pilasters, which incorrectly come in two thicknesses for the same height. They also carry Corinthian capitals of a rather quirky flatness. This house is similar to several works by Mahan and Broadwell, but it does not appear on Mahan's list of commissions. For that reason, it may well have been designed by James Broadwell, whose partnership with Mahan dissolved in 1924.

Morningside Park contains the Curtis King House, one of the great houses of Memphis.

F-140   Curtis King House
   11 Morningside Park
   Mahan and Broadwell, architects, 1917

Next to the names of the almost two thousand projects on his list of commissions, George Mahan made a notation about style only once: for this house. He called it a "Colonial Bungalow." The only part that belongs to the standard bungalow, as it developed in the United States, is the deep front porch that runs across the entire facade and moves forward at the ends to engage the house with its yard. The architectural forms of this remarkably original house are all drawn from classical architecture, even though in general the bungalow was supposed to be designed to suggest no particular historical style, and certainly not the stiffly formal classical. Perhaps Mahan understood this "Colonial Bungalow" to be something more in line with the original structures of this type: the houses the English built for themselves in India in the eighteenth and nineteenth centuries. Or perhaps by "Colonial" he only meant classical, as in the eighteenth-century architecture of the American Colonies.

Everything in the facade is tied together; even the graceful sculptural elements in the pediment are connected visually to the Ionic columns

F-140

below. Only the little statues that were placed on the urns above the roof line at a later date and the modern skylights in the roof mar the playful serenity of this house, which marks one of Mahan and Broadwell's happiest moments.

The house was a honeymoon bungalow for its original owners. The downstairs has a large living room that occupies the entire center and opens onto the back lawn. To the south are two bedrooms and to the north a dining room and kitchen. Upstairs, under the great roof, lurk a billiard room and a ballroom. American urban bungalows were meant as modest middle-class housing, but this one is upper-class all the way. For its high architectural qualities, however, the King House deserves to be more than just an aristocratic footnote in the history of the bungalow.

As soon as the Kings began to have children, they moved out. For them Mahan later designed a large Spanish-style house south of Park Avenue, of which, unfortunately, only the garage remains, behind the White Station Church of Christ, 1106 Colonial Road.

F-141 Francis W. Andrews House

> 66 East Parkway North
> Mahan and Broadwell, architects, 1923–24

A Tudor with brick laid around the doorway to suggest that the wall might be picturesquely crumbling away.

F-142 Noland Fontaine House

> 80 East Parkway North
> Mahan and Broadwell, architects, 1919–21

An elegant little classical pavilion, with doors and windows set directly into a stark stucco wall.

F-145

F-143 Abraham Goodman House

159 East Parkway North
1914

A correctly classical house, with everything done right, including having real sandstone shafts for the Ionic columns and real sandstone quoins at the corners. Because of its impressive scale, the house commands its site on a very wide and busy intersection with ease.

F-144 First John Sneed Williams, Sr., House

123 East Parkway North
Mahan and Broadwell, architects, 1921

F-145 John McClure House

65 East Parkway North
Jones and Furbringer, architects, 1920
Noland Van Powell, architect for renovations, 1950s

An eclectic house in which the disparate parts don't quite come to terms with each other. The whole is pseudo-Tudor, but the stone doorway is pure Early Renaissance, from fifteenth-century Florence, while the wrought-iron balcony suggests a production of *Romeo and Juliet* staged in New Orleans. The slender white window frames with tiny round ornaments, English Regency in style, were added to the house in the 1950s by Nowland Van Powell, who remodeled the interior extensively.

F-146

F-146   W.J. Crawford House

> 1 East Parkway North, corner of Madison
> George M. Shaw, architect, 1912–13

This house is one of the two or three finest Colonial revival houses in town. The bowed side bays, with shell niches over the triple windows, flank elegantly proportioned Ionic columns based on those of the Erechtheum in Athens. Inside the main porch is a one-story subsidiary porch, in which the same columns are repeated at a smaller scale. Particularly beautiful is the repetition of the curve over the main door in the curved center of this inner porch, which is sheltered under a noble canopy of coffers. Here shape, scale, and space are manipulated with consummate skill. Shaw's career is still something of a mystery, but this must be his masterpiece.

F-147   Dr. J.W. Monks House

> 191 East Parkway South
> Regan and Weller, architects, 1929

F-148   Oliver P. Hurd House

> 527 East Parkway South
> Mahan and Broadwell, architects, 1922–24

A big house, covered with sculpture, that strangely combines some of Mahan's favorite Mediterranean devices with the dark-red brick he usually used for his Anglophilic classical houses.

F-154

F-149   Harry A. Darnell Duplex

557 South Parkway East
Mahan and Broadwell, architects, 1921–23

A stripped, but nonetheless handsome, Spanish building built for invest-
ment purposes.

F-150   John M. Maury House

567 East Parkway South
Jones and Furbringer, architects, 1915

Although this house has no particular style, it hangs together in a far more
coherent fashion than the McClure House (F-145), by the same architects,
a few blocks to the north.

F-151   Horace H. Twiford House

550 East Parkway South
George Mahan. Jr., architect, 1927–28
Everett D. Woods, associate architect

F-152   John Sneed Williams, Jr., House

542 East Parkway South
1930

The best English cottage in town, and maybe one of the best this side of
England. The Williamses got the plans from a magazine, complete with
the wavy pattern of the roof shingles, the curving timbers inserted in the

brick walls, and the fake dovecote on the west gable. The small entrance porch is turned on a jaunty diagonal from the square tower that marks the meeting of the two main blocks. The little ogee arch over the entrance adds just the right wiggle at the right moment. The plantings are now so mature that it is hard to see the house, except in fragments.

F-153   Michael J. McCormack House
196 East Parkway South
1926

A Spanish fantasy, set on a terrace, with the entrance marked by a tower.

F-154   Memphis Theological Seminary
(formerly Joseph Newburger House)
168 East Parkway South
Hanker and Cairns, architects, 1912–13
D.T. McGown, architect for addition, 1982

Bayard Cairns put much of what he learned at the École des Beaux Arts into this house. Newburger was a cotton factor with offices all over the world and, in architecture, cosmopolitan taste to match. Particularly wonderful are the interiors on the ground floor, with elegant plasterwork on the walls and ceilings. Visitors once entered the house from a fountain-bedecked terrace, passed through an entrance hall big enough to be a narthex, and then emerged into a central hall with Ionic columns that hold up a pierced ceiling that allows a tantalizing glimpse of Doric columns on the floor above. This may be the best entrance hall in town. If Cairns had been a truly careful classicist, he would have put the Ionic upstairs, and the Doric down. But clearly he and Newburger wanted the fancier order for company, and the plainer for the family quarters.

The second-floor ballroom has been converted into a chapel. The Memphis Theological Seminary deserves kudos for taking good care of this house and for putting on a modern addition that is sympathetic to the house in form and clever enough to disguise a four-story, 70,000-volume library.

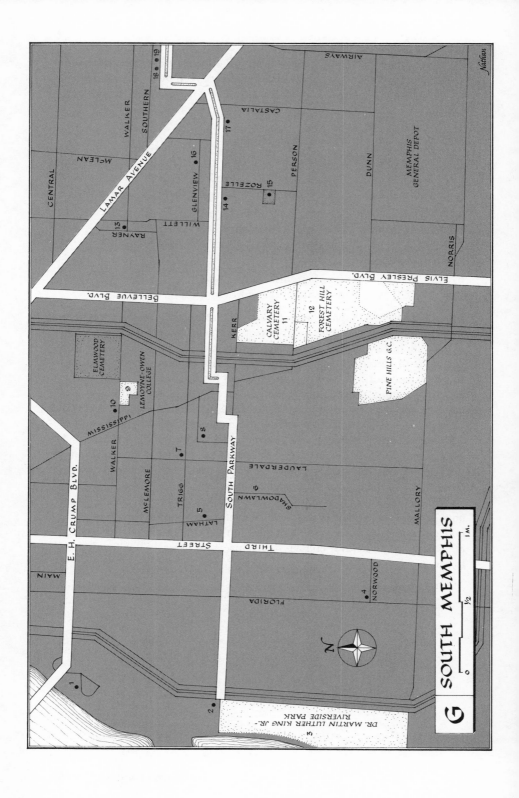

G SOUTH MEMPHIS

G South Memphis

South Memphis, the part of town south of Crump Boulevard and Lamar Avenue, is large and often architecturally pedestrian. There are, however, areas and individual buildings of the highest quality. The turn of the century working-class neighborhoods south of Crump and east of South Third Street are remarkably intact, having been spared the worst of the urban devastation that wiped out so much of Memphis south and east of the downtown. The vistas of columned porches on the fronts of rows of cottages are largely unchanged from when the area was newly built a hundred or so years ago.

G-1   United States Marine Hospital
360 West California Avenue

This complex of buildings contains two Italianate structures from 1884, the Laundry-Kitchen and the Executive Building. The exterior of the former is still largely in its original condition, while the latter had its original two-story wooden porch replaced in 1937 by the present classicizing appendage, which attempted to harmonize the nineteenth-century structure with the 1930s classical buildings nearby.

The largest brick structure consists of two parts. The straight north wing, by Regan and Weller, 1933, was put considerably in the shade by the Y-shaped south wing of 1936, for which Louis A. Simon was architect. The centerpiece of the south facade of the south wing features a Doric portico rising over brick piers connected by segmental arches. Over it floats a Doric tempietto. To the west of the main building, in the former nurses' quarters, one finds the National Ornamental Metal Museum, which has changing shows that frequently feature metal objects of architectural interest. North of the museum is a blacksmith's shop, with splendid nineteenth-century cast-iron window frames from a Texas courthouse applied to its facade. From the grounds of the hospital, one has a magnificent view of the river—some claim this is the best view of the river in town. Across the street, in De Soto Park, is a large mound erected by the native population of the Mississippi Valley long before Hernando de Soto set eyes on the river. How this mound fitted into the context of the Native American village that once stood on this site is made clear by the reconstruction of a similar village south of the city at Chucalissa (K-1).

G-2

G-2   Ford Motor Company Assembly Plant

1429 Riverside Drive
1924

One of an architect's main problems in dealing with a big, no-nonsense building is that what is simple and effective on a small building is usually boring when enlarged to giant size and repeated endlessly. This is a big building, with nearly a quarter of a million square feet inside, but the architect has managed to obviate most of the potential boredom of the design with some fancy ornamental footwork.

The building is essentially a sprawling, one-story industrial structure, with the roof jumping up in a sawtooth pattern to contain a series of light monitors. This being a factory (and one belonging to that eminently practical man, Henry Ford), the concern was first of all practical, and there wasn't much that could be done with the spatial arrangement. That left the architect the facade and the decoration to play around with. He marked the piers of the facade by facing them in brick. These carry a symbolic frieze of sandstone, which jumps up a little as it runs over each pier. He then stuck fancy "capitals" over the brick piers, with a chevron pattern of bricks set in stucco. In between these vertically-oriented areas are stretches of brick in a basket-weave pattern.

Faced with an immensely long south flank (it's eight hundred feet), he broke up the flat plane of its facade by pushing every seventh bay forward. This injected a little variety, and it also marked the doorways into the factory. The front facade, treated in a similar manner, has been wrecked by the addition of a cheap metal soffit.

G-3   Dr. Martin Luther King, Jr., Riverside Park

George Kessler, Kansas City, landscape architect, 1901

Kessler designed the two finest parks in the city, Riverside and Overton. They were planned as a piece and connected by the Parkways. The point of Riverside was to provide a place in which the natural terrain would be preserved and from which views of the river could be enjoyed by Memphians taking their leisure. The roads meander through the park in a delightful way, taking full advantage of the relatively hilly lay of the land. The river view, however, has been changed by filling in the channel between the mainland and President's Island, to create an industrial park served by the still waters of what was once the flowing river, but is now McKellar Lake.

G-4   Dr. Charles R. Mason House

10 East Norwood Avenue
Mahan and Broadwell, architects, 1921

In their pursuit of variations on the bungalow, Mahan and Broadwell left almost no style unturned. In this, one of their very finest designs, they created what one might call the hacienda bungalow. The flat roofs and white stucco walls are Spanish, but the big porch and porte-cochere, as well as the relaxed planning, are pure bungalow. The strong cubic massing of this relatively modest house is particularly impressive.

G-4

G-5   A.B. Hill School

1372 Latham Street
Jones and Furbringer, architects, 1909

Jones and Furbringer had their wild moments; a few of them can be seen here. The entrance pavilion, which rises through all three stories of the school, is grand and lets you know that you are about to go into someplace that is someplace. The stone ground floor is Doric, and it is done right. The next story boasts a window with a pair of fluted pilasters in what Philibert Delorme called the "French Order" when he invented it in the sixteenth century. The third story has weird volutes, and a big semicircular pediment with huge voussoirs and rosettes that look more like lion snouts than flowers, all sticking up over the facade. The corner pavilions are plainer, but even these have slightly wacky modillions above the cornice, with volutes outside and crosses inside.

G-6   Shadowlawn Subdivision

Shadowlawn Street, south of South Parkway
William Chandler, developer, c. 1920

A particularly characteristic street of bungalows, by one of the developers who did most to make Memphis a major bungalow city. The masonry posts at the entrance to the subdivision off South Parkway are there to make you take notice.

G-7   Fellowship Baptist Church

(formerly St. Thomas Catholic Church)
580 East Trigg Avenue
Regan and Weller, architects, 1925

G-8

G-7   St. Thomas Catholic School
580 East Trigg Avenue
Regan and Weller, architects, 1938

The church, in a North Italian Romanesque mode, has a particularly fine
tower that marks the corner of Trigg and Lauderdale, while the school
boasts a very large-scale diaper pattern in the masonry of its facade.

G-8   Lincoln Junior High School
(formerly South Side High School)
667 Richmond Avenue
Pfeil and Awsumb, architects, 1922

The rather severe facade of this school is relieved by a pair of charming
sculptural details: statues of two children, one reading and one musing
over a book.

G-9   Lemoyne-Owen College
807 Walker Avenue

Small urban colleges in America have it tough. They exist in cities, but
the very word "campus" (Latin for "field") implies a sort of rural expansion. It is no accident that the first college really to have a campus, and to
call it that, was Princeton, which in the middle of the eighteenth century
was truly out in the sticks. Lemoyne-Owen manages to put a lot of buildings on a restricted site and still retain the feel of a "campus." The key
elements here were the choice of a Colonial style for the main building,
Brownlee Hall, and the realization that the quadrangular scheme of collegiate design, which came to America with the Collegiate Gothic style in

G-9. Hollis Price Library of Lemoyne-Owen College.

the late nineteenth century, was not a part of Colonial classical campus planning. Thus Lemoyne-Owen has retained the big campus green between Brownlee and the street it faces.

Brownlee Hall (George Awsumb, architect, 1933–36) is a very fine Colonial collegiate hall, probably Awsumb's finest classical design. Its brick mass is set off by a plain Doric portico with four columns topped by a pediment with a bull's-eye window and some graceful swags. The body of the building is marked only by flat brick arches over the windows, with their stone keystones, and by brick quoins at the corners. The remarkable effect of elegance and grace that this building projects is less the result of ornament, then, than of proportion and a harmonious relation of parts.

The inside of the building continues the forthrightness of the exterior. There is a single transverse hall, intersected at the midpoint by the entrance hall and the main doorway. The proportions of the hall are generous but not ostentatious, the detailing is good, and the only false step is the introduction of out-of-place perforated acoustical tile for the ceilings.

Lemoyne-Owen College has not attempted to continue the Colonial style of Brownlee Hall in its other buildings. The firm of Gassner, Nathan and Browne, which is responsible for most of the other important buildings on campus, has designed them in a straightforward modern style. The Hollis Price Library (1963), the best of these new buildings, is essentially a floating cube of masonry and glass set in a concrete frame. The generous use of strip windows placed high up in the walls gives a feeling, from the inside, of being in a walled garden. The imagery here is of the Groves of Academe. The central core of the cube is open through both stories. This allows light to enter the center of the building from the top and provides a suitably impressive place for a big mosaic by Ben Shahn as well. This is one of the few pieces of large-scale public art anywhere in the city, and the only one by an artist with as widespread a reputation as Shahn. The text in the Shahn mosaic is Psalm 133, a celebration of brotherhood. Shahn was active in the civil rights movement, and he used this text in several works associated with that cause. The reclining figure, holding a symbol of the atom against a starry sky, is said to represent Shahn's hope for unification of the sciences and the humanities. A library, of course, is not a bad place to begin such an effort.

G-10   Second Congregational Church

764 Walker Avenue
1926–28

The Second Congregational Church, founded in 1868, is one of the oldest black congregations in Memphis. Its first church, at 239 Orleans Street, was abandoned when the present was designed and built by a group of "black artisans," whose names might well be uncovered by a search of the church's records.

Memphis has many substantial, rather plain, red-brick churches built by blacks to serve the numerous black congregations. Some have pointed-arch detailing, while others, such as Second Congregational, make use of round arches. What is most striking about these churches is their sense of solidity and permanence, which is often in striking contrast to the relatively impermanent appearance of the wooden shotguns and cottages in which the members of the congregation lived. Second Congregational is a particularly well-proportioned and satisfying example of these local vernacular churches.

G-11   Calvary Cemetery

1663 Elvis Presley Boulevard
Founded 1867

Calvary Cemetery holds the funeral monuments of the great Catholic families of the city. The layout of the oldest part, with drives arranged concentrically around major landscape features, is handsome.

Of the monuments, the most impressive is that of Eugene Magevney (d. 1873), Memphis schoolteacher and real-estate entrepreneur. On the right shoulder of the Risen Christ, who holds the cross in His left hand, leans a weeping angel. Diagonally opposite the angel is Saint Mary Magdalen. A second angel carries a communion goblet, a third the superscription and nails, while a fourth kneels at Christ's feet and holds the crown of thorns and the cross. The whole emphasizes the elements of Christ's Passion, the means through which He suffered and died to achieve

G-11

salvation for Christian believers. The presence of the discreetly placed Mary Magdalen (she was, after all, a prostitute) signals the redemption offered penitent sinners. Teaching school didn't provide Magevney the means for such a monument.

G-12 Forest Hill Cemetery

1661 Elvis Presley Boulevard
Founded 1892

It's not the oldest cemetery in the city, nor is it the biggest, but Forest Hill has some of the finest monuments. Remarkably, it seems to have been the first cemetery in the country designed *not* to have monuments. Small markers were to suffice for everyone. That intention lasted almost no time at all. In addition to the monuments, Forest Hill also has three very good buildings.

Entering the cemetery and taking the left fork, you pass, off to the left, a marble replica of Bernini's David, which looks a lot better from far away than from close up. To the right, at the top of the highest hill in the cemetery and now almost completely hidden by funereal-looking trees, is a Romanesque Revival chapel that once was used as a receiving vault. One of the original buildings, this little architectural fantasy has more than its

G-12a

share of powerful forms, particularly its columns and corner buttresses. A big barrel vault roofs the interior, and a round porch projects to the west, outside a triple window. The chapel has gone to seed, but it has more of the romantic aura of a cemetery for having been allowed to do so.

Going farther west, towards the expressway, there is the Fly column, a fine example of understated opulence. A big, florid Corinthian column rises over a pedestal with the name FLY on it. There is nothing on top, and there doesn't need to be.

Following the road around to the south, you will find the Van Vleet mausoleum on the left. This lowering mass of stone has a vaguely Egyptian feel to it, although no single motif used is actually Egyptian. The roof is a pile of stone slabs, held up in front by two massive, squat piers that define the porch. The piers are decorated with garlands and palm fronds, and out in front there are two bronze lamps with bronze flames.

Going down the hill to the right, you can see the office next to the original main gate, off Hernando Road. Like almost everything else in Memphis, Forest Hill used to face toward the river, but now it has turned around to look east. The office, also from 1890, is in a Romanesque style similar to that of the chapel on the hill. But it is even closer in style to R.B. Snowden's Ashlar Hall on Central Avenue (F-23), of 1896, and it would be tempting to see this as the first hometown undertaking of the young Princeton grad fresh from his architectural training. The exaggerated, blocky crenellations look a lot like those at Ashlar Hall, and the crazy, pointed horseshoe arch window in the second story looks like the work of someone who had not quite got his styles under control.

G-12b

Heading farther south, you come to a memorable bronze elk at a fork in the road. This is a World War I memorial, erected by the Benevolent and Paternal Order of Elks. The bronze clock in the base eternally marks the eleventh hour.

Still going south, and at the next fork in the road, is the William R. Moore Memorial (G-12a). This, one of the most elaborate of the Forest Hill markers, is a three-part affair: a rusticated, truncated obelisk topped by Mr. Moore; a low, bulging, rusticated sarcophagus surmounted by his wife, Charlotte Blood Moore; and a short, pink granite wall surrounding the other two. Memphis funereal sculpture tends towards stone rather than bronze, but the Moore memorial is an outstanding exception. Mrs. Moore is shown, *en deshabille*, as the Christian Soul, eyes heavenward, a cross clasped to her breast. You have to look twice to see that her billowy dress is decidedly classical in flavor. In stark contrast to his wife, Mr. Moore is turned out in very earthly fashion, with a long coat and a heavy mustache that makes him look not a little like Mark Twain. Their different positions and pedestals—he atop a tall obelisk and she on a low, rounded container—and their differences in dress provide (unwittingly?) a remarkable comment on male-female relations around 1900.

His figure is signed by S.A. Sbjornsen. On the obelisk below Mr. Moore is his parting shot: "He Did the Best He Could." He certainly did here. This monument makes up for the dullness of his big building downtown, which still stands at the corner of Third and Monroe.

Following the right fork of the road even farther south, almost to the bottom of the cemetery, you see on the left the memorial to J.R. Brinkley, M.D., a severely elegant green-marble column shaft, left unpolished and topped with a green-marble ball instead of a capital. Balanced precariously

G-12c

on the ball is a winged Victory, looking something like the Nike of Paionios. As she flutters down, she holds out the laurel wreath of victory, here surely a Christian victory over death.

Making the perfect backdrop to the classicized Christian Soul of Charlotte Blood Moore and the classically victorious Dr. Brinkley is one of the best classical revival buildings in the city. The Abby Mausoleum (G-12b) was built in 1914, possibly on a design by Charles O. Pfeil, who had done a design for the mausoleum in an Italian Renaissance style in 1913. Although that was rejected, he may have kept the commission. If the existing mausoleum is by Pfeil, it is one of his very finest buildings. It has the icy perfection of the best nineteenth-century German Neoclassicism, and it approaches the maddeningly simple classical definition of architectural perfection, as spelled out by Leon Battista Alberti in the fifteenth century: "A building, to which nothing can be added, and from which nothing can be taken away, without lessening the whole."

The two long, low wings of the mausoleum are joined in the center by a four column Doric portico with wreaths in the entablature and bronze fire pans standing above each column. The wings are kept from running out to boredom by a tight but subtle framework of extremely shallow Doric pilasters and entablature. The whole echoes the central portico, with wreaths in the entablature above each pilaster, but it is so delicate that it looks almost sketched in. Above this, on the edges of the roof, are antefixes and lion heads, which provide the only decorative effect on what is otherwise a very severe building.

Inside, the building is just as you would imagine it from the outside: all grey marble, shadowy and still. Even in a Memphis summer, the building seems to hold the chill of death. The final, indisputable proof of the power of this building, and of its perfection as a mausoleum, is that it terrifies children.

The Abby Mausoleum was the penultimate resting place of Elvis Presley. Since his body was moved to Graceland, quiet has largely been restored, but visitors still hang notes on the iron grate of the chamber in which he once rested. We found one from a Parisienne that read, *"Mon cher Elvis. Je t'aimerai toujours."*

On the way back out of the cemetery is the monument to J.T. and Mary Mallory Harahan (G-12c). Harahan is the man for whom the Harahan Bridge was named; it is ironic that he died in a railway crash in 1912. Mrs. Harahan died in a similarly romantic fashion: on board a steamer in Hong Kong harbor while on a world cruise. The monument is in a classical style that is almost as severe as that of the Mausoleum. The double sarcophagus is protected by a canopy of a single huge block of granite, held up by columns of the Ionic order, with capitals resting on plain granite shafts. The entablature and the short attic are both plain stone, so that the carved decorations on the sarcophagus itself stand out all the more. The garlands and ribbons and—nice classical touch—inverted torches contrast handsomely with the bare stone of the architecture.

G-13   Eli Rayner House

1020 Rayner Street
1856

Of the plantation houses that ringed Memphis in the mid-nineteenth century, the Rayner House is an elegant example in the super-slender proportions of its four-columned portico.

G-13

G-14 Ben J. Edwards House

> 1657 South Parkway East
> 1924

This is Memphis' only Lincoln Log bungalow. Such a rustic house may be a little out of place on an elegant boulevard like the Parkway, but the rural enthusiasm carries it all off. The standard masonry construction of the Memphis bungalow is here replaced by log-cabin construction. The two piers that hold the protruding roof up are battered like their masonry counterparts, but they look as if they were built by some giant's child industriously playing with his toys. Even the chimney on the eastern face of the house is given the Lincoln Log treatment up to the top of the gable. The final touch of rusticity occurs in the eaves brackets, which are just branches, *au naturel*.

G-15 Sam Abraham Chapel

> Baron Hirsch Cemetery
> 1536 South Rozelle Street
> George Awsumb, architect, 1941

This building would be impressive as a church, let alone as a funerary chapel. Built of local fieldstone, it is a remarkably convincing replica of a twelfth-century Lombard Romanesque church. The plain facade, of rough stone carefully laid and topped by an arched corbel table following the rise

G-15

G-18

of the gable, is all just right. The small porch which protrudes to shelter the door is barrel vaulted beneath a little gable. The columns on the capitals, not particularly Lombard in form, inject the only false note. But this is just a quibble, because the overall effect is so good. The tympanum over the door, with its sunburst behind the Tablets of the Law, and the rose window in the middle of the facade, with the Star of David, are the only clues that this is not a real medieval church.

G-16   Bungalow
    1780 Glenview Avenue

A place of literary rather than architectural pilgrimage. In the garden of this bungalow turned sideways to the street, Tennessee Williams saw the very first performance of a play he had written. The bungalows across the street, at 1791 and 1795 Glenview, used stone left over from the construction of the Cossitt Library downtown (A-63 [Lost Memphis]).

G-17   Robert Fagin House
    1979 South Parkway East
    Jones and Furbringer, architects, 1917–18

This elegant Beaux-Arts stone house is as urbane as 1657 South Parkway is rural. The smooth plane of the facade is broken only by the protruding porte-cochere and entrance porch. Both of these are supported by corner piers, against which snuggle Ionic columns. The front porch comes out of a slightly protruding frontispiece with a triple window above the porch. There is a slight classical *faux pas* here, in that Doric columns are used above Ionic, rather than the orthodox other way round. Finally, there is the signature Jones and Furbringer off-center dormer, sticking up to the left of the porch.

The stateliness of the house is compromised by the zero-lot-line townhouse development growing like poison ivy in its back and side yards.

G-18   H.N. Smith House

2170 South Parkway East
1916

After navigating what is probably the most confusing change of streets in the city, where South Parkway East turns north and becomes East Parkway South and then turns east and goes back to being South Parkway East (all in a few hundred yards), you come to a razzle-dazzle Arts and Crafts house. On such a large house, you might expect a projecting porch. Instead, the entrance is recessed, visually set between the battered brick piers of the porte-cochere on the left and the sunporch on the right. The most overwhelming feature of this house is the roof, which comes down off its center peak in one great swoop. The roof is so strong that it even engulfs the porte-cochere, and all the minor gables on the front of the house can do nothing but echo it. The architect, whose name unfortunately is unknown, knew that under a roof like this a plain wall would suffer irreparable eclipse, and so he salvaged a potentially weak part of the design by adding a two-story polygonal bay to the east, where it gives variety to the exterior and light to the inside.

G-19   Estes W. Mann House

2190 South Parkway East
Estes Mann, architect, 1926

Two doors east of the Arts and Crafts saltbox is an *elegantissima* Italianate house designed by Estes Mann for himself. This house does exactly what a city house should do: it turns its best face to the world. From the street the house looks wide but very shallow. The living room, in the left wing, opens up through a pair of French doors with urns in their fanlights. To the right, nestled in the angle between the living room and the projecting dining room, is a fine stone doorway with a parade of griffons in the lintel. The triple window of the dining room is marked by four spiral barber-pole columns, each surmounted by a graceful urn in silhouette.

The view from the east, however, is very different. This part of the house was not meant to be seen so readily. Here the fancy decoration dis-

G-19

appears, to be replaced by a much plainer mass. It turns out that there is really a lot more house here than is apparent from the street, but that is the whole point. As with people, houses are sometimes not exactly what they seem at first.

Mann was an extraordinarily prolific architect. He once told a reporter that in 1925 he had designed 350 houses, which meant (jokingly) that he had only two days off during the year! Mann's client-filled 1925 doubtless paid for this house of 1926. Such a volume of commissions often had an adverse effect on the quality of Mann's designs, but in this one he showed what he could do when he took his time.

H   Northeast Memphis

Northeast Memphis is a large area of mixed residential, commercial, and industrial use, bordered on the north by the Wolf River, which, together with its flanking bottomlands, forms a natural barrier to the expansion of the city northward. The major streets of the area are Chelsea, which is highly industrialized; Jackson, where industry stands side-by-side with commerce and housing; and Summer, an almost unbroken commercial strip of the Anywhereville, USA, variety.

H-1   Memphis Area Transit Authority

Bus Storage, Service and Maintenance Facility
1370 Levee Road
Walk Jones and Francis Mah, architects, 1981
Michael F. Finefield, principal designer

Here the typical Jones and Mah rectilinear system is replaced by a softer treatment of forms. Each building, no matter how wide, has a similar section. An east-facing pylon gives way to a double roof with a nine-inch air space inside that slopes away to the west. All of this has a solar point. In the summer months, the hot air that builds up under the roof is exhausted through the hood of the pylon. In the winter, the same warm air is trapped and forced down into the building to heat it. The administration building has four splendidly bug-eyed portholes in its east front, while the bus maintenance building can handle forty-one of the monsters at a time.

H-1

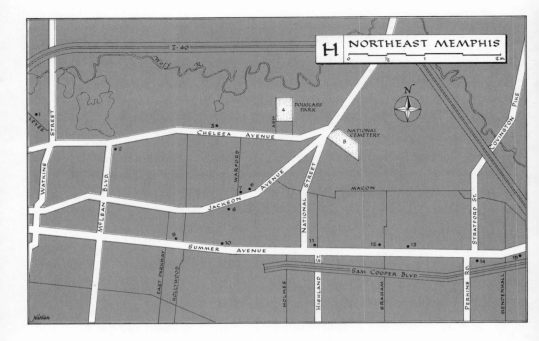

H-2   Buckman Laboratories

1256 North McLean Boulevard
Walk Jones and Francis Mah, architects, 1969–71

A building with a planned future, the Buckman Laboratories are laid out
with a circulation spine—the two-story glass block anchored by the two
concrete stair towers—from which spaces are to grow as needed. The
spaces off the spine are enclosed in aluminum-and-glass curtain walls,
designed just for this building, that can be demounted and remounted at
will. Despite the fact that the labs can change appearance with some ease,
they have been inserted sensitively in earth berms in such a way that they
look permanent, and that sense of permanence is enhanced by the concrete
podia from which the curtain walls rise. The crisp, clean lines of this complex are one of its strongest points.

H-3   Buckeye Cotton Oil Plant

Chelsea Avenue at Fairfax Street
1931 and later

This plant is the city's pre-eminent industrial complex, at least from a
visual point of view. Toward Chelsea, two enormous rectangular sheds,

H-2

H-3

clad in metal, rise parallel to the street. They are topped by precipitously steep hipped roofs capped dramatically by monitors that run the whole length of the ridge. Behind the shed is a row of seven gigantic metal cylinders, topped with cones and connected by steel truss systems. The best view of this group, where they appear all lined up in a staggering row, is from Fairfax. North of the cylinders are still more sheds of different sizes.

H-4   Douglass Park

Holmes Road, north of Chelsea Avenue
1913

Douglass Park was the first public park built in Memphis for the use of the black population. It was not put exactly in the center of things. Rather, it was shoved up against the Wolf River bottoms on the north edge of town. The park contains pleasantly rolling grounds and open woods, into which a public golf course has been woven.

H-5   Memphis National Cemetery

(originally Mississippi River National Cemetery)
Townes Avenue, just south of Jackson Avenue
1867

The cemetery was founded to take care of the Union soldiers who had died in battles along the Mississippi River. Of those Union soldiers buried here, 8,866 are unknown. Also buried here are the victims of the explosion of the steamer Sultana on 27 April 1865. The overburdened ship was carrying a huge load of soldiers recently released from Confederate prison camps. Just upstream from Memphis, its boiler exploded, and over 1,700 men died.

Worth seeking out is the State of Illinois monument, by Leon Hermant of Chicago, 1928. A bronze soldier, wrapped in a fringed flag, lies in state on top of a pink and black granite sarcophagus. The horizontality of the monument keeps it from having a false sense of rhetoric and makes it fit the flat landscape of the cemetery.

H-6   Schering-Plough Administrative and Research Center

3030 Jackson Avenue
Gassner, Nathan and Browne, architects, 1970

A cool six-story rectangle of concrete and glass. In 1983–84 the successor firm, Gassner, Nathan and Partners, placed the Scholl Corporation Headquarters inside a warehouse located on the same property. The remodeling job produced a particularly airy high-tech office suite.

H-7   Ford Motor Company Sales and Parts Distribution Center

2970 Jackson Avenue
1951

Although the yellow-brick front is not the happiest face ever put on an industrial building, the sides are a handsome adaptation of a system used often in the 1930s by Albert Kahn, of a brick curtain wall below and a steel-and-glass curtain above. These walls enclose a prodigiously large warehouse, covered by great steel trusses. This was the kind of American industrial architecture that Mies van der Rohe got excited about when he arrived on these shores in the late 1930s. This American industrial style continued to be popular after World War II.

H-8   Buckeye Cellulose Plant

2899 Jackson Avenue
1931 and later

The great metal cylinders, capped with cones, that we saw on Chelsea here make a return appearance, right alongside the Jackson Avenue viaduct that rises over the railroad serving the plant.

H-9   Paris Adult Entertainment Center

(formerly Luciann Theater)
2432 Summer Avenue
1941

The Luciann is one of the slightly retarded Art Deco theaters built in suburban sections of Memphis in the 1940s, both prewar and postwar. It may be the best of the lot. The quilted effect of the center of the facade is quite unexpected, and the two sunbursts to the sides of the centerpiece give the whole a certain theatrical bravura.

H-10   (Lost Memphis) Alamo Plaza Motel

(originally Alamo Plaza Tourist Courts)
2862 Summer Avenue
1939

The seventh in a chain of motels that originated in 1929 and spread across the southwest, the Alamo Plaza beckoned weary travelers, journeying on the three U.S. highways that make use of Summer, to seek rest and safety behind its double-arched Spanish Colonial frontispiece. (Never mind that

H-10

the original Alamo eventually fell to its attackers.) The false fronts antici-
pated Robert Venturi's notion of the decorated shed by three decades or so.
Here nostalgia coupled with comfort. Each unit boasted a tile bath, a
kitchenette, and innerspring mattresses. The arches shelter no more. This
important monument of American roadside architecture (it had a great
influence on Kemmons Wilson, founder of the Holiday Inns) fell in the
strip wars during the Christmas season of 1988.

H-11   Highland Heights United Methodist Church

3476 Summer Avenue
Mahan and Broadwell, architects, 1922

A brick and stone Gothic structure that does not show Mahan and
Broadwell at their best. Gothic was not their style.

H-12   Grahamwood Elementary School

3950 Summer Avenue
Estes Mann, architect, 1949
William Mann, associate architect

William Mann, Estes Mann's nephew, apparently did the lion's share of
the design work on this building, which attempted to put modern architecture to work in a suburban area that had had little previous experience of
the style. The original part of the school is the section to the east, and the
major elements of that building were repeated when an addition was put
on by another firm.

H-13   Memphis Consumer Credit Association, Inc.

4066 Summer Avenue
Roy P. Harrover and Associates, architects, 1987

The dreary strip-scape of Summer is seldom broken by buildings of quality. When something competent comes along, like the great sweeping
curve of the glass-block window in this facade, one feels inclined to celebrate it.

H-14   Grimes Memorial Methodist Church

4649 Summer Avenue
Nowland Van Powell, architect, 1960

Powell was a master of the cheap Colonial church. He could stretch a
modest budget into more architecture than that budget would seem ca-
pable of sustaining. Here the flat-roofed, yellow-brick mass of the
church—a seemingly unpromising beginning—gains authority from the

H-14

application of a skillfully-proportioned Tuscan portico, whose slender
columns rising from tall pedestals give everything around them grace.
Behind the columns Powell grouped his second set of strong architectural
forces: two square-headed windows, two round windows, and a central
door with a heavy curved pediment, all located at the back of a porch that
is inset to give breathing space before you enter. The flanks, in contrast,
are cost-conscious basic, relieved only by small round windows and panels
inset in the brickwork above the rectangular windows of the nave.

H-15   Royal Oaks Motel

> (formerly Holiday Inn Hotel Courts)
> 4941 Summer Avenue
> Eddie Bluestein, designer, 1952

Here is one of the most historic buildings in town, now a bit run down:
the first Holiday Inn that the local real-estate developer, Kemmons
Wilson, ever built. From this prototype the whole great international chain
of motels and hotels grew. There are two parts, an office and restaurant
building and the separate buildings that house the guest rooms. The former sported an enormous porcelain enamel sign that greeted travelers
entering Memphis from the east. That sign now lies under the one that
says "Szechuan Restaurant," and the original wide plate-glass windows of
the restaurant still peer out at us from under the later *chinoiserie*. To the
west of the little vertical glass tower, a fake mansard roof—a later form of
roadside architecture—and white paint cover the original yellow and green
enamel and buff-colored Roman brick.

   The simple shed buildings that house the travelers were designed to be
easy and cheap to build, so that any carpenter or developer, anywhere,
could duplicate them without a hitch. They were also meant to look like

H-15. Present and Past

home, or at least like the kinds of little ranch houses Wilson was building by the dozens in Memphis. The walls were brick, the roofs were low, the windows were flanked by shutters, and the porches were supported by thin vertical piers of fairly frilly wrought iron. For a middle-class traveler, this could be, visually, a home away from home. Wilson's idea caught on, and in a hurry.

The present motel sign is a weak substitute for the sock-'em-over-the-head original, which became the trademark of the chain. In the original Holiday Inn, the signs dominated the architectural forms, in contrast to the earlier Alamo Plaza, down the street, where the architecture itself was both sign and building. Wilson, however, has said that he learned a lot from the Alamo Plaza—that, indeed, it was an inspiration to him.

I   East Memphis

East Memphis began to be developed as a residential area of the city in the early 1920s, when population pressures created a need for new residential neighborhoods to supplement the Central Gardens and Evergreen neighborhoods, which were beginning to fill up. The older neighborhoods had been close enough to downtown to commute to work by trolley, but the development of East Memphis depended on the newly plentiful automobile to span the increased distance from home to office. Public transportation was provided, but to bring servants to work in the houses, not the owners to work downtown. By the late twenties, the bungalow had passed its heyday of popularity, and you find very few of them in this area.

The first major developments took place north and south of Central Avenue, which loses its character as a grand residential street when its passes east of Cooper but regains it once it has ducked under the railroad tracks in a great curve east of Flicker Street. Goodwyn Street, located on the western edge of the Memphis Country Club (which had been truly in the country when it was laid out in the teens), became a street of large houses. The largest house in Memphis, the Pink Palace, sprang up across Central from the country club golf course in the early twenties. Its builder, Clarence Saunders, intended to construct his own private golf course right across the street from that of the country club, but financial problems turned Saunders' greens into a pricey new subdivision, Chickasaw Gardens. Other subdivisions, Red Acres and Hedgemoor, also were laid out in the pre–World War II years. After the war, wholesale development for both upper and middle classes followed. Into this area came, right after the war, the Poplar Plaza Shopping Center, the first major commercial development outside the downtown area. Poplar Plaza signaled the beginning of the end for the downtown as the principal shopping district.

The area north of Poplar and east of Highland is a largely residential district that has grown up since the late twenties and early thirties. Walnut Grove Road, once barely two lanes wide, forms the central spine—and some may think the central race track—for the locals. Between Goodlett and Perkins, Walnut Grove Road boasts a collection of eclectic houses of the late twenties and thirties unrivaled in any other part of the city. In more recent times, Walnut Grove also has come to be the street on which a number of churches have chosen to build, but otherwise the street has not varied at all from its residential zoning. As such, it is one of the few main thoroughfares not to go commercial in a city whose real-estate interests are always mindful of potential commercial values.

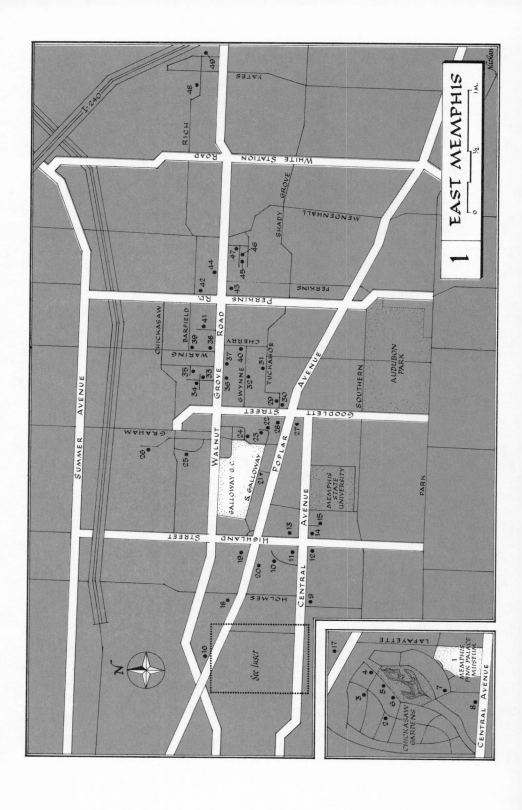

1 EAST MEMPHIS

I-1

I-1   Memphis Pink Palace Museum

(formerly Clarence Saunders House)
3050 Central Avenue
Hubert T. McGee, architect, 1922
Thorn, Howe, Stratton and Strong, architects for addition,
1976–77

Clarence Saunders, the founder of the modern supermarket through his
chain of Piggly Wiggly stores, began this extraordinarily ambitious building in 1922, the same year in which he eventually lost his fortune in a
Wall Street battle. Piggly Wiggly grew from a single store in 1916 to a
chain of 1,200 stores in 1922. Those figures alone should give a picture of
Saunders' ambition and energy. The house, designed to fit both, included
not only the usual rooms, but also a ballroom, a swimming pool, a bowling
alley, and a shooting gallery. All of this was wrapped in a package of pink
Georgia marble that Hubert McGee, the architect, described as a "Romanesque American Rambling Design," probably as good a description of the
house's style, or lack thereof, as you will find. The center of the building is
occupied by a great two-story hall that sports a variety of Italian Renaissance details, but most of the rest of the interior was never finished. When
Saunders lost it all on Wall Street, the house and its adjoining 160 acres,
on which Saunders had built a lake and on which he planned to lay out a
golf course, were sold to developers. They in turn donated the house and
about 10 acres to the city, which opened a museum there in 1930.

In the 1970s, the museum expanded into its new wing, an echo of I.M.
Pei's addition to the National Gallery in Washington—at least in its angu-
larity. The gallery spaces, without windows, form an exterior wall that
relates to the old house only in terms of the color of the masonry. The
addition's original Great Wall of China character has been softened considerably by lavish plantings that now have had time to grow up to cover it.

You enter this wall on the east face and, through a huge glass window, have a view, immediately, of a surprising forest outside. You feel that you have stepped back in time, from suburban Memphis of the twentieth century to the primeval forests that once covered this land. The forest is part of an exhibit of native vegetation arranged around a model of an ox-bow lake. The museum, which devotes itself to science and to the history of the Mid-South region, has on permanent display a number of items that will interest architecture buffs, such as James Dakin's original watercolor elevation of the first Gayoso House, a reconstruction of Saunders' first Piggly-Wiggly store that stood at 79 Jefferson, and a collection of nineteenth-century carpenters' tools.

CHICKASAW GARDENS
Harland Bartholomew and Associates, planners, 1926–27

The subdivision of the Saunders estate was laid out as a rambling English romantic garden, perhaps taking as a point of inspiration Frederick Law Olmsted's plan for Riverside, Illinois. The center of the area is occupied by a lake, whose shape creates wave-like reverberations in the paths of the surrounding streets. The streets mostly bear Native American names, but some strangers, such as Lombardy, creep in.

I-2   Second Clyde Van Fossen House

2925 Natchez Lane
George Mahan, Jr., architect, 1928–31
Everett D. Woods, associate architect

Here Mahan, joined by the talented young Everett Woods, turned from a more clearly Spanish kind of Mediterranean house to one that was Italian, particularly in the stone door, which looks as if it could have been taken off an Italian palace of the late sixteenth century, and in the two blind windows that flank the large round-arched window in the center of the facade. That window lights a sunken living room with a beamed ceiling and a stone fireplace that is more medieval than Renaissance. East of the living room is a groin-vaulted sunporch, which opens in the back onto a handsomely balustraded terrace, pleasantly irregular in plan.

I-3   Dr. D. Harbert Anthony House

2968 Iroquois Road
George Mahan, Jr., architect, 1929–30
Everett D. Woods, associate architect

A half-timbered Tudor of stucco and wood that seems to have gotten hold of a bit of the stone from the newly built Southwestern (now Rhodes) College campus.

I-4 Mrs. Alex Scott House

3020 Iroquois Road
Lucian Minor Dent, architect, 1940

Dent here did a careful replica of the Josiah Gorgas House in Tuscaloosa, Alabama, designed by William Nichols in 1829. In the 1930s and 1940s, under the influence of the Williamsburg reconstruction, clients and architects began to want reconstructions of genuine earlier American houses, rather than fanciful recreations of Jolly Olde England or Never-Never Spain. J. Frazer Smith's book, *White Pillars*, did much to bring the early-nineteenth-century architecture of Tennessee, Alabama, Mississippi and Louisiana to the attention of discriminating Memphis clients. Dent, who had worked at Williamsburg, was an appropriate architect to choose for such a job. Budgetary concerns caused some problems here, but in general the house is a convincing copy.

I-2

I-4

I-5   Dr. W.L. Howard House

91 West Chickasaw Parkway
George Mahan, Jr., architect, 1927–29
Everett D. Woods, associate architect

A somewhat reduced version of a James River plantation house, with the Baroque doorway Mahan consistently favored in such Georgian endeavors.

I-6   James D. Robinson House

101 West Chickasaw Parkway
Nowland Van Powell, architect, 1966–67

In Memphis, at least since the early twentieth century, the classical tradition has successfully withstood the onslaughts of every new architectural style. This design of Powell's is a particularly elegant example of that staying power, particularly in its careful, sparing use of architectural details.

I-7   Dr. Henry Stratton House

220 Goodwyn Street
J.O.E. Beck, designer, 1985

While Chickasaw Gardens contains a few large examples of houses based loosely on the ideas of Frank Lloyd Wright (they belong to a style one might call Wronged Wright), only this one actually dares to go even farther in announcing a new sense of domestic form. Stucco panels enclose a series of flat-roofed boxes that insure privacy for the inhabitants and tell us almost nothing about what goes on inside. The home here is not so much a man's castle as an ensemble of enigmatic, closed cubes that open onto generous and very private courtyards on the inside.

I-8

I-8   John Kimbrough House

2956 Central Avenue
Lucian Minor Dent, architect, 1940

1940 was a vintage year for Dent, who produced this house and the nearby Scott House (I-4), two of the best small classical houses in town, at the same time. The Kimbrough House has a dominating two-story Doric portico *in antis* that leads onto a recessed porch. The hefty columns and the *antae* that cling to the porch corners are made of cast concrete, which contrasts strongly with the brick of the rest of the house. In the frieze, Dent placed an elegant linear meander, instead of the more complex arrangement of triglyphs and metopes a pure Doric style would demand. Although his work at first seems pure, Dent was perfectly happy to break the rules when it suited him. The central section is flanked by one-story wings that are symmetrical, save for the garage on the west side that is pushed so far back, and treated in such a minor key, that there is little sense of its compromising the symmetry of the facade. Recent developers who fling garages in the faces of passersby should take note.

I-9   St. John's Episcopal Church

Central Avenue and Greer Street
Lucian Minor Dent, architect, 1950 on

The church and the accompanying parish buildings, completed over a number of years, form one of Dent's two finest ecclesiastical groups. St. John's nostalgically looks back to Bruton Parish Church in Williamsburg as its prototype. The simple brick volumes of the exterior are handled

I-9

surely, and the play of roofscapes and arcades in the parish buildings produces an ensemble that is both richly varied and serene. The church interior is vaulted, and the severely planar brick walls are interrupted by a series of murals by John Henry de Rosen, 1951. These paintings, in which one can feel simultaneously the influences of Salvador Dali, Sandro Botticelli, and the English Pre-Raphaelites, are certainly far from Williamsburg in style, but they give the interior quite a grand sense of scale.

I-10   Frederic Thesmar House

273 Windover Road
1938

The Thesmar house was one of the earliest in Memphis to take the modern movement in architecture seriously. It has almost all the characteristics of the International Style of architecture that grew up in Europe in the 1920s and received its official debut in this country under the auspices of the Museum of Modern Art in New York in an exhibition of 1932. The Thesmar House has the requisite flat roof; metal-sash windows; taut, planar stucco or concrete walls with no decoration; and white color.

I-11   Ramelle Van Vleet King House

3481 North Central Park
George Mahan, Jr., architect, 1937
Everett D. Woods, associate architect

A handsome and rather grand exercise in a Louisiana plantation-style house, now beset by condominia that have been developed on the King House's land (and on the land of King's brother's now-destroyed house to the west, the McKay Van Vleet House, 3460 Central, one of Mahan's most finely-crafted Tudors). By stealing the segmental arches from the Central Avenue side of the King House, the condominia have played the contextual game. They have not played it very well.

I-12   Day Foundation Headquarters

(formerly the Boyce-Gregg House)
3475 Central Avenue (formerly 317 South Highland Street)
Jones and Furbringer, architects, 1919–21

One of Jones and Furbringer's grandest, most satisfying designs, this is a sober house that indulges in a few Italian, or at least Mediterranean, delights, particularly on the main facade, which faces east toward Highland. The broad two-story facade is flanked by projecting porches that have Doric columns set inside strong corner piers. The center, however, switches to the richer Ionic order in the main portal and also makes use of real marble for the shafts and capitals. The columns support a round arch

I-12

I-13

that contains a beautifully-wrought, rather flat shell that stands out from the wall to give itself a halo of shadow. To either side of the arch are roundels with representations, in relief, of painting and music as nubile young women with appropriate attributes. Was this a house where painting and music were treasured? On the second floor, more young women in relief appear in oval frames, accompanied by elegantly thin swags and garlands. These figures actually repeat themselves across the upper story, twice over the main door and once to each side.

I-13   Luther Towers

274 South Highland Street
Walk Jones and Francis Mah, architects, 1970–71

This high rise structure for the elderly was erected in eighty-nine days, using the Mah-LeMessurier structural system that its designer and a Boston engineer, William LeMessurier, perfected. The projecting vertical piers, which form the vertical structure, are made up of eight-foot prestressed concrete modules that contain the bathrooms. The horizontal members were then hung on the verticals to produce the floors and also the wind bracing. The verticals, clear echoes of Louis Kahn's servant spaces, produce strong shadow patterns that considerably enliven the otherwise plain walls.

I-14   Second Church of Christ, Scientist

3535 Central Avenue
Lucian Minor Dent, architect, 1955

Dent here strove for effects richer and more sculptural than in St. John's a few blocks to the west. The facade is most powerful from a head-on view. The curving entablature of the porch, supported on hefty Ionic columns, pushes boldly forward. Its outward thrust is reinforced by the fact that the doorway also moves forward from the plane of the wall behind it. Even Dent's choice of where to use which ancient order underscores his point here. The frame of the doorway, only one story tall, uses the rich Corinthian order, although it would have been correct to use the plain Doric here under the taller Ionic columns of the porch. In the wings, which he wanted to de-emphasize, Dent did use the Doric, as custom dictated.

Above all this, the curve of the porch is continued in the circular base of the tower, which carries a circular Corinthian temple with a very tall witch's cap. Unfortunately, the main view from the parking lot to the west packs less of a wallop. The entire facade is based fairly closely on John Nash's All Soul's Church, Langham Place, in London.

I-15   "Radio Home"

347 Central Cove
J. Frazer Smith, architect, 1941
Chandler and Chandler, developers

To attract buyers to this small Williamsburg-esque subdivision, William Cullen Chandler turned this into a talking house. Visitors were greeted in the driveway by a 1941 Nash that talked to them about itself and hinted at things to come. Inside, all the appliances and rooms were wired to explain their wonders via loudspeakers. The trick apparently

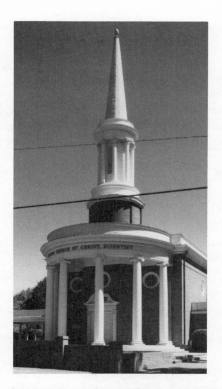

I-14

I-15

worked; the house sold the first day it was on view. This may be a paradig-matic account of what most Americans look for in houses: outside, nostal-gic fantasies about times and places gone by; inside, the latest gadgets. The facade, with the two side bays pulled forward ever so slightly, shows Smith's skill at turning an inexpensive house into something that looks good.

I-16   Memphis Light, Gas and Water Division, Poplar Substation

2904 Poplar Avenue
Walk C. Jones, Walk C. Jones, Jr., architects, 1939

For twenty years the firm of Jones and Jones, Jr., had a monopoly on the design of the electric substations of Memphis Light, Gas and Water, building nearly one a year. For such buildings the Joneses frequently adopted a simplified Art Deco style. Here the nicest detail is the wrought-iron gate that guards the main doorway. Watery lines, alluding to the building's function, flow up and down it.

I-17   Chickasaw Oaks Village Mall

3092 Poplar Avenue
Nowland Van Powell, architect of the interior, 1972
W.D. McKinnie, Jr., associate architect for design

The bland commercial exterior of this mall in no way gives away the surprise and delight one experiences on entering. Most shopping malls induce visual numbness; here the opposite happens. Powell lined the street of the mall with two-story house facades reminiscent of Williamsburg, New Orleans, and other wonderful places where classical architectural fronts

I-17

work their charms on the street. Some fronts project boldly, others recede, so that this interior street has a pleasant meander, rather than the dull, straight shot at an oversized neon sign that is the visual climax of most shopping malls. You even feel like a human being here, because everything is at human scale, including the ornament that makes each front work. (Powell didn't pull the Main Street, Disneyland, trick of using seven-eighths scale, to make the architecture seem cuter, and us a bit grander.) This mall is one of the city's hidden treasures. It deserves not only to be better known locally, but also more widely. Other malls like this were built around the country in the seventies, but none, one suspects, is more lovingly and knowingly detailed than this one.

I-18   East High School

3206 Poplar Avenue
Everett D. Woods, architect, 1946–48
Robert E. Brown, associate architect

East High was built to accommodate the eastward expansion of the city that burgeoned immediately after World War II, and to house the new school population in an architectural grandeur appropriate to the children of the well-to-do. Woods must have been thinking not only of earlier Memphis schools that were large in scale and classical in style, such as Memphis Technical High School (C-44), but also of much grander places, such as Blenheim Palace. The plan is certainly eighteenth-century baroque, with a strong centerpiece flanked by long wings that terminate in pavilions not quite as striking as the main frontispiece.

The building is highly visible from all four sides. Woods invented facades for the east and west which are equal to each other, but subordinate to the main south front. On the north, however, which was the least important of all, he expended relatively little effort. He achieved his effect of grandeur by gluing large classical members onto a simple structure with flat brick walls and large metal sash windows. The stone detailing—par-

I-18

I-19

ticularly those pediments that raise their heads over the utilitarian roof to challenge the sky—gives the flat silhouette and walls a character that belies the plain building beneath. Some of the ornament, closeup, is far from lacking in elegance, particularly the shallow reliefs of urns and swags over the secondary doorways of the south front.

I-19   Poplar Plaza Shopping Center

Poplar Avenue between Prescott and Highland Streets
Everett D. Woods, architect, opened 1949

Poplar Plaza is of some significance nationally. According to a considerable authority on the subject, Kenneth T. Jackson, it was one of the first complexes of stores to be built off-street following World War II. It is of historical importance in Memphis because it was established to serve the new and affluent East Memphis population and also because its founding put the first nail in the coffin of the downtown as the prime shopping area of the city. A few big structures, housing several enterprises, front directly on Poplar, with parking originally mostly to the front and to the sides. Later the center expanded to the north.

Architecturally there was considerable ambition. If Woods could give us his own version of the English baroque in East High, he gave us his own version of the modern in the Poplar Plaza Shopping Center. The Plaza Theater is faced with travertine, and it boasts a stainless-steel grid of decorations that culminates in a stainless steel acroterion, designed by Woods, that might be seen as the unfolding Spirit of the Cinema.

Farther east, the original Lowenstein's Department Store, now Dillards, was once a one-story building with Lally column porticoes that sported two giant ears, diagonally placed for best visibility from passing cars. In these ears lavish advertising displays were mounted. The east ear is still diagonal, but the west one has been straightened into the line of the now extended south wall. The strength of this design has been seriously com-

I-20

promised by the addition of a second story and by joining the store to the one to its west, faced in green and white stone to suit an entirely different original client. Don't miss, however, the rear entrance to this latter store, with its *fantasia*, somewhat dubious in form and taste, on New Orleans wrought iron.

I-20   Sunshine Home for Aged Men

3411 Poplar Avenue
Walk C. Jones, Walk C. Jones, Jr., architects, 1940

A Jeffersonian revival building designed to enable impecunious men to live out their days in a dignity equal to that of the architecture. The Joneses chose to make the home suggest a large Virginia plantation house, at least in terms of its central four-columned portico. Flanking the portico are broad terraces that connect to the embracing wings and provide ample opportunities for porch sitting and for watching the world go by on Poplar Avenue, seen through a lush screen of magnolia trees. The Sunshine Home is one more example of the high level of straightforward classical architecture practiced in Memphis around 1940 by the Joneses and Lucian Dent. When Jones, Jr., came to do the Mary Galloway Home (J-24) for elderly women in the 1960s, he abandoned the classical mode for a modern one—handled, however, with equal finesse.

I-21

I-25

I-21 Second Walk C. Jones, Sr., House

3833 South Galloway Drive
Walk C. Jones, Sr., architect, 1930

Jones combined four materials—stone, brick, stucco and wood—in this Tudor house with a very handsome chimney, and he used these materials to underscore different planes in space. The light-dark play of the stone blocks that outline the brick doorway in a snaggletooth pattern is repeated, in reverse, in the bricks that outline the stucco plane of the chimney. The diamond shape produced behind the chimney by the gable and the descending roofs is a particularly happy piece of geometric playfulness. The Jones House overlooks Galloway Golf Course, named for Robert Galloway, who had been chairman of the Memphis Park Commission. The land for the course was given to the city by H. W. Brennan, the developer of the surrounding subdivision, Red Acres, to be developed into a park that he hoped would make his lots more attractive to buyers.

I-22   Thomas M. Garrott House

4001 South Galloway Drive
Oscar Menzer, architect, 1981

Menzer is a contemporary architect who takes the classical styles very
seriously, even though almost no-one can now afford the lavish materials
and ornament such buildings would have had in earlier times. Here he
does a very simple French-Provincial house, relying on the appropriate
shapes, rendered in proportions true to the style, to carry the idea.

I-23   Hugh Sprunt House

4036 South Galloway Drive
John F. Staub, Houston, architect, 1955

A simplified Georgian brick two-story with a projecting central pavilion.
The details are handled with considerable care. The chimney breaks out
into the angle created by the pavilion and the south wing, so that we can
understand that the chimney rises from the ground up. The two brick
string courses that separate the lower and upper floors are neatly inte-
grated into the whole. The lower single-brick course marks the tops of the
first-floor windows, while the upper, three bricks wide, continues the
cornice line of the garage wing.

I-24   Hugh Brinkley House

170 South Rose Road
John F. Staub, Houston, architect, 1960

Rose Road has a handsome collection of classicizing houses, some of
which deliberately recall the architecture of Williamsburg. Staub broad-
ened the geographical boundaries of the architecture of the street by adding this echo of provincial France.

HEDGEMOOR SUBDIVISION
1936

An English-Romantic-garden subdivision laid out in a cornfield,
Hedgemoor took its Anglophilia so seriously that the streets have veddy
British names, such as St. Andrew's Fairway and Devon Way.

I-25   Walker Wellford, Jr., House

135 St. Albans Drive
George Awsumb, architect, 1948–49

Mrs. Wellford has described this stone-faced house aptly as "a modern
house by a Gothic architect." Awsumb was the designer of Idlewild Presbyterian Church (F-117), of which the Wellfords are members. The house

has a steel-frame structure, reinforced concrete floors, and a roof terrace. Le Corbusier himself would have approved of those aspects of the design, but other details might not have pleased him quite as much. The house also had the first heat pump in use in the city and was apparently the first fully air-conditioned two-story house in town. All these refinements reflect the interests of its owner, an engineer.

I-26 Laurence Bloch House

333 St. Andrew's Fairway
Nowland Van Powell, architect, 1959

The center of this house is quite assertive. Its roof rises up above the wings, the main block moves forward, and the centrally-placed doorway advances an additional plane to join steps that flow in two circles into the front yard. The detailing over the door and the flanking windows is more nineteenth-century Neo-Grecque than it is actually Greek. Once again Powell's classicism is highly personal.

I-28

I-27   Second Presbyterian Church

4055 Poplar Avenue
Harold Waggoner, Philadelphia, architect, 1951
W.D. McKinnie, Jr., architect for additions

Presbyterian Day School

W.D. McKinnie, Jr., architect, c. 1973

Second Presbyterian Church occupies a prominent piece of land between Poplar and Central, on the corner of Goodlett. The parish buildings and the school structures of Presbyterian Day School are dominated by the church, which sits on the eastern end of the site, the better to hold sway over the surrounding streets. The church, a classical building of brick and grey stone, suggests that Waggoner had more than a passing acquaintance with some of the works of the English baroque of the late seventeenth and early eighteenth centuries. At the entrance end, there is a suggestion of a transept, the kind of suggestion that Sir Christopher Wren was wont to make in his London churches, and the tower moves skyward with a ponderosity that also suggests baroque prototypes. Waggoner didn't really have his heart in the exuberance and joy of the style he was imitating, however, so that it comes out a bit dour, as perhaps a Presbyterian adaptation of an English idea should.

I-28   Mrs. Frank M. Crump House

4030 Poplar Avenue
George Mahan, Jr., architect, 1927–28
Everett D. Woods, associate architect

Behind the generally impenetrable walls that protect the high-priced condos on the northwest corner of Poplar and Goodlett stands Mahan and Woods' most grandiose classical revival house. Mrs. Crump was one of the first to build a large house on ample ground far out from the center of town. The J.P. Norfleets on Walnut Grove Road got a similar if less elaborate house from Jones and Furbringer about the same time (I-45), and the Dabney Crumps, Mrs. Frank Crump's brother and sister-in-law, built a large New England–style house, also by Mahan, across Goodlett (I-29). All of those estates have now been subdivided, but fortunately the main houses, some of the city's best, have been allowed to stand.

The Crump House is a large rectangle with a two-story, four-columned portico in front. On the back wall, a very grand Palladian window lights the main staircase. Everett Woods' drawing of 1927, reproduced here, shows the portico complete with automobile. One cannot help but compare this to the photographs Le Corbusier staged, in the same years, of his Villa Stein at Garches, with an automobile conspicuously parked in the driveway. For Corbusier, the automobile symbolized the new machine age, and it was an analog for the machine aesthetics of his architecture. Through technology, represented by his architecture and by the automobile, he hoped a better future for humanity could be achieved. In Woods' drawing, the automobile is also the symbol of a new age, which made the ten-mile drive from Poplar and Goodlett to downtown Memphis easy, but the style of the house is hardly the product of a machine aesthetic. Rather, it is a deliberate look back to what were seen as better times. Technology and architecture are presented as serving different rather than the same ends. The one offers convenience and the thrill of being up to date, while the other offers traditional symbols of wealth, domesticity, and the power of a landed southern aristocracy. When you drove your car into the driveway of the Villa Stein, you drove toward a vision of the future. When you drove under the Crump portico, you drove into the shelter of the past.

I-29   Dabney Crump House

4110 Tuckahoe Road
George Mahan, Jr., architect, 1926–27

The Dabney Crump house is actually a bit earlier than the larger Mrs. Frank Crump house across Goodlett. The Crumps had been struck, on their travels, by the late-eighteenth- and early-nineteenth-century houses of New England. They asked George Mahan to fashion them a house after such buildings. Mahan gave them the large rectangular block that he customarily produced when asked to do a classical house, only here he gave them one in wood, painted white. In the center of the facade he added one of his grand doorways, which in this "New England" case makes particular sense, because just this kind of doorway is found on the eighteenth-century houses of the Connecticut River Valley. The Crump House joins the house at 1785 Harbert (F-94) as one of the few Yankee architectural imports in Memphis.

I-30

I-30   Charles Freeburg House

4105 Tuckahoe Road
Lucian Minor Dent, architect, 1951

Opposite the stark New England grandeur of the Dabney Crump House sits one of Lucian Minor Dent's most modest but most successful houses. Stripped bare of ornament, its effect depends entirely on the symmetry of the central block and the carefully proportioned alternation of the solids and voids of the walls, windows, and door. It is a traditional red-brick Williamsburg house, elegantly (as they said of Ziegfeld girls) undressed.

I-31   Oscar Menzer House

4310 Tuckahoe Road
Oscar Menzer, architect, 1977

If you follow the winding course of Tuckahoe, you eventually come to the house that Dent's son-in-law and one-time partner built for himself. Menzer in some ways is heir to Dent's tradition of careful classicism. In his own house he shows his penchant for flat, unadorned surfaces in which the shapes of the windows themselves form the only ornaments. Here even the forms of the window frames—casements, not the double-hung windows of the standard classicizing house—count for much, since there is almost nothing else in the facade to compete with them.

The front is actually a story and a half. The upper windows rise into the roof line (or seem to sink down from the roof into the wall below) in a way that is particularly noticeable because they are the only elements that cross a border between one area and another in this facade. Menzer here was playing a reductionist game similar to the one Dent had played in the Charles Freeburg House twenty-six years earlier. It is a game one longs to see the designers of houses in the new subdivisions of River Oaks and Southwind learn to play, even just a little bit.

I-32   Myron Garber House

4217 Gwynne Road
Lucian Minor Dent, architect, 1949

An Ionic cottage with brick walls and white trim. The projecting central pavilion is emphasized vertically by the dormers that pop out of its roof. The wrought iron is very delicate, in keeping with other thin, small-scale elements that Dent used here in one of his best houses.

I-33 Robert M. Crump House

42 Wood Grove Road
Nowland Van Powell, architect, 1956

The center of this one-story brick house is organized by the application of five blind arches that create a strong, even rhythm. Into the central arch Powell inserted an elegant white doorframe, flanked by two pairs of extremely thin engaged columns and topped by a delicate fanlight. The door is reached by a handsome staircase with two curving flights that lead up to a central landing, which once again emphasizes the central bay. These major elements of the facade are freely adapted from the east and west fronts of Moor Place, Hertfordshire, England, completed in 1779 from the designs of a little-known architect, Robert Mitchell. Powell knew Moor Place from illustrations that appeared in *Country Life* for 26 January and 2 February 1956.

Refined details are what make Powell's houses stand out from run-of-the-mill suburban dwellings such as the ones on all sides in this neighborhood. In this section of town there is a sameness of design—one story brick houses with white columns or white trim—that pleases some and numbs others. Powell and Dent were the two architects who consistently satisfied with style and verve the local taste for houses of classical inspiration.

I-34 J. Everett Pidgeon House

4202 White Oaks Road
George Mahan, Jr., architect, 1931–32
Everett D. Woods, associate architect

The Pidgeon House once dominated a large estate, now subdivided into many small lots. Mahan and Woods gave it a grand Mount Vernon porch, but unlike that at Mount Vernon, the roofline is made interesting by dormers that poke up into its edge.

I-35 Nellie Pidgeon House

4275 Nellwood Road
George Mahan, Jr., architect, 1933
Everett D. Woods, associate architect

Everett Pidgeon's mother installed herself, a year later, to the east of her son in a rambling stone house that suggests Bucks County horsefarms more than Tidewater Virginia. Her estate has also been subdivided, and one of the appendages to her house can still be seen at 4304 Nellwood.

I-33

I-34

I-36

I-36   Second Dr. Harry Schmeisser House

4225 Walnut Grove Road
George Mahan, Jr., and Nowland Van Powell, architects,
1939–40

When Powell returned to Memphis at the end of the 1930s, after working
for almost a decade in St. Louis, he teamed up briefly with George Mahan,
after Everett Woods left Mahan to strike out on his own. Mahan and
Powell made a great pair, as two very different houses on this street, the
Schmeisser House and the William Fisher House, testify. The Schmeissers,
for whom Mahan and Broadwell had done a Tudor cottage on McLean (E-
51), here built probably the best Tudorbethean house in town (the competition is the Carrier House on Willett [F-81]). The massing of the Schmeisser House seems probably mostly the work of Mahan, but a lot of the detailing must belong to Powell. The exterior combines any number of materials—brick, stone, stucco, wood, slate—in picturesque combination.
Equally mixed-up are the historical styles on which this house draws. The
main entrance, in orange stone with a coat of arms above, is late medieval,
but immediately next to it, to the east, is a grey stone Palladian window
set into a dark brick wall. Such mixing of historical styles, of course, was
exactly what English designers in the late sixteenth century were wont to
do. There is also ample play with texture—rough and smooth stone, rough
brick, smooth stucco—as well as play with pattern, in the diaper patterns
in some of the brick parts of the wall.

Inside, there is a grand, dark oak staircase that winds up against the
front wall and creates a low entrance area just inside the front door. The
staircase dominates an enormous rectangular entrance hall that opens not
only into dining room and living room to west and east, but also directly
into the large garden, laid out with an informal romanticism that one also
suspects is due to Powell's skills. This is one of the city's great houses.

I-37   Allen Cox, Jr., House

4315 Walnut Grove Road
Walk C. Jones, Walk C. Jones, Jr., architects, 1939

If the Schmeissers got a dream of Elizabethan England, the Coxes got their
own version of Tara of *Gone with the Wind*. The house is a large brick
rectangle, with a square columned, two story porch attached. The plantation here comes to the suburbs, which, of course, were being populated
with all kinds of versions of larger country houses reduced to relatively
small lots. That, of course, is what suburbs are all about—giving the inhabitants the illusion of living in the country, while actually being quite
close to the city.

I-38

I-38 First J. Frazer Smith House

20 Waring Road
J. Frazer Smith, architect, 1927

Smith, who was to design the Dixie Homes in the thirties, built for himself in the twenties one of the best Italian villas in the city. The blocky
two-story mass of the house is broken by asymmetrically-placed elements
that are knowingly adjusted in terms of scale. The two-story round-arched
window on the southwest corner gives the house a grand sense of scale as
you approach from the driveway. It also lights an interior staircase.
Around the corner, the smaller main doorway is emphasized by a projecting pediment, while the living room window, farther to the east, is given a
different scale still, in keeping both with its relative importance in the
facade and with the scale of the room it lights. To the east an ample terrace comfortably snuggles into a ravine, while to the north the house is
connected to its garage by a handsome arcade. Smith was a thoughtful
architect who could manipulate the elements of the design to get just the
effect he wanted. It's instructive to compare Smith's essay in the Mediterranean style with the many Italo-Spanish houses George Mahan designed
in the same decade. Smith is bolder and more direct, while Mahan is often
more convoluted and given to a kind of surface decoration that did not
attract Smith's fancy.

I-39 A.L. Aydelott House

150 Waring Road
A.L. Aydelott, architect, 1962

Aydelott was an important father figure to most of the young architects
who arrived in Memphis in the late 1950s intent on practicing the kind of
modern architecture they had been taught in school, particularly at Yale,
where Aydelott himself taught briefly. This house was a kind of mani-

festo, a gauntlet thrown down in the faces of all those brick imitations of Williamsburg and other sentimental southern sites that one finds at every turn in this neighborhood. Aydelott chose to do a house that looks, perhaps, more like a modern church than a place someone would live. (Was there some pride at work here?) The building is eccentric even its its placement, which is diagonal to the street line, a line that every other house maintains assiduously. Having broken the mold in these ways, Aydelott then proceeded to make a house that was not all red-brick walls, but rather all metal roof. Its four gables that sweep low to the ground intersect at right angles to form a cross shape. The whole suggests, at least just a bit, something out of the head of Buckminster Fuller, whom Aydelott doubtless encountered at Yale. This is a house of willfully a-traditional forms.

I-40   Peter Pettit House

111 North Cherry Road
Oscar Menzer, architect, 1980

To move from the self-conscious modernity of the Aydelott House to the careful evocation of a real Williamsburg house here requires a radical shifting of critical gears. Menzer's house deliberately does not challenge its neighbors, but rather fits the residential environment in which it sits. The house is so modest that you might well pass it by without remarking the competent way all the parts have been put together. But well crafted they are, and well proportioned and well thought through, so that the house, after a careful look, reveals itself to be just as different from the ordinary houses around it as Aydelott's.

I-41   Lucian Minor House

54 Cherry Lane
Lucian Minor Dent, architect, 1955

A Doric cottage, somewhat beefier and less refined than Dent's Ionic cottage on Gwynne (I-32) of six years earlier, the Minor House boasts a bold portico with a wider space between the two middle columns to call attention to the entrance. The segmental arches over the windows repeat, in their sameness, the rhythm of the porch columns, but they offer variety as well through their curved shapes. It is instructive to compare this house with one of its neighbors, such as 7 Cherry Lane to the north, to see the difference between a house whose every element has been organized by a thoughtful architect and a house to which a builder has simply attached some columns and a pediment to give it a "Colonial" air.

I-42   Nowland Van Powell House

130 North Perkins Road
Nowland Van Powell, architect, 1950–52

Powell's small house for himself has been compromised by an unsympa-
thetic addition—the lattice carport to the north. Remove this, however,
and you get back to what Powell designed: a U-shaped plan with two low
wings projecting toward the street from a slightly higher brick wall with
three tall shuttered openings. The opening on the right is the front door,
while the other two light the living room. The north wing housed Powell's
office, which could be reached either from the house or from the courtyard. The central pavilion is given a flat brick parapet that conceals the
steel truss roof that spans the main "company" spaces in the front. Inside,
Powell indulged himself in marble floors and tall ceilings in the living
room and in the hall, which he further adorned with *putti* painted by his
own hand and with portraits of the geniuses who presided over his architecture, Andrea Palladio and Robert Adam. The steel truss that makes it
all possible is nowhere to be seen.

I-43   Church of the Holy Communion

4645 Walnut Grove Road
Walk C. Jones, Walk C. Jones, Jr., architects, 1949

Holy Communion was the first large church to appear on Walnut Grove
Road, and it did so on a commanding rise at the corner of Perkins. The
church is straight out of eighteenth-century England, and out of copies of

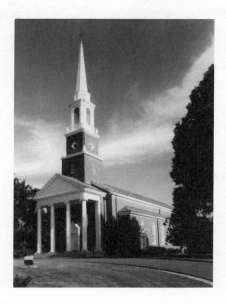

I-43

those English churches built in America. A tall tower rises dramatically over a four-columned portico. The tower begins with a square base. On the next level, the corners of the towers are pulled back into reveals, which in the next level become beveled edges that in turn lead skillfully into the low octagon that supports the tall, eight-sided steeple. The Joneses did a very similar steeple at Evergreen Presbyterian Church across University Street from Rhodes College.

I-44   William H. Fisher House

4680 Walnut Grove Road
George Mahan, Jr., and Nowland Van Powell, architects, 1938

The Fisher House is the classical counterpart to the Second Schmeisser House (I-36), by the same architects, down the road. The center of the

Fisher house is a five-bay, two-story wooden-walled porch recessed into the brick block of the building. The generally rectilinear character of the house is intensified by the use of square, instead of round columns for the order of the porch. Indeed, even the straight lines of the metal roof count as integral parts of the whole design. In all of this rectilinearity, the segmental pediments over the first-floor windows in the center take on an absolutely crucial importance. Their downward curves pick up the triangular shapes of the separate hipped roofs over the two brick end bays of the house. These roofs make the end bays read as separate wings, even though they do not project beyond the plane of the porch columns. The only break in the symmetry of the facade comes from the bay window at the west, but you may be thankful for this slight irregularity. It inserts a sense of the messiness of life into this house of classical order and repose.

I-45   J.P. Norfleet House

4795 Fleetgrove Avenue
Jones and Furbringer, architects, 1924

The Norfleet estate was the grandest on Walnut Grove Road, and Norfleet descendents still maintain part of the great garden that once had this house as its center. The estate has been subdivided, however, and the house relegated to a small lot. Even so great a loss of territory cannot undo the power of Jones and Furbringer's architectural conception. The house is large, but simple in massing and detail—a big white rectangle with a porch cut out of the center. All of this seems straightforward, and even easy, but it took some care to make so little work so well.

I-46   E.J. Goldsmith House

4827 Fleetgrove Avenue
Lucian Minor Dent, architect, 1968

I-47   Mel O'Brien House

"Berryhill"
4840 Fleetgrove Avenue
Mel O'Brien, architect, 1972

Vertical wood siding, painted grey, encloses the cube and diagonally-truncated cylinder that make up the geometry of this very geometric house, which looks as if it might have been designed for a beach site in one of the Hamptons. Whatever the site, this house clearly reflects the work of such New York architects as Gwathmey and Siegel, who in the 1960s consciously revived the cubic geometry and flat roofs of the International Style of the 1920s. O'Brien was one of the architects closely involved in the replanning and rebuilding of Beale Street.

I-48

I-49

I-48   Richland Elementary School

5440 Rich Road
Mann and Harrover, architects, 1957

Richland Elementary was the first truly modern school built in Memphis.
(The modernism of Mann's Grahamwood School on Summer, 1949 [H-12],
is relatively cosmetic.) Mann was sufficiently skilled as a salesman to
persuade the Board of Education to let the architects do what they wanted,
as long as they stayed within the budget. The result is a handsome building, made up of rectangular boxes that clearly show the concrete structural
frame. A series of low gables in the center marks the multi-purpose room;
they are the only vertical projections in an otherwise long, low, and clean
design. One of the best buildings from the 1950s in town.

I-49   Anshei Sphard–Beth El Emeth Synagogue

170 East Yates Road
Walk Jones and Francis Mah, architects, 1969–70

The squared-off, blank brick exterior in no way prefigures the excitement
provided by the interior of the sanctuary, which is one of Jones and Mah's
finest works. The entrance to the rectangular sanctuary is in the middle of
one of the long sides, and the windows are concealed in setbacks on the
side opposite. Visually, however, the rectangle quickly disappears. A
curved stalactite of a wall drops down from the ceiling to frame the semicircular arrangement of seats. These, upholstered in a dusty pink, are set
on what was once a brilliant purple carpet. Opposite the door, the walls lit
by the concealed windows are painted blue. All of this is reflected in the
other walls, covered in their entirety by a silvery aluminum foil and vinyl
film that takes on the character of whatever is reflected in it. The room
dissolves in a shimmer of light and color. The space seems to have no
boundary, because the silver walls cannot be perceived for themselves.
Because there is nothing on the walls that suggests what the real size of
the room is, there is also no true sense of scale. The result is an interior of
color, light, and reflections that is softly dazzling—if we can be forgiven
such an oxymoron—and mysteriously insubstantial. Even the furniture
and the handrails have been dissolved into light and air by making them
out of clear Lucite. When the sanctuary first opened, some who were not
ready for the modernity of its interior dubbed it the spaceship synagogue.
This room does have to do with space, but space of a profoundly spiritual
nature.

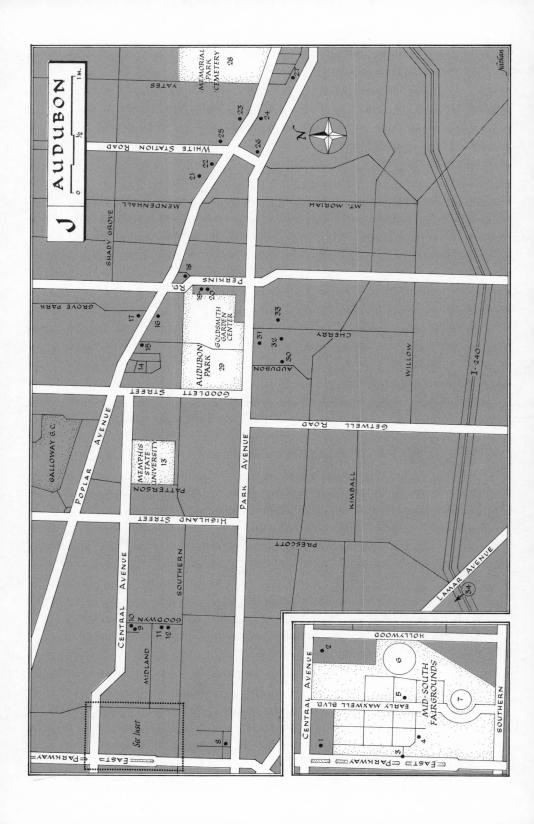

J AUDUBON

0   ½   1 M.

J Audubon

J-1   Fairview Junior High School

750 East Parkway South
E.L. Harrison, architect, 1930
Nowland Van Powell and John F. Hozier, associate architects

Built at a time when Memphis city schools were expanding east with the rest of the city, Fairview is the architectural gem of the school system and one of the finest buildings in the whole city. The architect of record was E.L. Harrison, but it seems that the real mind behind Fairview was Nowland Van Powell's, and it is fair to say that this is his surviving masterpiece. The style is Art Deco, and this is an early example for Memphis— the building was right up to date as far as the rest of the world was concerned.

The architects made full use of the location. A sweeping curve of an entrance drive led in from the Parkway, and the school buses unloaded the kids on this drive, on axis with the school. For the elect, another oval drive intersected the upper edge of the bus drive and led right up to the entrance.

The front facade is divided into five parts: the projecting corner classroom blocks, the two hallway wings, and the central entrance tower. This last exists on four separate planes, receding as it goes up four stories. There is the two story entrance porch, the terrace above it with flanking pylons, and above that a huge cupola with a pyramidal roof. The pylons are deco-

J-1a

J-1b

rated at their tops with reliefs representing Night and Day, left and right, who are identified in French and Latin (!). The carvings, as Art Deco as the rest of the building, flank the reading terrace of the school's library.

The windows of the porch wings are surmounted by four wonderfully carved reliefs illustrating agriculture and industry: purple mountains' majesty and amber waves of grain on the left, and a fantasy celebration of the city of tomorrow, as conceived in 1930, on the right. Here one sees steamships, airplanes, and skyscrapers—all the right stuff for a glorious urban future (J-1b).

Lots of schools, including most of the others in Memphis, put all their architectural power on the outside and leave the inside to the students. At Fairview, however, the outside part of the entrance is just half of the experience of coming into the school. Once through the doors, there is a two-story stair hall, with dark green-terrazzo floors and stairs and slick, pinky-gold and black marble walls. It is amazing, and perhaps even a bit miraculous, that so much of the original decoration is left. Even the lighting fixtures in the ceilings are original equipment, as is the trophy case that you can just make out on the floor above.

The plan of the school is ingenious and compact. Directly beyond the entrance is the auditorium, the stage of which doubles as a basketball court, with great folding doors to close it off. Above the entrance hall, on the third floor, front and center, stands the library. The central of its three rooms opens out onto the terrace above the entrance porch. Here students could sit in the sun and read, or just sit and look at the allegorical figures of Day and Night, which one can see close up from here.

Fairview is a wonderful building. It takes a difficult architectural problem, the American secondary school, and does great things with it.

J-2

J-2　National Guard Armory

Central Avenue and Hollywood Street, southwest corner
Walk C. Jones, Walk C. Jones, Jr., architects, 1941–42
Herbert M. Burnham, Lucian Minor Dent,
associate architects

A decade later, and just east of the Fairview Junior High School, the great wartime National Guard Armory in Memphis also arose in Art Deco style. But what a difference from Fairview! That school celebrates knowledge and learning with joyous exuberance. The armory is a much more obviously "serious" set of buildings. There was war in Europe and the Far East when it was designed, and America had entered the war by the time it was completed. No time for fun and games, and there is no humor in these buildings. The armory is expansive—six buildings instead of the standard one—but it's tightly organized. The main building facing Central is an almost standard armory hall, but its strong diagonal buttresses mark it as something distinctive. It is flanked by a pair of lower, blocky buildings, branded forever on their facades as the Assembly Hall and the Administration Building. To the southwest stretches a very long pair of buildings which mark the western edge of the parade ground. The sunburst window grates added at a later date to the southern of these are, miraculously, wholly in keeping with the spirit of the complex. They actually even make the building look better. The south end of the complex is closed by motor-pool structures.

All of these buildings are constructed of concrete, cast using horizontal wooden shuttering and allowing the concrete to ooze out between the shuttering boards to create a strong surface texture. This is common enough nowadays, but almost no-one was doing it in the thirties and early forties, except the builders of TVA dams.

J-3   Mid-South Fairgrounds

East Parkway South Entrance
1908

This grand entrance to the fairgrounds, on the east side of East Parkway, is the best neoclassical entrance in the city, but now it only leads directly to parking lots. The fairgrounds were originally designed so that the view from this gate was down a street to the entrance of the Shelby County Building, far across the grounds. Thus the "grand drive" of the fair led from an impressive entrance to an impressive building. To the right of the gate, Libertyland, an amusement park with a carousel worthy of being on the National Register, is tucked away.

Of the various permanent buildings, in a bunch of different architectural styles, only two are exciting enough to liven up a trip to the fair.

J-4   The Woman's Building

2375 Mississippi Avenue
George Awsumb and Sons, architects, 1950

This red-brick rectangle leans toward the Italian side of things with the red tile roof, big three-arched entrance, patterned brickwork, and, most of all, a huge Palladian window that fills up the end of the east wall.

J-5   The Shelby County Building

904 Early Maxwell Boulevard
1908

This is the only Spanish Renaissance public building in town. It may not be the Escorial, but it does dominate the area with its great four-story

J-6

central tower rising over what used to be an impressive entrance. The corner pavilions with their octagonal towers echo the main tower. Most of the architectural ammunition is, or was, saved for the entrance. The Park Commission, which owns this building, boarded up the great arched entryway (along with all the windows along the sides within reach), covered the nameplate of the building with a squat little porch, and replaced the original doors with mean steel traps with little plexiglass portholes. This is enough to make you miss the delights still left. Above the wrecked entrance, a coat of arms with bees and a hive still celebrates agricultural industriousness, and at the top of the telescoping octagons of the tower, a lantern with marvelous shell half-domes says, "Come to the fair."

J-6   Liberty Bowl

Yeates, Gaskill and Rhodes, architects, 1965
Hellmut, Obata and Kassabaum, St. Louis, architects for addition, 1987–88

The Liberty Bowl bowl has a particularly graceful profile against the sky, to which the later rectilinear addition on the northeast side is not very sympathetic. Inside, there is a clever disposition of seating. The field is displaced to one side of the circular shape, to provide much greater seating area for the home-team rooters on one side, and much less for visitors, who are bound to be fewer, on the other.

J-7   Mid-South Coliseum

Furbringer and Ehrman and Robert Lee Hall and Associates, architects, 1964

J-8   Orange Mound Community Day Care Center

Grand Street and Saratoga Avenue, southeast corner
Walk Jones and Francis Mah, architects, 1971

The Orange Mound neighborhood, laid out in the first years of this century, was the first subdivision in Memphis built for blacks by blacks. It was the black equivalent of Annesdale Park, which it followed by only a few years. The houses, not expensive in their day, have not aged as well as their pricier white counterparts closer to town, but the area still has a strong sense of being a coherent neighborhood.

Jones and Mah's daycare center, an attempt to give the neighborhood a modernist focus, is not necessarily sympathetic to the small scale and domestic character of the surrounding houses, and the fortress-like aspect of the exterior can hardly seem welcoming to impressionable kids. The inside, filled with light and color, is much more kindly disposed, visually, toward its users.

J-9   Walk C. Jones, III, House

360 Tara Lane
Walk C. Jones, III, architect, 1968–69

Jones' own house is just as different from its neighborhood as the daycare center is from Orange Mound. You will have no problem picking it out among the undistinguished houses on this short dead-end street. Its red brick is a traditional Memphis material, but that is the only thing traditional about it. Jones looked to the architecture of Louis Kahn for inspiration rather than to standard domestic formulae.

It's a tough house, with uncompromisingly planar walls, flat roofs, and geometrical blocks bridged at two levels by glass-walled hallways. The living room, in the central block and on the first floor, is surmounted by a terrace which peers out at the street through a big porthole. The house is meant to be private all around, even on a small lot. On the north side, a free-standing brick plane protects glass walls from neighbors, while the little front yard, sunk into the ground, sports a magnolia tree that shields the big windows from passersby.

J-10   Charles O. Pfeil House

333 Goodwyn Street
Charles O. Pfeil, architect, 1913

This big stucco two-story is remarkable in that it is an architect's house with almost no discernable style. It has extremely thin detailing on the eaves, and the upper balcony gives a vaguely Swiss-chalet effect, but beyond that it is hard to say what Pfeil had in mind. This house suggests, however, that the most visually arresting buildings in which Pfeil had a hand may have been designed by his partners.

J-11   Buntyn-Ramsay House

487 Goodwyn Street
1864

One of the few remaining nineteenth-century country houses in Memphis, this one has been absorbed into a high-priced suburban street. Indeed, this is the house that gave the street its character, since most of the later houses approximate its setback from the road. When the house was built in the 1860s, it was old-fashioned, more Federalist than anything else. Its symmetrical central block, the original part, is preceded by a square two-story portico. The columns of the portico relate to the bay division of the house, rather than to the idea of a porch, with consequent confusion. The paired columns in the center of the porch are just where the entrance door should be, and so the door itself has to be offset to the right. What might

J-9

J-11

J-12

have been an impressive, centralized, plantation-house entrance turns into something less. But the relationship of part to part in the house is generally good. Nineteenth-century builders, even when they didn't get something as important as the front door quite right, still had an intuitive feel for correct proportions.

J-12   Cecil M. Norfleet House

517 Goodwyn Street
Mahan and Broadwell, architects, 1922

This is an early but spectacular version of Mahan and Broadwell's Spanish mode. The white stucco block of the house is preceded by an open arcade with twisted columns on the right. Visually, the arcade is pulled through the central entrance block by continuing its elements into the sunporch on the left. The door in between is typical Mahan, with two arched windows, a relief roundel, and swags above.

J-13   Memphis State University

Memphis State was founded in 1912 as the West Tennessee State Normal School, an institution for teacher training. It became State Teachers' College in 1925, Memphis State College in 1941, and Memphis State University in 1957.

Mynders Hall

Mahan and Broadwell, architects (?), 1912–13

The college began modestly enough as a red brick campus with a restrained classical style used for ornament. One of the earliest surviving buildings is Mynders Hall, located west of the main Administration Building. It has continued to serve its original function as a women's residence hall. This building shows most clearly what the early campus was like. It is an E-shaped structure, with its main facade looking west onto Patterson Street and its entrance marked by a stone frontispiece. Inside, the main transverse hall still retains its original glazed tile floor, and, despite a shabby dropped ceiling, it is possible to get a real sense of the spacious and airy quality of the public parts of the building. The end wings projecting from the main block are residential. The central wing, immediately behind the western entrance, houses a common parlor and shows a control of classical detailing. The proportions of the room are residential, although the scale is large. The ceiling beams are supported on curved brackets and have very fine egg-and-dart moldings. All around the walls are double French doors leading out to the deep covered verandah which girdles the parlor and extends north and south to the projecting residential wings. The brick piers, jigsawed projecting rafters, and green tile roof here continue to emphasize residential qualities. Through such skillful uses of detail, the designer created an institutional dormitory with many of the characteristics and feelings of a spacious southern house.

Scates Hall

Everett Woods, architect, 1921

Straight east, across the center of the oldest part of the campus is Scates Hall (J-13a), originally an athletic dormitory. The real excitement in the building comes from the projecting one-story entrance porch facing what used to be the center of campus. Each of the three sides of this porch has triple arches separated by strips of brick wall. On the front, the arches are carried on stone columns with cast-ceramic capitals of a vaguely Corinthian order, each side equipped with a mischievously grinning face, presumably of undergraduates plotting (innocent?) pranks. The arches are framed by a string course of ceramic blocks with rosette decoration. This string course continues across the facade of the main block of the building and serves to tie the porch to what is behind it. In the upper walls of the porch the brickwork goes wild, and there are medallions and lozenges of marble set into the surface.

The early twenties saw the beginning of the Spanish revival craze in Memphis, and there are hints of that here, although the style is essentially Italianate. Too, there may have been some looking westward toward the campus of Stanford University in California, which Scates resembles in a lot of ways.

J-13a. Scates Hall

J-13b   Manning Hall

Manning Hall

George Mahan, Jr., architect, 1929
Everett Woods, associate architect

The entrance to Manning Hall, which now faces a parking lot, has probably the best baroque frontispiece in town, and certainly the greatest of
Mahan's numerous white baroque doors on red brick buildings. Pairs of
big, muscular Doric columns flank what is now a crummy little aluminum-and-glass door. Above this is a strong entablature and balustrade. The
window on the next floor is framed by Ionic columns and surmounted by a
segmental pediment, enthusiastically broken by a shield and stuffed with
all manner of foliage and fruits of the earth.

The Mall

Like many big college and university campuses, Memphis State's has little
coherence to its plan. Buildings appear to have been put up wherever there
was space for them. Stylistic unity was largely abandoned, and new buildings paid little attention to their older neighbors. The classical style of the
early MSU buildings essentially disappeared in the 1950s. In the early

sixties, however, there was a conscious attempt to emulate America's greatest classical revival campus: Thomas Jefferson's University of Virginia. South of the Administration Building, a mall was envisioned, similar to the one at Virginia, to be lined with big academic buildings. Between 1962 and 1966 the Mall was formed by the construction of Mitchell (1962), Ellington (1963), Clement (1965), and Smith (1965) Halls and the University Center (1966). Unfortunately, the open central space is lumpy and confused, and it ends not with a vista but a parking lot. There is even a serpentine brick wall, just like the ones Jefferson designed for the back gardens at Charlottesville, but it's hidden at the southeast corner of the campus, next to the Campus School.

The Temples

Although architectural coherence at MSU was abandoned early on, the practice, necessary in a public institution, of giving building commissions to many different firms instead of sticking to one or two favorites has resulted in occasional reversions to something like variations on the original architectural idea.

The Patterson Building

Robert Lee Hall, architect, 1966

Hall, who also did the Clark Tower at 5100 Poplar Avenue (J-21), seems to have looked to New York architects a lot. Here he was obviously thinking of the bastardized classicism of New York's Lincoln Center. But this is also the first time any modern architect seems to have remembered that MSU began as a vaguely classical campus, and that the quintessential classical building is the Greek temple. Hall's concrete frame plays the part of the columns, and the projecting top story acts like the heavy entablature. In order to give himself a level area to put this on, Hall built up a strong floating stylobate that hides the unevenness of the site.

Psychology Building

Thorn, Howe, Stratton and Strong, architects, 1968

This "Temple of the Mind" revives again the idea of the Greek temple. The concrete frame, acting as the peristyle, is emphasized by placing strips of glass on either side of the vertical elements to separate the concrete from the brick walls. In this architectural allegory, brick walls stand for empty space. The temple idea weakens considerably at the east and west ends, where consistency is sacrificed for different effects, but the view from the south is the view of a temple.

J-14a

J-14b

J-14   The Village

Williamsburg Lane, south of Poplar Avenue
and east of Goodlett Street
J. Frazer Smith, architect, designed c. 1938
William C. Chandler, developer

The name of the principal street of this small development tells everything there is to know about the stylistic source for the houses: Williamsburg, Williamsburg, Williamsburg. During the Depression Frazer
Smith turned from his grand Italianate manner of the twenties to a much
more modest Colonial style, evident in his Rosemary Lane development
(F-25), his own house on Peabody (F-57), and especially here. The houses
are for the most part brick cottages set on broad lawns cut by shady, curving streets. The intended effect was, as the Smith drawing (J-14b) shows,

J-16

to recreate a village, and Smith was largely successful. It is the sort of place where kids and dogs play in the streets. The taste for the American Colonial house, particularly of red-brick with white classical ornaments, established a major beachhead in the city here in the late thirties and then took over much of East Memphis in the post–World War II years.

J-15   Twelve Oaks Condominiums

Twelve Oaks Drive, south of Poplar Avenue
Taylor and Crump, architects, 1975

This was the first condo development in this part of Poplar, and Taylor and Crump worked to give a residential scale to their buildings that would help them fit into the neighborhood. In this they were successful. There is, however, a sociological point of some importance to be made through a comparison of the Village and Twelve Oaks. The Village houses open up to each other across their level lawns. They welcome visitors with columned porches or relatively elaborate doorways. Here, instead of front doors facing each other across the central common, garages go head to head with other garages. The dwellings for people have retreated behind the anonymity of undecorated brick walls, lowering roofs, and shelters for cars. This is not the sort of place where kids play in the street, or where a visitor feels particularly welcome. The architectural style comes from 1960s resort condos instead of from images of early American domesticity, and perhaps that is part of the problem.

J-16   Econocom

4385 Poplar Avenue
The Crump Firm, architects, 1988

This is Memphis's post-mod baroque palace. Like a baroque palace, the facade builds up to a grand central effect. End pavilions flank wings that in turn enfold a central entrance with not one but two pediments. From the lobby a slick double staircase curves up to a skylit hall that leads to Memphis' only *Kaisersaal*—where, fittingly, the Econocom Tetrarchy, the four who run the company, have their offices. (In certain late baroque palaces in eighteenth-century Germany and Austria, the principal room on the upper floor, overlooking the garden, was called the *Kaisersaal*, because it was the room in which the *Kaiser*, or emperor, would be entertained, should he visit.)

Downstairs, a lobby runs through the building past a reception area and an art gallery to what, in a baroque palace, is the *Sala Terrena*, or garden room. Here a curved glass wall looks out onto a garden unfortunately truncated by a curving road, off axis, that the architects couldn't control. The Econocom Tetrarchs look out their strip windows onto this road and somebody else's parking lot, where their great garden axis, *à la Versailles*, ought to have been.

J-17   Christ United Methodist Church

4488 Poplar Avenue
Office of Walk C. Jones, Jr., architects, 1959–64
Thorn, Howe, Stratton and Strong, architects for additions, 1972 and 1982

This big church shows that the Jones office could do a lot more than red-brick, white-columned Colonial revivals. The church has a symbolic front that faces onto Poplar and says "Church Here," but the real business of going in and out of the building is done elsewhere: at the side, by the parking lot.

The sanctuary is like some huge, mendicant order preaching barn from the late Middle Ages: a single uninterrupted space, with its roof held up by a big concrete-and-steel frame, the vertical members of which are accentu-

J-17. Grant Building, detail

ated by their placement between pairs of vertical stained-glass windows that throw bands of pretty but distracting multi-colored light across the pews. Joseph's coat couldn't have had more colors. Since the sanctuary space is unitary, the circulation for the church has been put outside, in the form of low aisles that run along the sides of the sanctuary wall.

Behind the main church building is a rectangular courtyard enclosed by various education buildings and the church hall, all unashamedly modern in conception. The Grant Building, the one to the west, has a great double trumpet bell of a curved brick wall that protrudes from its ground floor. The rest of the construction is Miesian, with exposed steel frames filled in with glass. The suspended steel walkways around the perimeter of the building tie together the two separate blocks and create screens that define planes, but at the same time the screens are transparent and allow your view to carry through to the other side. Too many different directions of screening, however, compromise the effect of the whole in busywork.

J-18   Theater Memphis

630 Perkins Road Extended
George Awsumb and Sons, architects, 1975
Lawrence Anthony, sculptor, 1979

The lumpy grey-brown brick building isn't worth a stop, but the sculptural group, *Dramatis Personae*, by Lawrence Anthony is. Anthony, a Memphis sculptor, has a gift for caricature and gesture, and his over-life-sized, plate-steel figures representing the likes of Cleopatra, Cyrano, and Medea, are remarkable for capturing just the right dramatic effects. Anthony's original intention was to have the figures placed as a group, so that they would

J-18

appear to be theatergoers chatting during intermission. The present arrangement, carried out without the artist's consent, scatters the figures and destroys that idea completely. Luckily, the individual figures are still strong enough to stand on their own. It may be some small consolation for Anthony that even Rodin had similar problems with clients.

J-19   Whitworth House

711 South Perkins Road
Office of Walk C. Jones, Jr., architects, 1958–59

Few houses in Memphis make any attempt to deal with modernism. The ones that do ought to be noted. The abstract modernist effect here is created by playing verticals and horizontals against one another. The house is not very open toward the street; you get the impression that it has turned away to look at its own back yard.

J-20   Walk C. Jones, Jr., House

727 South Perkins Road
Walk C. Jones, Jr., architect, 1951

The houses architects build for themselves are always revealing. This brick Colonial Revival, painted white, is very unassuming, but it doesn't sink to dullness. It is one of the few Colonial Revival houses in Memphis that bases itself more on the architecture of the northeastern Colonies— seen most clearly in the big centrally-located brick chimney—than of the southern ones.

J-21   Clark Tower

5100 Poplar Avenue
Robert Lee Hall, architect, completed 1971

Memphis has the misfortune of having a dud as its only skyscraper between downtown and the eastern reaches of the city. The inspiration comes from Yamasaki, especially works like his Woodrow Wilson School at Princeton of the mid-1960s or, closer to home, from Mann and Harrover's Memphis Airport. But both of these buildings are delicate and depend for their effect on a proper use of scale. Hall has stretched Yamasaki up to the sky, and it doesn't work. When Yamasaki designed tall buildings like the World Trade Center in New York, he left off most of his spacy Venetian Gothic effects and built relatively severe boxes, appropriate to their scale. The Clark Tower even misses a chance to be cool and elegant at ground level; there is only a pathetically small patch of green marble around the entrance. Hall also gave us the 100 North Main Building, the tallest structure downtown and one of the least interesting.

J-22

J-22   Dryve Cleaners

5180 Poplar Avenue
O.T. Marshall, architect, 1987

This is one of the wildest pieces of roadside architecture in town. Its big tent roof, a bit indebted to Frei Otto, swoops down from two masts rising from two Art Deco revival stepped pylons. The tent roof spreads out to shade the driveways on either side with such generosity that you hardly notice that the rest of the building is just a simple shed. Under the tent, on the west side, you can stop your car out of the weather and have your clothes brought out to you.

J-23   E.H. Crump Building

5350 Poplar Avenue
Gassner, Nathan and Browne, architects, 1974

This can be seen almost as a revival of the architecture of the 1950s, with particular reference to the surface of the Lever House on Park Avenue, New York. There is the same emphasis on a glass skin, stretched tightly over the whole building, with the thin metal window frames scarcely protruding at all.

J-24   Mary Galloway Home for Aged Women

5389 Poplar Avenue
Office of Walk C. Jones, Jr., architects, 1961

A modernist pendant to Jones' Sunshine Home for Aged Men in the 4300 block of Poplar (I-20). The building is placed directly on the ground, so that there are no steps to deal with. The ground-hugging character of the building is emphasized by the low segmental barrel vaults that form its main

J-24

structural elements. These recall Le Corbusier's so-called Catalan vaults on his Maisons Jaoul at Neuilly of the 1950s, or, better, on his Weekend House outside Paris of the 1930s. Le Corbusier thought of these vaulted forms as feminine, and that may have had some influence on the Jones office. The concrete frames of the bays are filled in with glass and brick. Each vault forms a room for one of the ladies, who has her own little patch of garden just outside her window. The scale here is homey, not grand. Grandeur is provided by nature, in the towering trees which surround the building.

J-25   766 South White Station Road
John Millard, architect, 1987–88

Most buildings erected to house commercial operations show about as much interest in architectural issues as Scrooge in raising Bob Cratchett's salary (and for the same reason). Millard's carefully-detailed, historicizing *ménage à trois* displays no such disinterest.

J-26   930 South White Station Road
Lindy and Associates, architects, 1987–88

This building also shows a lot of spunk for a speculative office job. A slick two-story white-and-blue triangle, it sits aggressively on its corner lot and looks expensively new. The pass-through underneath its north point is an impressive gateway, but it leads you only to a parking lot and a neighboring building that is a pastiche of almost every postmodern cliché. This is a building that implies more than it actually delivers. There is, for example, no stairway inside the big blue half-cylinder underneath the pass-through, even though the shape suggests something more than the little elevator that's there.

J-27　The Bell Building

5545 Murray Avenue
1975

This speculative office building also shows signs of architectural thought. Essentially a three-story rectangular block, it proclaims its structural system by detaching the concrete frame from the glass walls of the lower floors to create a two-story loggia around the bottom of the building. The corners make a big deal of not being supported, something a concrete frame allows a designer to do. Where the dark windows fill in the concrete frame, they seem to provide a row of giant television screens for the neighbors to look at.

J-28　Memorial Park

Poplar Avenue and Yates Road, northeast corner
Founded 1924
Dionicio Rodriguez, sculptor, 1935–41

In the center of Memorial Park is a collection of concrete sculptures by the Mexican artist Dionicio Rodriguez that constitutes one of the most remarkable groups of three-dimensional objects in the city. Rodriguez could make concrete do things that most people don't think concrete can do. Some of the works are based on biblical themes. In Rodriguez's hands, the Cave of Machpelah (see photo), where Abraham and Sarah were buried, becomes a mannerist grotto of rusticated stone, more appropriate, perhaps, to a sixteenth-century princely garden in Italy than to a biblical cave. Nearby is Abraham's Oak, a great blasted tree trunk of considerable Romantic power—the kind of trunk that nineteenth-century landscape painters such

J-28

as Thomas Cole loved to depict. Behind the oak is the Crystal Shrine Grotto, a more genuinely cavelike experience. The whole complex is reached by crossing a concrete covered bridge that masquerades as a hollow log. It is all a delightful combination of personal fantasy and extraordinary technical skill.

J-29   Audubon Park

Audubon Park was laid out in the 1950s at the behest of E.H. Crump to provide a large public space in a part of the city that was sure to experience considerable growth. While the planning can't compare with George Kessler's masterful Overton and Riverside parks, Audubon does provide a major horticultural amenity:

Goldsmith Civic Garden Center
750 Cherry Road
Eason, Anthony, McKinnie and Cox, architects, 1963

This building is a modern version of a Japanese garden pergola on a giant scale. The concrete frame of the structure is treated as if it were wood, and there is an especially open and spacious entrance pavilion. Behind the main building is a big cubic greenhouse covered with an array of metal screens that looks suspiciously like a lot of vines in a jungle, somehow trained into geometric shapes.

Behind this pavilion is a large public garden that contains, among its delights, a wildflower trail, a Japanese garden, a lavish plantation of azaleas, and particularly strong collections of irises and roses.

J-31

J-30　　Ex-Elvis Presley House

1034 Audubon Drive

Elvis lived in this house, the first he bought in Memphis, for about a year before he acquired Graceland. The house bears Elvis' mark in the brick-and-wrought-iron wall he built in front. The roundels, containing musical staffs that originally held musical notes, prefigured the famous musical gates of Graceland. The notes have long since disappeared, sold by a subsequent owner to Elvis' fans.

J-31　　Dixon Gallery and Gardens

(formerly Hugo Dixon House)
4339 Park Avenue
John F. Staub, Houston, architect, 1940
Hope Crutchfield, landscape architect
Donald Bingham, architect for additions, 1977 and 1986

Staub was a Houston architect who had a good practice designing big houses for wealthy Texans. The Dixons, who had lived in Houston before coming to Memphis, knew Staub from there and commissioned him to design their new house in Memphis. The original part of the house can be seen on the right as you go toward the main entrance to the gallery. It is a restrained classical design, with a Doric doorway under an Ionic portico, all a bit reminiscent of Belle Meade, a great antebellum house in Nashville. The central block was flanked by one-story wings, both of which have now been modified. The west wing was given a second story, and the east wing was absorbed into Bingham's first enlargement in 1977. The 1986 addition consists of the present entranceway, which leads to the main gallery spaces, and the block nearest the street, which houses an auditorium. These maintain the restrained red-brick impression of the original house.

Hugo and Margaret Dixon, who left their estate to the city, owned a small group of nineteenth-century paintings that form the core of the permanent collection of the Dixon Gallery. The furnishings of the ground floor of the house are largely intact, so that here is preserved the taste of a mid-twentieth-century cotton merchant and his wife, just as the Mallory-Neely House (C-1) preserves such tastes from an earlier era.

The really spectacular part of the estate is the gardens. They were designed by Hope Crutchfield, Dixon's sister, in a series of three parallel *allées* that stretch south from the house to join a fourth corridor cut through the native trees perpendicular to the first three. The gardens are worth a visit anytime, but especially in early- to mid-April, when the azaleas and dogwoods bloom. Then, low-lying clouds of pink and white blossoms float beneath a high, pale-green canopy of budding oaks. The swimming pool, now covered over, and the pool house were designed by George Mahan, Jr., in 1941.

J-32   Holiday Corporation Headquarters

(formerly Everett Cook House)
1023 Cherry Road
Everett Woods, architect, 1938
Jones, Mah, Gaskill and Rhodes, architects
for the addition, 1987
Francis Mah, principal designer

The retreat of corporations into suburban locations, into what have been called corporate villas, has been going on since the 1950s. The Holiday Corporation headquarters is a recent and successful addition to the list of such structures. The original building on the site is a handsome stripped-down Tudor house of the late 1930s, set into a landscape designed to look much more informal than the gardens of the Dixon House immediately to the north, although the same types of plantings are used in both. Into this ambient, which also contains a pool house and kidney-shaped pool of the 1950s, the much, much larger office building of Holiday Corporation has been placed with great sensitivity.

The big mirror-glass tail that now wags the Tudor dog is set discreetly apart from the house by a gallery, painted white like the house, that forms a transition between the two parts, separating them visually while connecting them physically. The office wing is not one huge, solid block. Rather, it is broken up into many facets that march diagonally across the grounds and down into a ravine to help conceal their bulk. The first view of the office wing from the east, as you drive up the drive, shows a set of cubes that house the offices of the vice-presidents. The mirror glass reflects the landscape, particularly beautifully in April at dogwood and azalea time, while the metal frame that holds the glass in place suggests, appropriately for the garden setting, large-scale latticework.

The offices of the most important executives are in the house, which

J-33a. From the North

also contains a collection of works of art on the theme of hospitality. The house serves as entrance to the new wing. In the office wing are paintings and sculpture collected from countries in which Holiday Corporation does business. The play of the diagonal vice-presidential offices, preceded by secretaries, against the rectangular grid of supports is particularly effective. The structural system employed by Francis Mah consists of reinforced-concrete columns that support a series of coved vaults. In the Kahnian fashion that Mah frequently adopts, the interior thus consists of a series of discrete bays that open into each other.

J-33 Harding College Graduate School of Religion, Administrative Building

(formerly Leroy King House)
1000 Cherry Road
Bryant Fleming, Ithaca, New York, architect, 1931–33

Like other out-of-town architects who worked in Memphis, Fleming didn't come in for a single job. The web of associations connecting him to rich Memphis families is still discernable. He worked in Louisville with W.J. Dodd, who designed the C. Hunter Raine house at 1560 Central. He also did work for Robert Carrier, who lived in Louisville before he came to Memphis. When Carrier moved to Memphis, he called on Fleming to design his new house at the corner of Harbert and Willett (F-81), built just a few years before King hired Fleming to do his estate in the wilds east of town. Fleming actually was a landscape architect who had expanded his work to include designing the houses that went with his gardens. This doesn't mean that he was a second-rate architect; indeed, this is the finest Georgian Revival house in the city.

It is often said that this house is based on Westover, a real eighteenth-century colonial Georgian house near Jamestown, Virginia. There are obvi-

J-33b. From the South, original state

ous similarities between the two houses, especially in the central block with its four tall chimneys in the corners. But Westover itself was based on English houses, and Fleming, not too long before he began this project, had been to England to look at houses and to collect architectural tidbits to reuse in America. Since the King house is not an exact replica of Westover, it is more reasonable to assume that Fleming based his design for the house on several real English Georgian houses, rather than on one Colonial version of Georgian architecture. In any event, the perfect symmetry of the north front of the central block ceases with the one-story wings (living room to the left, dining room to the right), which are treated differently. The stableyard area to the right of the main house sheltered no horses, but a fleet of Rolls Royces inside a brick wall with arched openings punched in it.

Fleming was a sensitive architect, aware of climate and local tradition, and so the resemblance to Georgian houses, whether in America or England, holds only for the main facade of the house. Gracious living in Memphis needed spaces different from those required in, say, Devonshire, or even along the James, and so the historicizing front gives way to a real southern house out back. Fleming knew that he had to provide a lot of spaces open to breezes but protected from the sun. The ground floor is defined by a five-bay arcade of strong brick arches that screen a porch. (Fleming wanted to site the house on a hill, but the flat terrain was uncooperative. He solved this problem by building his own hill and then cutting away the back of it to open the bottom story of the house to the southern vista.) Above this arcade a two-story porch cuts into the body of the house behind two giant columns. This porch now has been closed in, but it is easy to see how it once worked. Originally, there was scarcely a room in the house that did not have immediate access to a cooling porch, and usually a shaded one at that. One real surprise is that the house is so shallow. Originally, the front door led almost directly into a transverse entrance hall that opened, through French doors, onto the lower part of the two story south porch.

When institutions move into private houses, it usually means bad news for the house, but in this case the Harding Graduate School of Religion is to be congratulated for doing a good job of maintaining, as much as possible, the interior of the house. Especially authentic are the downstairs breakfast and dining rooms, and Mrs. King's dressing room upstairs, which has six free-standing columns of an astonishing slenderness found generally only in Roman wall-painting.

J-34

J-34   High Fashions in the Shoe

2995 Lamar Avenue
1965

This is one of Memphis' best piece of roadside architecture—almost road-side sculpture. This is truly a duck, to use Robert Venturi's word for a building that looks like what it sells. He had in mind a duck-shaped poultry market on Long Island. What better way to advertise shoes than by putting them inside a giant boot (here gunnite, not leather) with a crooked chimney on top? If there is anyone who can look at this without thinking, "There was an old woman who lived in a shoe . . . ," he or she deserves to be discalced.

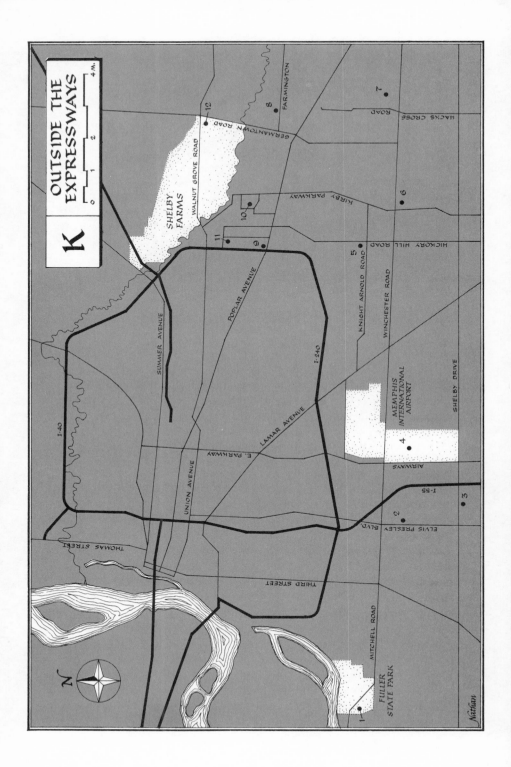

OUTSIDE THE
EXPRESSWAYS

K

0   1   2   4 w.

K   Outside the Expressways

Although the city of Memphis has spread far outside the belt of expressways that encircled it in the 1960s, the area beyond the belt is not yet rich
in architecture of quality. It also simply requires a lot of time to make
one's way from Frayser on the north to the Hickory Hill area on the south
to Chucalissa Village in the southwest. For that reason, we have chosen to
cite only those buildings that we feel are, in the language of the Michelin
guide to French restaurants, worth a detour.

K-1   Chucalissa Indian Village and Museum
1987 Indian Village Drive, off Mitchell Road
Clark Jones and Harold Thompson,
architects of the museum, 1968

When the Spanish explorer, Hernando de Soto, came to the banks of the
Mississippi River in the early sixteenth century, he found the area inhab-
ited by native Americans who had been there for many centuries. Around
1500, these people lived in villages like Chucalissa, which has been exca-
vated and partly reconstructed by anthropologists from Memphis State
University. Settlement at this site seems to date back to c. 1000 A.D., but
de Soto would not have seen Chucalissa, for it had been abandoned a bit
before he arrived. Like all the other villages in the area, Chucalissa was
centered on a rectangular open area dominated by earth mounds. The
largest mound, to the north, was the one on which the temple and the
ruler's house were erected. (A similar mound can be found inside the city
limits in De Soto Park.) Around the square are lower rectangular mounds
on which important members of the community had their houses. Others
lived in houses outside this regularly planned center. Their livelihood, in
part, came from farming the rich floodplain of the Mississippi located just
below the bluff on which the village stood. The floodplain has now grown
a giant TVA steam plant.

The reconstructed houses offer us a good sense of the early architecture
of the Memphis area. Posts were driven into the ground on a square or
rectangular plan and connected by cane mats plastered with mud and grass
to form walls. Across the posts, horizontal logs were laid, and from these
rose the rafters of the roof, which was covered with thatch that hung down
close to the ground to protect the mud walls from the weather. The resulting silhouette, as we see it in the reconstructions, is imposing, and the

K-1

combination of the cubic base and the pyramidal roof, softened by the curved edges of the thatch, produces a visually satisfying form that carries a clear message of shelter. The house of the chief, atop the largest mound, was by far the most imposing. Because it was much larger, it had not only an outer wall of posts and mud-covered mats, but also an inner group of posts that were necessary to support the much greater span of the roof rafters. The result was a kind of house within a house, not entirely unlike the configuration of the megaron of a Mycenaean palace, which had a square plan with four columns placed in a smaller square toward the center to support the ceiling.

The village is entered through a small museum which, in the battered shape of its exterior walls, recalls the shape of the great mound of the chief's house. Inside there is a modest exhibition that explains life in the area at the time Chucalissa flourished. Chucalissa brings into focus the fact that the great cities we now know along the Mississippi replaced other settlements, built by another civilization whose memory the new cities have almost totally erased.

K-2 Graceland

(formerly Dr. Thomas D. Moore House)
3797 Elvis Presley Boulevard
Furbringer and Ehrman, architects, 1939
Purchased by Elvis Presley, 1957

The name Graceland is an old one, first given in the nineteenth century to a house belonging to the Toof family that occupied the site. That house was replaced in the 1930s by the present one, but the name continued. It goes on today not only in the house, but also in the title of a Paul Simon album. One wonders what the nineteenth-century lady called Grace, whose name started it all, would think of what her name means now.

Elvis chose to buy a house that deliberately copied the early-nine-

K-2

teenth-century architecture of the Middle South. In so doing, he bought himself a bit of southern history, even southern mythology, complete with the white columns of a plantation house. To a young man who was born in a shotgun in Tupelo, Mississippi, and who first lived in Memphis in the Lauderdale Courts public housing project, Graceland must have seemed a special place. He had achieved the ultimate southern domestic status symbol.

To protect himself from his fans, Elvis erected the ten foot wall that surrounds the house and its grounds, and he installed the famous wrought-iron gates with guitars to guard the driveway. Visitors to Graceland now pass through these gates in small buses that carry them from the ticket office across the street right up to the white columns of the stone house itself. At the porch, a tour guide, one of many you encounter on this visit, ushers you into the house for the beginning of the tour.

Inside, the house is pretty much as Elvis left it, although there are said to have been some changes in appointments. The interior is closed in; the drapes and blinds are drawn against the world. The walls are covered with "antiqued" mirrors that reflect, through a dark golden haze, the life inside and turn that life back on itself. Despite their fancy decor, the playroom and pool room in the basement feel even more closed in, even more bunker-like. The outside world came into Graceland only through the television sets that Elvis put in every room. He watched these sets constantly, we are told.

The decor in the main rooms on the first floor might be called Louis V, as in Vegas, rather than Louis XV or Louis XVI. But the precise period is beside the point. The great crystal chandeliers and the gold and white of the walls and furniture are opulent; they suggest the lives of aristocrats of ages past and the newly rich of today. Those were the lives that Elvis, in his own way, wanted to rival or emulate.

The most startling room in the house is the den out back, sometimes known as the Jungle Room, which Elvis furnished with neo-Polynesian furniture of staggering proportions. The largest chair is so big that a window had to be taken out to get it inside. The fantasy here is different from the fantasy of the front rooms. There, the elegant life of the French aristocracy of the late eighteenth century is recalled and indeed reconstructed for Elvis on his own terms. Here the fabled languid leisure of the South Seas is summoned up for Elvis to relax in, again on his own terms. Ultimately, there is little difference between the historical and geographical fantasies that Elvis created for himself at Graceland and the Spanish fantasies that George Mahan created in midtown for his clients in the early twenties, or the Colonial fantasies of Lucian Minor Dent in the forties and fifties. Elvis simply subscribed to the notion, hardly restricted to Memphis, that a man's home should suggest some place other than where it is and some time other than the present.

The trophy room, in a separate building, is one of the most moving experiences of the Graceland tour. All of the gold and platinum records hung on dark-blue walls suggest a dim chapel in an Italian church where hundreds of the faithful have hung silver hearts as thank offerings to a benign Virgin Mary. This is a reliquary space, and even a devotional space. You leave it with a sure sense of the achievements of the man memorialized.

Outside in the garden at the south side of the house, Elvis, his parents, and other family members are buried radially in a semicircle. We walk around them, elevated on curved steps that suggest ancient theater seats, to become the audience at this final theatrical event in which Elvis continues to play a part. Like a hero in a Greek tragedy, he was a good man brought down by circumstances and by his own weaknesses.

After the graves, you have to get back on the bus, with its wired music, and go back across the street to the tackiness that surrounds the commercialization of Graceland. There is much of significance to learn about American life and culture from studying the way Elvis chose to live. The way his memory is merchandised across the street may also suggest, if only indirectly, some of the reasons for his fall.

K-3   Broadway Baptist Church
1574 East Shelby Drive
Nowland Van Powell, architect, 1966

The residential areas south of the expressway are full of churches. A few of them, such as Nowland Van Powell's Broadway Baptist, are buildings worth making a trip to see. It is Powell's most powerful church, with a massiveness of wall rarely encountered in his work. The brick piers of the porch carry segmental arches that accentuate the broad proportions of the church behind. Inside, thick piers, painted white, support similar arches that move down the nave with dignity. To the west of the church, the subsidiary buildings stretch out to end in a chapel that mimics the church in a minor key and suggests that the church has spawned an offspring.

K-4   Memphis International Airport
Mann and Harrover, architects, 1959–63

Memphis International Airport is one of the architectural success stories of the city. Planned before many of the great American airports we now use were conceived, Memphis continues to provide an entrance and exit for the city that combines dignity with a sense of the joy of travel—or at

K-3

K-4

least travel as it used to be before our air system reached its current state. The architects wanted to give us a sense of a safe haven and a prelude to flight. They did not want to emulate what they viewed as the excessive imagery of Eero Saarinen's TWA terminal at Kennedy. They wanted something a little more conservative and classical, yet something lofty and airy, with at least one great space. They achieved what they wanted.

The central part of the present terminal was built first, but the wings were included in the original plans in order to provide for orderly expansion. The lower story is a big brick podium, sitting firmly on the ground, that supports the glazed two-story upper concourse. There the structural system consists of reinforced concrete piers that mark the corners of bays forty by forty-four feet. Each pier supports a forty-foot-square "umbrella" that is independent of its neighboring "umbrellas." These forms are reinforced concrete hyperbolic paraboloids that gain sufficient strength through their curvature to be reduced to a thickness of five inches. They were cheap to build, and they provide, according to the architects, the effect of a great porch that they wanted. Saarinen himself, for Dulles International Airport outside Washington, designed a similarly porch-like air terminal only two years later.

The terminal building is equally effective at night; concealed lights at the tops of the piers wash over the undersides of the vaults to create glowing white planes that hover over the dark, flat landscape of the airport. For the airport, Mann and Harrover won a *Progressive Architecture* award in 1961. Tragically, Mann died of cancer while the project was still in the design stage. He was only in his late thirties.

K-5   Church of the Holy Apostles

3185 Hickory Hill Road
Taylor and Crump, architects, 1973

From the outside, this church doesn't look like a church in standard Memphis terms. The primary view from Hickory Hill Road is dominated as much by the serrated silhouette of the three north-facing monitors that light the school building as by the taller bulk of the church proper to the south. One might take this to be a wooden-clad industrial building that somehow made its way into a residential quarter. On the other hand, the scale is right for the neighborhood, and the board-and-batten siding gives it a small-scale, humane texture.

Inside, the church is all white walls rising up to a complicated wooden truss that supports the shed roof and the long, narrow monitor that rises over the center of the nave. In an industrial building, this monitor would have had windows all around its rising walls, but here the openings are skylights that give a direct view into heaven, if you will. The quality of the light, falling through the skylights and throwing shadows from the trusses on the walls, is probably the nicest characteristic of this interior,

K-5

which, with seemly modesty, never tries to be anything more than it is. For its abstinence from rhetoric, fancy architectural tricks, and the architectural clichés of its day, this church deserves several good words. Holy Apostles fits splendidly the description a great architectural historian once coined to describe early churches of the Franciscans and Dominicans in Italy—preaching barns. It has something of their ascetic quality.

K-6 Central Church

6655 Winchester Road
Thomas Gregory of Ingram, Paires, Gregory, Architects, Valdosta, Georgia, architect, 1981

Centrally-planned Central Church has the biggest interior space of any church in the city, some 450 feet in diameter. It seats 4,200, and if more pews were to be added, the capacity could be raised to 6,000. The church stands isolated in a large plot of ground, surrounded by parking lots. There is no single front door. Churchgoers can enter the building by numerous doors that ring the structure and go directly to their seats in the sanctuary. This plan accommodates the way the modern suburban faithful arrive in automobiles for services. The sanctuary itself is surrounded by a two-story ring of corridors, called by church officials "the Mall," a revealing choice

K-6

of words. What else should the contemporary suburbanite enter from a huge parking lot? The Mall not only offers access to the church but also provides space for offices, gathering spots, and classrooms. The Mall is broken up visually by the pools of light entering from skylights and from staircases that provide access to the enormous interior balcony.

The sanctuary is polygonal rather than round, but there are so many sides that it is hard to tell the difference. From one side of the polygon, the choir projects into the space and pushes out the speaker's platform so that the lectern stands directly under the center of the dome, where it is almost totally surrounded by the seats. Above, in the dome, an oculus admits the light of day, symbolically the Light of God, directly over the speaker. Otherwise, the interior is lit by large windows in the outer walls. The vault is ribbed, so that you can see where the major and minor structural elements are located.

Unfortunately, this relatively clear expression of the structure inside is not carried through in the rest of the church. From the outside, you get no sense of what holds the building up. Flat exterior walls, of no apparent strength, rise up to a curved roof with thin ribs that lead to a central crown. These visually slight elements tell us all too little about the actual structural forces at work. An opportunity for a building as visually exciting as it is huge unfortunately was missed.

K-7 Southwind

Players Club and Tournament Drives, off Hack's Cross Road
1987 ff.

This is probably the priciest new residential development in the city's
history. The golf course setting, the *raison d'etre* for the development, is
splendid. Many houses have direct views of greens where great golf players
one day will compete in nationally-televised tournaments. Southwind
offers opportunities for building houses of high architectural quality, because the owners have to have the means to afford them. A tour of these
houses, however, reveals that high quality has not yet been achieved. The
houses that use elements of the classical tradition use those elements
poorly. Proportions are wrong, massing is incoherent, and ideas that come
from great European country houses are squeezed onto lots too small to
hold them. Perhaps most egregious in its wrongheadedness is the Pi Kappa
Alpha Fraternity Headquarters, 8347 West Range Cove (Byron Carson,
architect, 1988), because it so thoroughly trashes a noble prototype, Thomas Jefferson's Monticello. Monticello was deliberately chosen as the
prototype here, because the fraternity was started at the University of
Virginia, which, of course, Jefferson founded. So far, not one house has
been built that we feel we can admire for architectural excellence. Instead,
we see Southwind as a cautionary tale, instructive of the fact that although great architecture often requires money, money alone never as-
sures great (or even good) architecture.

K-8 Germantown Post Office

7776 Farmington Avenue, Germantown
Gassner, Nathan and Partners, architects, 1977

Germantown has grown from a sleepy village dotted with horse farms into
what some suburbanites consider the true social, cultural and economic
center of the Memphis metropolitan area. You hear tales of Germantown-
ers who rarely venture west of the expressway and have never been downtown. In its new community center, which includes a town hall and a fire
station, Germantown has a building of considerable quality, the U.S. Post
Office. The building faces its parking lot with a row of slender brick piers
that support a lacy steel truss system, painted white. The piers and the
roof form a portico that offers shelter before you enter the post office
proper. The walls at ground level are made of mirror glass, and the walls
up inside the trusses are clear glass. The mirrors reflect the trusses, and
the clear glass lets us see the continuation of the trusses inside, all in a
way that delightfully confounds our sense of where we are, or what we are
looking at. Inside, the truss system provides a large, lofty, open space subdivided into two parts, a smaller window area and a larger box area. The

K-8

trusses continue on the north, through a glass clerestory, to hold up the lower roof of the work area behind the public space. The whole is handled with a clarity and directness, and yet with a playfulness, that are exemplary.

K-9   Omni Hotel,

(formerly Hyatt Regency Hotel)
Hyatt Ridgeway Parkway and Ridge Lake Boulevard
Walk Jones and Francis Mah, architects, 1974

The Omni sits on the southwest corner of a large tract of land that was once the golf course of the Ridgeway Country Club. With the opening of the intersection of I-240 and Poplar, the land became too valuable for mere sport. Thus the construction, in the mid-1970s, of a complex of office buildings, all by Jones and Mah, for which the Omni is the landmark tower. A pure mirror-glass cylinder attached to a rectangular elevator tower, the hotel rises from a reflecting pool bordered by a terraced garden. The entrance, on the west side, is a bit hard to find. From this vantage point, the tower rises behind a series of concrete terraces that curve toward it. Inside, the space under these terraces is shaped like a fan, with the

K-9

roof above split into fan sections, each raised above the other to allow daylight to pour into the interior. The outer rim of the fan is a corridor, surrounding a bar that tapers down to the great post that is the common support for all the planes of the roof. The corridor sweeps around to enter a low, square area with skylights and a fountain, a complete architectural change of pace that in turn leads to the darker square area of the reception desk. Here mirrors on the ceiling replay the skylights of the adjoining room in a minor key. From the desk area one goes to the elevator lobby, which is connected by a glass bridge to the tower. The bridge offers the chance to watch the waters of the reflecting pool simultaneously reflect off the walls of the tower and reflect the reflective tower. The glass elevators open your view to the surrounding landscape as you go up to your room, thus providing the final panorama in this clever promenade of changing spaces and perceptions. There are variations on several John Portman themes here, but the variations are played very well.

K-10

K-10   Temple Israel

376 East Massey Lane
Gassner, Nathan and Partners, architects, 1976

With regret, the members of Temple Israel abandoned their great Jones and Furbringer building on Poplar for a new suburban location, closer to where they now live. They acquired the Raymond Firestone estate, and into that parklike setting they settled their new synagogue. To protect the beauty of the site, even the parking lots are terraced and provided with trees in regular intervals between the parking spaces. The building itself is a very large brick structure with three major parts—the sanctuary, the entrance area, and the office and school block. The sanctuary, semicircular in plan, forms one end of the building, showing on the outside a large, flat wall topped by a roof that is half an inverted cone. The forms are strong.

The entrance porch offers a considerable surprise. The flat porch roof that runs along the driveway seems totally detached from the wall of the building far behind it. Only after you pass under the porch do you realize that it is attached to the building by an enormous sloping glass plane that protects you from rain but allows light to flood the entrance area in such abundance that at first you think you are still outside. The whole is strongly reminiscent of the same architects' Boatmen's Bank Building (A-104) downtown, with its entrance conservatory under a steeply sloping glass roof. In both buildings, the gesture is dramatic.

K-11   River Oaks Subdivision

River Oaks was the first large, truly upscale subdivision laid out in Memphis since the 1920s, when Chickasaw Gardens and Red Acres were planned. It has all of the faults of Southwind without the advantage of the golf course, but with the advantage of beautifully rolling land into which the streets were sensitively set. Unfortunately, that sensitivity was not matched in the architecture of most of the houses that have been built there. We suggest a treasure hunt for architectural *faux pas* while you visit River Oaks. Which street might be called the Street of the Two Gaping Maws? Which house has columns that look as if they had been stretched on the rack and then strangled at their necking? Which house has the engorged, or blow-fish, frieze? Which house is most aptly labeled "French Pretential"? Which house is so ill-suited to its steeply sloped lot that in the rear it has enormous French windows looking out on a tall retaining wall only a few feet away? There is, however, one fine house in River Oaks:

Dr. Randolph McCloy House

5842 Garden River Cove
Oscar Menzer, architect, 1984

Menzer designed a Louisiana plantation house (see photo K-11), usually found on flat land near water, that fits its sloping site beautifully, because the requisite staircases in the front rise here to reach the main floor, which lies at the level of the ground in the back. The driveway opens up the vista of the house and introduces the curves taken up in the staircase. The proportions and the details are right; there are no lapses here. Even the fact that the house is essentially asymmetrical inside has been concealed by putting the outward signs of that asymmetry toward the back, where they cannot interfere with the power and conviction of the image of the house in the front. Menzer put the garage in back too, where it ought to be, instead of out front, as it is in some neighboring houses where the desire to show off the exhaust pipes of the Mercedes overcame any impulse there may have been to embellish this street with a graceful facade.

K-11

K-12   Agricenter

7777 Walnut Grove Road
Rudolph Jones, Jr., architect, 1986
Edward Wheeler, associate architect

East of I-240 Walnut Grove Road leads out into Shelby Farms, an open area
once given over to the Shelby County Penal Farm, a correctional institution that put prisoners to the labor of farming. Now Shelby Farms, planned
by Garrett Eckbo and Associates of San Francisco, is being given over to
recreational purposes and to experimental agricultural endeavors. The
architectural focus of the latter is Agricenter, a powerful steel-and-glass
building that is one of the most exciting structures built in Memphis in
recent years.

Agricenter has many functions, one of the principal being exhibitions
relating to agriculture, and it is the exhibition space that forms the core
and provides the dominant shapes of the building. The center of the complex is an enormous metal roof, held up on large steel trusses, that forms
two sides of a four-sided pyramid; the other sides are open. With its monitor projecting from the top, this roof suggests a host of different types of
farm buildings, blown up to gigantic scale. Under this open roof is a second, smaller pyramid, made of glass, that has been rotated forty-five de-
grees in relation to the larger one. The smaller seems to be a jewel protected by the bigger, whose metal roof is an umbrella that shades the glass
pyramid from the sun. Under the glass pyramid, one floor below grade, is
the main exhibition space. As you approach these pyramids from the parking lot to the north, a low wall moves away to the left in a gradual curve
that betrays the presence of an auditorium behind it. To the right, the
corresponding wall is straight, with jagged chunks cut out of it to let light
into offices. This play of opposites is held together by the geometric
strength and huge scale of the pyramids in the middle.

K-12a

K-12b

From the south, the appearance of the building changes considerably. The tall metal roof is still there, but the lower pyramid has a metal roof on this side, painted orange to make a strong contrast. (The lower, orange roof is there to keep the southern sun from overheating the inside.) There is a splendid play of transparent and opaque forms in this smaller pyramid. On the south, the roof is solid metal, while the walls are glass. On the north, the roof is glass, but the walls, below grade, are solid.

Inside there are equally wonderful surprises. From the exhibition floor you look through transparent planes at the skeletal forms of the structure and the shadows those forms cast. The four corner piers that support the large pyramid are hollow towers, with staircases inside crowned by pyramidal ceilings.

Somewhere back of all this stand the changing-rooms of Louis Kahn's bathhouse at the Trenton, New Jersey, Jewish Community Center of the mid-1950s. The structure is basically the same: four hollow piers that contain circulation spaces and hold up a pyramidal roof. But Kahn's idea has been so enlarged and so transformed through the use of fragmentation, rotation, transparencies, and opacities; through the use of the imagery of farm structures; through a careful study of Russian Constructivist architecture and the early works of James Stirling; and through shifts in scale and materials, that this powerful architectural statement only remotely depends on the original prototype. Here Shelby County has turned its attention to its agricultural origins with a thoroughly up-to-date building that, like modern agriculture, combines tradition and innovation. Architecturally, this is a much more interesting essay in pyramid-building than The Pyramid promised to rise downtown on the river.

Glossary of
Architectural Terms

Abacus A block set at the top of the capital of a column under the architrave.

Acroterion On classical buildings, a statue or other ornament placed at one of the angles of a pediment.

Adamesque In the style of Robert Adam, an English architect of the second half of the eighteenth century.

Airplane Bungalow. See **Bungalow.**

Aisle A lateral subdivision of a church or other building, divided longitudinally from the main part by rows of columns or piers.

Antefix In classical architecture, an ornament at the eaves.

Anta The thickening of the end of a lateral wall in a Greek temple. **In Antis**, inside the antae, or between the ends of the lateral walls of a temple.

Apse A projecting part of a building, especially of a church, usually semicircular or polygonal in plan and covered by a half dome.

Arcade A series of arches and the columns or piers which support them, either freestanding or attached to a wall.

Architrave In classical architecture, the lowest division of an entablature, or that part which rests immediately on the column.

Art Deco A fashionable style of design of the 1920s and 1930s based on stylized, abstract, geometric shapes, often representing humans or flora or fauna.

Ashlar Hewn or squared stones; also, masonry of hewn or squared stones.

Balustrade A row of short pillars, or balusters, topped by a handrail and serving as an open parapet, as along the edge of a balcony, terrace, or staircase.

Bargeboards Projecting boards placed against the slope of a gable under a roof to hide the ends of the horizontal roof timbers. Bargeboards are a popular place for carpenter decorations.

Barrel Vault A continuous arched structure with a semicircular or pointed section. The top of a rural mailbox is a good example of a barrel vault.

Bas Relief Literally, low relief, in which figures are only slightly raised above the background.

Base The lowest element of a column.

Basilica An oblong building, typically with a broad nave flanked by colonnaded aisles and sometimes by galleries, often terminated in an apse. A building type of Roman origin, utilized in Early Christian church construction.

Batten   A strip of sawed timber used for covering the joints between wider wood planks.

Battered Wall   A wall sloping inward toward the top.

Bay   A clear subdivision of an architectural space or of a wall, marked off by orders, windows, buttresses, vaults, etc.

Beaux-Arts   Artistic style named after the École des Beaux Arts, the chief official art school of France from the late eighteenth through the early twentieth century. Works produced in this style generally were in a classical vein.

Berm   A narrow, sloping shelf, often made of earth.

Blind Arch   Arch with no opening, so that neither light nor passage is possible. Usually attached to a wall as decoration.

Blind Window   Window with no opening for light.

Boss   A projecting block or mass, as an ornamental block used at the intersection of the ribs in Gothic vaulting.

Bracket   A projection from a wall or pier to support an overhanging weight.

Bull's-Eye Window   A circular or oval window.

Bungalow   In the United States, a small house of a single story, usually made of "natural" materials such as wood, stone, brick and stucco, surrounded by porches and covered by low roofs with deeply projecting eaves. Its plan features an interpenetration of interior and exterior space. In Memphis, after c. 1910, the bungalow became the most popular form of middle-class housing. It reflected a desire for informality in living. An **Airplane Bungalow** is a variant with two porch "wings" in the front and a small second story, generally placed toward the rear, that forms the "tail."

Buttress   A projecting structure, generally of masonry, to support or stabilize a wall or vault.

Cantilever   A projecting beam or member supported only at one end.

Capital   The head or crowning member on a column or pier.

Cartouche   A scroll shaped ornament with curling edges; any tablet of ornamental form.

Castellated   Decorated with crenellations.

Cavetto Cornice   A concavely curved cornice typically found in ancient Egyptian architecture.

Chamfer   To cut off a corner, to bevel; to cut a furrow in, as in a column; to groove; to flute.

Chancel   The part of a church, often separated from the rest, reserved for the clergy. In it the altar or communion table is placed.

Chevron Pattern   An ornament consisting of two broad bands meeting in a V-shaped pattern.

Chicago Window A three-part window consisting of a large plate glass window in the center, flanked by two narrower double-hung windows. The Chicago window was designed to fill one bay of a steel-frame building.

Clapboards Long, thin boards, overlapped horizontally to form an exterior surface on a building.

Clerestory In church architecture, the upper part of a wall containing windows.

Coffer A panel recessed in a ceiling.

Colonnade A series or range of columns placed at regular intervals.

Colonnette A small decorative column.

Colossal Order An order of columns or pilasters that rises through more than one story.

Column In classical architecture, an upright supporting member, usually circular in plan, that consists of three parts: the base, the shaft, and the capital.

Composite Order In classical architecture, a Roman order that superimposes Ionic volutes on a Corinthian capital covered with acanthus leaves.

Console An ornamental element, having a compound curved outline, that supports a projecting weight. Also, sometimes the decorative element applied to the keystone of an arch.

Cor-Ten Steel A high-strength, low-alloy steel that does not need to be protected by paint or other substances because it forms its own protective coating of rust on the surface.

Corbel A bracket projecting from the face of a wall to support a weight above it.

Corbusian In the style of Le Corbusier, a leading twentieth-century architect and proponent of Modernism.

Corinthian Order The most ornate of the Greek orders. Its capital is bell-shaped and enveloped in acanthus leaves, and the shaft is fluted.

Corner Block Any stone that forms a corner or angle of a building.

Cornice A horizontal member which crowns a wall or other vertical surface. Also, the uppermost member of a classical entablature.

Corona The projecting part of a classical cornice.

Crenellation A notched parapet, consisting of alternating solids and voids, on the top of a fortified building.

Cupola A small, generally domed structure, on a circular or polygonal base, that crowns a roof or turret.

Curtain Wall A nonstructural wall used, generally, in buildings of steel or reinforced-concrete construction.

Dentil A small rectangular block in a series projecting like teeth under a cornice or forming a molding.

Depressed Arch An arch whose curve has been flattened.

Diaper Pattern A diamond-shaped overall surface pattern.

Diaphragm Arch   A transverse arch that does not form part of a vault but divides one part of a space from another.

Doric Order   The simplest of the classical orders. The Greek Doric has a slightly convex, fluted column shaft, no base, and a capital with the echinus, curved in profile, supporting a square, undecorated abacus. The Roman Doric has a base. Both orders have an entablature in which triglyphs and metopes alternate in the frieze.

Dormer Window   A window with its own gable set into the slope of a roof.

Double-Hung Window   A window consisting of two vertically-sliding parts, or sashes.

Dovecote   A small house having compartments for domestic doves and pigeons.

Drip Molding   A molding which projects beyond a window or door to protect it from rain running down the wall.

Egg-and-Dart Molding   A classical molding with egg-shaped ornaments that alternate with others in the form of darts, or tongues.

Ell   An addition to a house, usually set at right angles to the original structure.

Engaged Column   A column partly embedded in, or bonded to, a wall or pier.

Entablature   In classical architecture, the horizontal element resting on the capitals and, at the gable end of a building, supporting the pediment. It is divided into three parts: architrave, frieze, and cornice.

Entasis   A slight convexity of the shaft of a column.

Eyebrow Ventilator   A low, ventilating dormer over which the roof is carried in a wave-like line that looks something like an eyebrow.

Facade   The face or front of a building.

Fanlight   A semicircular window, with radiating sash bars like the ribs of a fan, generally placed over a door or window.

Fasces   A bundle of rods, holding an axe with the blade projecting, carried before Roman magistrates as a symbol of authority.

Finial   The knot, bunch of foliage, or other ornament that forms the upper extremity of a pinnacle, canopy, gable, or the like. A terminating ornament.

Fluting   Incised parallel grooves of curved section in a column or pilaster shaft.

Foursquare   A popular early-twentieth-century house type. In its simplest form, it is a two-story cube topped by a pyramidal roof. Generally, there is a porch on the front and along one side. The plan usually consists of four rooms downstairs and four rooms upstairs.

Frieze   In classical architecture, the middle division of the entablature. Also, a horizontal decorative band on a building.

Gable   The triangular upper portion of a wall under the end of a pitched roof.

Gambrel Roof A four-part, ridged roof, with the two lower parts steeper and the upper flatter. Barns often have gambrel roofs.

Golden Section A proportion in which a straight line or rectangle is divided into two unequal parts so that the ratio of the smaller part to the greater part is the same as that of the greater to the whole. Expressed numerically, the ratio is 1 to 1.618, or roughly 3 to 5. A 3x5-inch note card gives a good approximation of a Golden Section ratio. Since antiquity the Golden Section has been thought to possess inherent aesthetic value, and it is frequently used in classicizing architecture.

Greek Cross A cross with all four arms of equal length.

Groin Vault A vault formed by the intersection, at right angles, of two barrel vaults. The groins are the lines of the intersections of the barrels.

Gunnite A form of concrete sprayed over a support of wire mesh.

Guttae A series of peg-like ornaments hanging below the triglyphs in a Doric entablature.

Half-Timbering An exposed timber frame with the spaces between filled with brick, plaster, or other material. In modern domestic architecture, the half-timbering is always decorative rather than structural.

Hammer-Beam Ceiling A ceiling supported by short horizontal beams or cantilevers projecting from the tops of a pair of opposite walls, especially in Gothic buildings.

Herm A stone pillar, tapering toward the ground and surmounted by a head or torso.

Horseshoe Arch An arch with the shape of a horseshoe.

I-Beam A rolled-steel beam with a section shaped like the letter "I." For construction, it has a very advantageous strength-to-weight ratio.

Ionic Order A classical order distinguished by paired spiral volutes on the front and rear of its capital. The shaft, rising from a base, is fluted, and the frieze of the entablature is continuous, rather than interrupted as in the Doric.

Jacobean A style of architecture and decoration prevailing in England in the early part of the seventeenth century, during the reign of James I. Jacobean gables are scrolled, or composed of curves.

Keystone The voussoir at the center or crown of an arch, which, being the last set in place, binds the arch together and makes it self-supporting. Keystones are often decorated.

Lintel A horizontal member, carried on posts or walls, that spans an opening. In classical architecture, the entablature is the lintel carried by the posts of the columns.

Loggia A roofed gallery or passage open to the outdoors through one or more arcades or colonnades.

Lunette A semicircular or crescent-shaped opening or surface.

Machicolations Projecting arches or brackets near the top of a wall that carry a parapet.

Mansard Roof A roof with two slopes, the lower being much steeper than the upper. Popular in French architecture from the seventeenth century on, and in late Victorian architecture in the United States.

Marquee   A canopy extended from a building.

Masonry   In general, any construction using bricks or stones set in mortar.

Meander   A decorative pattern of angular, interlaced lines.

Megaron   The great central hall of a Mycenaean house, in the center of which four columns surrounded a circular, open hearth.

Metope   The space, generally square in shape, between two triglyphs of the Doric frieze, often adorned with relief sculpture.

Mezzanine   A low story between two high ones, especially between the ground floor and the story above.

Mission Style   Architecture based on the architecture of the Spanish Colonial missions in North America, particularly California.

Modillion   The ornamental bracket generally found in series under a cornice of the Ionic, Corinthian, and Composite orders.

Molding   Strip of wood, stone, metal, or other material used to cover a joint, or for decoration.

Monitor   A raised central portion of a roof, generally with low windows along its side or sides.

Narthex   A transverse hall preceding the nave, or main space, of a church.

Nave   The main, central space of a church. In a cross-shaped church, the nave is the space between the front door and the point at which the transept intersects.

Niche   A recess in a wall.

Obelisk   An upright four-sided pillar, gradually tapering as it rises, and terminating in a pyramid. Usually made of one block of stone.

Oculus   A round window or opening.

Ogee Arch   A pointed arch having on each side a reversed curve, or ogee, near the top.

Orders   In classical architecture, systems of interdependent parts that are carefully proportioned, so that a change in the sizes of one part necessitates a change in the size of all the others. Generally, an order consists of the base, the shaft, the capital, and the entablature. The ancient Greeks had three orders, the Doric, Ionic and Corinthian. To these the Romans added the Tuscan and the Composite, as well as their own version of the Doric.

Palladian   A classical architectural style based on the works of Andrea Palladio, a North Italian architect of the second half of the sixteenth century.

Palladian Window   A three-part window, with the side lights topped by horizontal elements and the central light capped by a round arch that rises above the sides.

Palmette   Architectural ornament with narrow divisions that form the shape of a stylized palm leaf.

Parapet   A low wall or similar barrier placed as a protection where there is a sudden dropoff.

Pediment   In classical architecture the low triangular space formed under the sloping planes of the roof. Also, a similar form used over doors, windows, porticos, etc., sometimes triangular and sometimes segmental, that is, in the shape of a segment of a circle.

Pendentive   A curved triangular vault which springs from the corners of a square or polygonal plan to support a circular element, such as a dome. In terms of solid geometry, pendentives are spherical triangles.

Pergola   An arbor or trellis treated architecturally.

Peristyle   In classical architecture, a colonnade surrounding a temple, court, or other structure.

Permastone   A trade name for a popular brand of artificial stone.

Pier   A pillar, that is, a vertical, solid masonry support for an arch or lintel.

Pilaster   A vertical architectural member, projecting slightly from a wall surface and treated like a column, with capital, shaft, and base.

Piloti   A post or stilt used in modern architecture to raise the bottom story above the ground, thus leaving the ground beneath the building free.

Pointed Arch   An arch formed by two segments of a circle intersecting to form a point.

Pop Art   An artistic movement of the 1960s that used the imagery of consumerism and popular culture.

Porte-Cochère   A covered space for vehicles, which allows passengers to enter or leave a building out of the weather.

Portico   A porch with a roof supported by a colonnade.

Pylon   In Egyptian architecture, the great gateway to a temple, with sloping or battered walls on each side of the door. Also, a large, freestanding, monumental form.

Quoin   A piece of material, often stone, by which the corner of a building is marked. Quoins are often laid so that they alternate in size between long and short.

Reinforced Concrete   Concrete with steel rods placed inside it to provide the tensile strength that concrete by itself lacks.

Reredos   A decorated screen or partition wall placed behind an altar.

Reveal   The side of a window opening or doorway between the glass or the door and the outer surface of the wall; or, where the opening is not filled with a window or door, the whole thickness of the wall.

Richardsonian Romanesque   In the round-arched style of H.H. Richardson, a late-nineteenth-century American architect.

Rinceau   Foliate ornament with sinuous, branching scrolls, elaborated with curving leaves and plants.

Roman Brick   A brick that is longer and thinner than the standard modern 2x4x8-inch brick.

Romanesque   The architectural style which developed in Western Europe in the eleventh and early twelfth centuries. Romanesque architecture has a heavy feeling of masonry, and frequently it makes use of round arches, barrel and groin vaults, and small windows.

Rosette   A sculpted circular ornament with an arrangement of parts resembling a rose.

Round Arch   An arch whose curve forms half of a circle.

Roundel   A small, circular panel, niche, or window.

Rustication   Roughly-finished masonry laid with deep joints, to give a rough-hewn, boldly-textured effect.

Sash Window   A window formed from sliding glazed frames which run in vertical grooves.

Sawtooth Frieze   A horizontal band of bricks set diagonally on their sides to make an ornamental pattern resembling the teeth of a saw. Also called a Dogtooth Frieze.

Scrolled Gable   A gable whose sloping sides are formed of curled volutes.

Segmental Arch   An arch that forms a curve less than half of a circle.

Shaft   The vertical element of a column, between the base and the capital.

Shingle Style   An American style, primarily developed in domestic architecture in the late nineteenth century, that makes extensive use of unpainted wood shingles on both roof and walls. Shingle Style houses are often asymmetrical and endowed with ample porches.

Shotgun   A house type that is one room wide, two or more rooms deep, with a porch on one of the gable ends.

Skeletal Construction   A method of construction using a self-supporting iron or steel framework and an outer covering that bears no weight. Skeletal construction forms the basis of modern skyscraper design.

Soffit   The finished underside of a lintel, arch, or other spanning member.

Spandrel   The triangular surface defined by the side of an arch, a horizontal line drawn from its apex, and a vertical line drawn from the point of its springing. Also, the surface area between two arches, or the surface between two ribs of a vault.

Steel-Frame Construction.   See **Skeletal Construction**.

Stringcourse   A horizontal band in a building.

Strip Window   A window or series of windows forming a horizontal strip across the facade of a building.

Stylobate   In a Greek temple, the top step of the base from which the columns rise. Also, the raised platform on which a classical building is built.

Swag   A kind of ornamental festoon, draped in a curve between two points.

Tempietto   Literally, a small temple, sometimes round, as in the Tempietto of San Pietro in Montorio, Rome, by Bramante.

Terra Cotta   Literally, cooked earth. A fired, unglazed clay, brownish red or yellowish red in color, used for architectural reliefs, sculptures, etc. Terra cotta may also be glazed with various colors. Flowerpots are made of terra cotta.

Terrazzo   A floor surface consisting of marble chips embedded in cement. The surface is ground and polished after the cement has set.

Tracery   Decorative stonework set in window openings in Gothic architecture; similar ornament applied to architectural or other surfaces.

Transept   In a cross-shaped church, the transverse part that crosses the nave at right angles.

Transom   A horizontal crossbar in a window, over a door, or between a door and a window above it; hence, a window above a door or other window, built on and commonly hinged to a transom.

Travertine   A relatively low-quality marble, yellowish tan in color and filled with holes, that is easily cut and polished. A building stone particularly popular in Rome.

Trefoil   An ornamental figure of three lobes, or foils.

Triforium   In a High Gothic church, the arcaded passage above the nave arcade and below the clerestory windows.

Triglyph   In the frieze of the Doric order, the projecting vertical block, divided into three sections, that alternates with the metope.

Triumphal Arch   A form of Roman victory monument, consisting either of one giant arch or of three giant arches abutting one another, the center one being larger than the others.

Truss   An assemblage of wood or metal members that form a rigid, self-supporting framework of triangles.

Tudor   An English architectural style of the sixteenth century characterized by flattish, pointed arches, shallow moldings, and a profusion of paneling on the walls.

Tuscan Order   A Roman variation of the Doric order, supposedly derived from Etruscan temples, with an unfluted column shaft that rises from a base.

Tympanum   In classical architecture, the recess in the triangle of the pediment. In medieval architecture, the space above a door framed by a lintel and an arch.

Volute   A spiral, scroll-shaped ornament, especially the chief feature of the Ionic capital.

Voussoir   A tapering or wedge-shaped piece used to construct an arch or vault. The middle voussoir is the keystone.

Williamsburg   Restored Colonial city in southeastern Virginia.

Further Readings

No serious study of Memphis architecture can be carried out without making use of the extensive collections on local history in the Memphis and Shelby County Room, Memphis and Shelby County Public Library and Information Center, and in the Mississippi Valley Collection, Memphis State University. The books listed here are the standard works with which any such study has to begin. We have not included a list of books on American architecture. For excellent recent bibliographies of that subject, the reader is directed to Dell Upton and John Michael Vlach, eds., *Common Places: Readings in American Vernacular Architecture*, and to Virginia and Lee McAlester, *A Field Guide to American Houses*. In the 1980s, several very fine studies of domestic architecture and suburbanization appeared. We have included some of the most interesting here.

Art Work of Memphis, Chicago, 1912.
Art Work of Memphis, Tennessee, Chicago, 1900.
Art Work of the City of Memphis, Chicago, 1895.
The Blossoming of the Century Plant: Memphis Centennial Celebration, May Nineteenth to Twenty-fourth, 1819–1919, Memphis, Tenn., 1919.
Capers, Gerald Mortimer, Jr., *The Biography of a River Town: Memphis: Its Heroic Age*, Chapel Hill, N.C., 1939. 2d ed., New Orleans, 1966.
Church, Annette E., and Roberta Church, *The Robert R. Churches of Memphis*, Ann Arbor, Mich., 1974.
Church, Roberta and Ronald Walter, *Nineteenth Century Memphis Families of Color*, Memphis, Tenn., 1987.
Clark, Clifford Edward, Jr., *The American Family Home, 1800–1960*, Chapel Hill, N.C., 1986.
Coppock, Paul R., *Memphis Sketches*, Memphis, Tenn., 1976.
Crawford, Charles Wann, *Yesterday's Memphis*, Miami, Fla., 1976.
Davis, James D., *History of Memphis*, Memphis, Tenn., 1873. Rev. ed., James E. Roper, ed., Memphis, Tenn., 1972.
Gowans, Alan, *The Comfortable House: North American Architecture, 1890–1930*, Cambridge, Mass., 1986.
Hamilton, Green Polonius, *The Bright Side of Memphis*, Memphis, Tenn., 1908.
Harkens, John E., *Metropolis of the American Nile: An Illustrated History of Memphis and Shelby County*, Woodland Hills, Calif., 1982.
Hughes, Eleanor D., *Two Master Architects of Early Memphis*, Memphis, Tenn., 1971.
Jackson, Kenneth T., *Crabgrass Frontier, The Suburbanization of the United States*, New York, 1985.

Keating, John McLeod, and O.F. Vedler, *History of the City of Memphis and Shelby County, Tennessee,* 2 vols., Syracuse, N.Y., 1888.

King, Anthony D., *The Bungalow: The Production of a Global Culture,* Boston, 1984.

Lanier, Robert A., *Memphis in the Twenties: The Second Term of Mayor Rowlett Paine, 1924–1928,* Memphis, Tenn., 1979.

LaPointe, Patricia M., *From Saddlebags to Science: A Century of Health Care in Memphis, 1830–1930,* Memphis, Tenn., 1984.

Lee, George Washington, *Beale Street, Where the Blues Began,* foreword by W.C. Handy, New York, 1934. 2d ed., College Park, Md., 1969.

McAlester, Virginia, and Lee McAlester, *A Field Guide to American Houses,* New York, 1986.

McIlwaine, Shields, *Memphis Down in Dixie,* New York, 1948.

McKee, Margaret, and Fred Chisenhall, *Beale Black and Blue: Life and Music on Black America's Main Street,* Baton Rouge, La., 1981.

McNabb, William Ross, *The Architecture of William Nowland Van Powell—Southern Classicist, 1904–1977,* manuscript, Mississippi Valley Collection, Memphis State University.

Magness, Perre, *Good Abode: Nineteenth Century Architecture in Memphis and Shelby County, Tennessee,* Memphis, Tenn., 1983.

Memphis Brooks Museum of Art, *Memphis 1948–1958,* Memphis, Tenn., 1986. Exhibition organized by J. Richard Gruber, foreword by Denise Scott Brown.

Miller, William D., *Memphis during the Progressive Era, 1900–1917,* Memphis, Tenn., 1957.

Morrison, Andrew, *Memphis, Tenn., the Bluff City,* St. Louis, 1892.

Morgan, William, *Collegiate Gothic, The Architecture of Rhodes College,* Columbia, Missouri, 1989.

Patrick, James, *Architecture in Tennessee, 1768–1897,* Knoxville, Tenn., 1981.

Plunkett, Kitty, *Memphis: A Pictorial History,* Norfolk, Va., 1976.

Priddy, Benjamin Hugh, *Nineteenth Century Architecture in Memphis: Ten Surviving Structures,* M.A. thesis, Vanderbilt University, Nashville, Tenn., 1972.

Ray, Laurence Allen, *Victorian Material Culture in Memphis, Tennessee: The Mallory-Neely House Interior as Artifact,* Ph. D. thesis, University of Tennessee, Knoxville, 1988.

Sigafoos, Robert Alan, *Cotton Row to Beale Street: A Business History of Memphis,* Memphis, Tenn., 1979.

Smith, J. Frazer, *While Pillars: Early Life and Architecture of the Lower Mississippi Valley Country,* New York, 1941.

Tennessee: A Guide to the State Compiled and Written by the Federal Writer's Project of the Works Progress Administration for the State of Tennessee, New York, 1939.

Upton, Dell, and Jon Michael Vlach, eds., *Common Places: Readings in American Vernacular Architecture*, Athens, Ga., 1986.

Williamson, James, and Carl Awsumb, *The Central Gardens Handbook*, Memphis, Tenn., 1981.

Wright, Gwendolyn, *Building the Dream, A Social History of Housing in America*, New York, 1981.

Young, John Preston, *Standard History of Memphis, Tennessee, from a Study of the Original Sources*, Knoxville, 1912. 2d ed., Evansville, Ind., 1974.

Credits for Photographs

(Unless otherwise indicated, all photographs are by the authors.)

Fig. 1   William Lawrence, survey map of Memphis, 1819 (Memphis Room, Memphis/Shelby County Public Library and Information Center)

Fig. 2   Memphis in the 1840s, seen from the Mississippi River (Memphis Room, Memphis/Shelby County Public Library and Information Center)

Fig. 4   Mario Bacchelli, View of Beale Street, oil on cavas, 1949 (Memphis Brooks Museum)

A-22   (Lost Memphis) North Side of Madison Avenue between Main and Front Streets, c. 1890 (Memphis Room, Memphis/Shelby County Public Library and Information Center)

A-26a   Jones Mah Gaskill and Rhodes Office, Brinkley Plaza, elevator lobby (photo courtesy of Jones Mah Gaskill and Rhodes)

A-26a   Jones Mah Gaskill and Rhodes Office, Brinkley Plaza, central hall (photo courtesy of Jones Mah Gaskill and Rhodes)

A-43b   (Lost Memphis) Gayoso House, 1842 block, left, and addition of 1855-57, right, from northwest (Memphis Room, Memphis/Shelby County Public Library and Information Center)

A-43c   (Lost Memphis) Second Gayoso Hotel, from west (Memphis Room, Memphis/Shelby County Public Library and Information Center)

A-63   (Lost Memphis) First Cossitt Library, from southeast (Memphis Room, Memphis/Shelby County Public Library and Information Center)

A-64   (Lost Memphis) First United States Customs House, from southeast (Memphis Room, Memphis/Shelby County Public Library and Information Center)

A-73   (Lost Memphis) First Temple Israel, from north (Memphis Room, Memphis/Shelby County Public Library and Information Center)

A-75   First Presbyterian Church, old photo showing original spire (Memphis Room, Memphis/Shelby County Public Library and Information Center)

A-90   Burch, Porter and Johnson Offices, photo c. 1900 (Memphis Room, Memphis/Shelby County Public Library and Information Center)

A-98   (Lost Memphis) Cotton Exchange Building, from southeast (Memphis Room, Memphis/Shelby County Public Library and Information Center)

A-101   (Lost Memphis) First Goodwyn Institute Building, from northeast (Memphis Room, Memphis/Shelby County Public Library and Information Center)

A-102   (Lost Memphis) Napoleon Hill House, from south (Memphis Room, Memphis/Shelby County Public Library and Information Center)

A-113	Peabody Hotel (Memphis Room, Memphis/Shelby County Public Library and Information Center)
A-116	(Lost Memphis) Central Baptist Church (Memphis Room, Memphis/ Shelby County Public Library and Information Center)
B-18	(Lost Memphis) Old Shelby County Jail, from southeast (Memphis Room, Memphis/Shelby County Public Library and Information Center)
C-11	(Lost Memphis) Robertson Topp House (Memphis Room, Memphis/ Shelby County Public Library and Information Center)
C-30	(Lost Memphis) Memphis Steam Laundry, from northeast (Memphis Room, Memphis/Shelby County Public Library and Information Center)
C-38	Dixie Homes Public Housing Project, aerial view from south (Memphis Room, Memphis/Shelby County Public Library and Information Center)
D-19	(Lost Memphis) Church Park Auditorium (Memphis Room, Memphis/ Shelby County Public Library and Information Center)
D-26	Tennessee Brewery, photo c. 1895 (Memphis Room, Memphis/Shelby County Public Library and Information Center)
D-28a	Frisco Bridge, photo c. 1895 (Memphis Room, Memphis/Shelby County Public Library and Information Center)
D-37	Arcade Restaurant, interior in 1938 (photo courtesy Arcade Restaurant)
D-41	(Lost Memphis) Union Station, from north (Memphis Room, Memphis/ Shelby County Public Library and Information Center)
D-53	Mt. Nebo Baptist Church, project drawing by James B. Cook, 1894 (Memphis Room, Memphis/Shelby County Public Library and Information Center)
D-54	(Lost Memphis) Robert R. Church House (Memphis Room, Memphis/ Shelby County Public Library and Information Center)
E-45a	(Lost Memphis) George Mahan, Jr., House, from southwest (photo courtesy of Elizabeth Mahan Ballenger)
E-45c	(Lost Memphis) Levy-Block Duplex, from northwest (photo courtesy of Elizabeth Mahan Ballenger)
H-10	(Lost Memphis) Alamo Plaza Motel, from south (Memphis Room, Memphis/Shelby County Public Library and Information Center)
H-15	(Lost Memphis) First Holiday Inn, from northeast (reprinted with permission of Holiday Inns, Inc.)
I-28	Mrs. Frank Crump House, drawing by Everett Woods, 1927 (photo courtesy of Elizabeth Mahan Ballenger)
I-49	Anshei Sphard-Beth El Emeth Synagogue, interior of sanctuary (photo courtesy Jones Mah Gaskill and Rhodes)
J-14	The Village, project drawing, office of J. Frazer Smith, 1938 (collection of Sue Cheek Smith Hughes)
J-33	Hardin College Graduate School of Religion, Administration Building, south facade in original state (Memphis Room, Memphis/Shelby County Public Library and Information Center)

Index

Where buildings are cited by more than one page number, the main entry is given in bold face.

Memphis: *An Architectural Guide* was designed by Dariel Mayer and composed at the University of Tennessee Press on the Apple Macintosh IIcx with Microsoft *Word* and Aldus *PageMaker*. Linotronic camera pages were generated by AM/PM, Inc. The book is set in Trump Mediaeval and printed on 50-lb. Glatfelter Natural. Manufactured in the United States of America by McNaughton & Gunn, Inc.